The HOLY SPIRIT

A Pentecostal Perspective

Anthony D. Palma

Stanley M. Horton, Th.D.
General Editor

Gospel Publishing House
Springfield, Missouri
02-0468

Chapters 7 through 10 originally published as *Baptism in the Holy Spirit.*

2nd Printing 2008

Logion Press books are published by Gospel Publishing House.

Library of Congress Cataloging-in-Publications Data

Palma, Anthony D.

The Holy spirit: a Pentecostal perspective / Anthony D. Palma; Stanley M. Horton, general editor.

p. cm

Includes bibliographical references and index.

ISBN 978-0-88243-786-6

1. Holy Spirit. 2. Pentecostal churches—Doctrines. I. Horton, Stanley M. II. Title.

BT121.2 .P34 2001

231′.3—dc21 00-052063

Printed in U.S.A.

Contents

Foreword

Several years ago an older believer told me about the first memory she had of me: I was six years old. She had made her way back to her pew after an intense time of prayer at the altar. With all the wisdom that a little boy raised in a Pentecostal preacher's home could muster I asked her this very adult question, "Well, Sister, are you satisfied with your experience?"

As Pentecostals, our emphasis on having a personal experience with the Holy Spirit has sometimes brought us into a great deal of criticism from other members in the Christian family. Many have perceived us as basing reality upon the subjectivity of our own experience rather than upon the objectivity of God's Word.

Sometimes our critics have forgotten that even the people of the Bible had great experiences in God before they were able to articulate a theology placing their experience within the greater context of God's revelation. Moses met God at a burning bush before God taught him the lessons of the Pentateuch. Isaiah experienced God in the temple long before he understood the panorama of history and prophecy God would later reveal to him. Saul of Tarsus encountered Jesus on the Damascus Road well before he could have passed an examination on the relationship of law to grace.

I say all this because you have before you a superb, systematic, and thoughtful biblical theology of the Holy Spirit, written by one of our preeminent scholars, Dr. Anthony D. Palma.

There are two things you should keep in mind as you study his work.

First, if you have already had a powerful experience or experiences in the Holy Spirit, this work will put a biblical floor underneath your feet. It will provide you with a thorough understanding of the person and work of the Holy Spirit, as revealed throughout the Scripture—our totally trustworthy source for truth. A great Pentecostal leader of another generation, Thomas F. Zimmerman, remarked that the relationship of the Spirit to Scripture is like a river to its banks. "The Holy Spirit," he said, "is the river, but the Spirit will only flow within the banks of Scripture." This book will help you know those banks, better enabling you to "walk in the Spirit."

Second, if you have not already encountered the person of the Spirit through conversion, baptism in the Spirit, exercise of spiritual gifts and fruit—this book cannot substitute for such experience. Dr. Palma's desire is to help you know the Spirit, but an intellectual apprehension of what the Bible teaches about the Holy Spirit can never replace your own personal experience with Him. May this wonderfully helpful textbook on the Spirit only whet your appetite for His presence and power in your own life.

Finally, a word about Pentecostal scholars. We owe a great debt to people like Dr. Palma who have dedicated their entire lifetime to understanding and teaching God's Word. I have known Dr. Palma and his wife, Betty, for many years. They are single-minded people, with a great love for the Lord, gentle dispositions, sacrificial and plain lifestyles, a deep care for students, and a passion that the Church today be a mirror image of the Church in the New Testament—full of the Holy Spirit and power.

George O. Wood
General Secretary
The General Council of the Assemblies of God

Preface

This study of the Holy Spirit is an outgrowth of several things: numerous articles I have written on various aspects of the Spirit's ministry; a monograph titled *The Spirit—God in Action,* which was used throughout the Assemblies of God in the mid-1970's as a training course for Sunday school workers; three theses I wrote for my graduate degrees in theology; notes for classes I have taught at the undergraduate and graduate levels; and extensive research for the past several years. The three theses are titled: "Glossolalia in the Light of the New Testament and Subsequent History" (S.T.B./M.Div); "Tongues and Prophecy—A Comparative Study in Charismata" (S.T.M.); and "The Holy Spirit in the Corporate Life of the Pauline Congregation" (Th.D.).

Notes and Abbreviations

In line with the usage of both the KJV and the NIV, "Lord" is used in capitals and small capitals where the Hebrew of the Old Testament has the personal, divine name of God, Yahweh (which was probably pronounced yah-wā).[1]

In quoted Scripture, words the author wishes to emphasize are in italics.

For easier reading, Hebrew, Aramaic, and Greek words are all transliterated with English letters.

These abbreviations have been used:

KJV: King James Version
NASB: *New American Standard Bible*
NIV: New International Version
NKJV: New King James Version
NRSV: New Revised Standard Version
BAGD: Bauer, Arndt, Gingrich, and Danker, *A Greek-English Lexicon of the New Testament and Other Early Christian Literature*
BDF: Blass, Debrunner, and Funk, *A Greek Grammar of the New Testament and Other Early Christian Literature*
TDNT: Kittel, *Theological Dictionary of the New Testament*

STANLEY M. HORTON
GENERAL EDITOR

[1]The Hebrew wrote only the consonants YHWH. Later traditions followed the New Latin JHVH and added vowels from the Hebrew for "Lord" to remind them to read *Lord* instead of the divine name. This was never intended to be read "Jehovah."

Introduction

This book is a study of the Holy Spirit from a Pentecostal perspective. It does not speak for all Pentecostals, but I believe it represents the thinking of classical Pentecostals and many charismatics in its main theses.

"What does the Scripture say?" (Rom. 4:3; Gal. 4:30) has been my motto from my mid-teens when, as a Roman Catholic, I began to study the Scriptures and, as a result, decided to leave the Roman Catholic Church. The Reformation watchword of *sola Scriptura* (Scripture alone) has guided virtually all I have written in this book. I have chosen to delimit the book's scope chiefly to an investigation of Scripture. Matters related to ongoing church history and to some contemporary extrabiblical phenomena, important as they are, would detract from the book's primary purpose.

Because of the book's perspective, the reader will understand why I have given a disproportionate amount of space to matters dealing with Pentecostal theology. But it is not because those matters are more important than others, except for the intent of this book.

Part 1 is a general treatment of matters about the Holy Spirit on which there is little disagreement among theologically conservative Christians. By design, therefore, the style and documentation are less interactive than one finds in the rest of the book.

Part 2 deals with the much-debated Pentecostal teaching on baptism in the Holy Spirit. I have tried to complement the traditional Pentecostal apologetic with insights I have gained from personal study and from colleagues. I readily admit that complete objectivity by me is virtually impossible. But I am hopeful that the readers will make a similar admission about themselves and maintain an openness of mind and spirit.

Part 3 deals with spiritual gifts. Even among conservative scholars, disagreements exist as to the nature of some of the gifts and whether the so-called extraordinary gifts were withdrawn after the first century. Readers must draw their own conclusions.

The distinctive theology of Pentecostals should not be a barrier to fellowship between them and other Christians. My seminary training was at an interdenominational school where the faculty members' church affiliations ranged from Free Methodist to Lutheran. My advanced theological studies were at a Lutheran seminary. In addition, I served as a Naval Reserve chaplain for many years. As a result, I have been personally enriched by fellowship with Christians of all major traditions.

Part 1

General Pneumatology

Chapter 1

The Spirit and the Godhead

Who, or what, is the Holy Spirit? This question was not raised in the Apostolic Church, but within a few centuries it was necessary for the Church to give attention to the matter. Some leaders in the Church were teaching that the Holy Spirit was created by the Son of God, and as a created being could not be considered a member of the Godhead. This was actually a denial of the doctrine of the Trinity—that God exists eternally in three Persons whom mainstream Christianity commonly designate Father, Son, and Holy Spirit.

This chapter will deal with two main topics—the personhood[1] of the Holy Spirit and the deity of the Holy Spirit. It will also include a brief survey of early church history as it relates to these matters.

The Personhood of the Holy Spirit

The Scriptures teach clearly that the Holy Spirit is a personal being. Yet some Christians misunderstand this, referring to the Spirit as "It," rather than "He."

Reasons for Confusion

The following are among the main reasons for this misunderstanding:

[1]The term "personhood" is preferable to the more common term "personality" because the latter term has a variety of meanings. The "-hood" suffix conveys the idea of condition, character, or quality.

(1) In Scripture the Spirit is the least mentioned member of the Godhead. There are considerably more references to the Father and the Son than to the Holy Spirit. Consequently, less is known about Him than about the others.

(2) The word "spirit" suggests absence of personhood. The idea of personhood has no difficulty attaching itself to the words "Father" and "Son"; but in English the gender of the word "spirit" is neuter, which means that, strictly speaking, the appropriate pronoun to be used is "it." We shall see, however, that in spite of this accident of the English language, there is abundant evidence in Scripture that the Holy Spirit is indeed a Person.

(3) The biblical languages are also partly responsible for this problem. Our word "spirit" is a simple and valid translation of the Hebrew word *ruach* and the Greek word *pneuma,* which are common words in those languages.

Originally, the words *ruach* and *pneuma* were used for inanimate and impersonal forces like wind and breath. Later, they were applied to what native speakers of English understand by the word "spirit." In Hebrew grammar the word *ruach* is predominantly in the feminine gender.[2] Greek, on the other hand, assigns the neuter gender to *pneuma.*

The point of these comments is to show that both in the biblical languages and in English, the personhood of the Holy Spirit may be misunderstood because of linguistic limitations.

(4) Translations of the Bible are sometimes inadequate. This may be due to the translators' desire to give what they consider a "strict" translation or to their unawareness of the overall biblical teaching about the Holy Spirit. For instance, Romans 8:26 in the King James Version reads, "The Spirit itself maketh intercession for us." "The Spirit itself" may be *technically* correct because of the neuter gender of both the noun and the intensive pronoun *(auto),* but it is better to follow the *theologically* correct reading which says "the Spirit *himself*" (as in the NIV; see also NASB and NKJV).

[2]It is masculine in a limited number of passages. The Heb. language does not have a neuter gender.

(5) The Spirit is often associated in Scripture with the idea of power. Consequently, some think of the Holy Spirit only as an impersonal force. But when Jesus promised the disciples that they would receive power when the Holy Spirit came upon them (Acts 1:8; see also Luke 24:49), He meant that the Spirit himself would come in fullness and that the Spirit, who is all-powerful, would provide them with the necessary means for effective ministry.

(6) Figures of speech often used in Scripture for the Holy Spirit may imply the idea of inanimate or impersonal objects. A few suggestions will suffice to illustrate this point. He is likened to

- water—John 7:38–39
- oil—Acts 10:38 (Throughout the Bible, anointing was done with oil.)
- wind—John 3:8; Acts 2:2
- fire—Acts 2:3; Rev. 4:5
- a dove—Luke 3:22

Most of these symbols will receive attention at appropriate points in the following chapters. Here it is simply necessary to state that often the purpose of a figure of speech is to help one understand something about a person. It draws an analogy using a common object that readily expresses some characteristic or attribute of the person, and is not to be pressed literally.

Biblical Proof of the Spirit's Personhood

Many lines of evidence in Scripture point to the Holy Spirit being a Person, and not an inanimate object or impersonal force. Our main concern here is to establish this by a survey of the biblical material. Further treatment of many of these matters will be given in subsequent chapters.

(1) He possesses personal attributes, which are associated with the mind, the will, and the emotions.

Paul speaks of "the mind of the Spirit" (Rom. 8:27), and says further that only the Spirit of God knows the deep things of God (1 Cor. 2:10–11). The intellectual activity of the Spirit is further seen in gifts of the Spirit such as a word of knowledge, a word of wisdom, distinguishings of spirits, and prophecy (1 Cor. 12:8–10). There is also the matter of the will, or volition. Sovereign actions of the Holy Spirit are one aspect of this. He distributes gifts "to each one, just as he determines" (1 Cor. 12:11). He directs God's people in setting some apart for special ministry (Acts 13:2) and in the choice of fields of labor (Acts 16:6–7). Finally, the Holy Spirit has emotions. He may be grieved or vexed (Isa. 63:10; Eph. 4:30); He also manifests love (Rom. 15:30).

(2) He performs personal acts. The following is a sample listing:

- He creates—Gen. 1:2; Job 33:4; Ps. 33:6
- He re-creates, or regenerates—John 3:5; Titus 3:5
- He strives with men—Gen. 6:3
- He convicts, or convinces, unregenerate men —John 16:8
- He intercedes—Rom. 8:26
- He performs miracles— Acts 8:39; Heb. 2:4
- He raises the dead—Rom. 1:3–4; 8:11
- He speaks—John 16:13; Acts 8:29; 10:19; Rev. 2:7
- He teaches—Luke 12:12; John 14:26; 1 John 2:27
- He testifies—John 15:26; 1 Pet. 1:11

(3) He may be personally offended. Stephen charged his persecutors with always resisting the Holy Spirit (Acts 7:51). Peter accused Ananias of lying to the Holy Spirit (Acts 5:3) and stated further that both Ananias and Sapphira had put the Spirit of the Lord to the test (v. 9). Paul admonishes Christians not to grieve the Holy Spirit (Eph. 4:30), probably recalling how Israel had so offended Him in the wilderness (Isa. 63:10). Furthermore, believers are warned of the possibility of insulting or outraging "the Spirit of grace" by denying their blood-bought salvation (Heb. 10:29).

In one of the most solemn passages in all of Scripture, Jesus warned against blaspheming, or sinning against, the Holy Spirit (Matt. 12:32; Mark 3:22–30; Luke 12:10). Bible scholars disagree on the precise nature of this sin, but at least two points are quite clear when one examines the context of each passage: (a) It consists of *knowingly* and *persistently* attributing to Satan what is obviously the work of the Holy Spirit. (b) It is a rejection of Jesus Christ as God's chosen and anointed One for the deliverance of humankind. (Christians need not be preoccupied or distressed with the thought that they have committed this sin. The very fact that they are concerned about it is a clear indication that the Holy Spirit has not forsaken them.)

(4) Jesus called Him the Paraclete. This term transliterates the Greek *paraklētos,* and is translated variously as "Comforter," "Helper," "Counselor," "Advocate." Its root meaning is "one called to the side of." The passages where this title is found (John 14:16,26; 15:26; 16:7) indicate clearly that Jesus is talking about the Holy Spirit as a Person.

A further indication of the Spirit's personhood is in Jesus' words identifying Him as "*another* Paraclete" (John 14:16, my translation). Jesus himself was the first Paraclete. The apostle John says that "we have an Advocate *[paraklētos]* with the Father, Jesus Christ the righteous" (1 John 2:1, NASB). The clue is in the Greek word for "another," *allos,* which usually means "another of the same kind." Just as the Lord Jesus Christ came to the aid of His disciples and encouraged them, so too would the Holy Spirit, helping, encouraging, and interceding for them (and those who would believe their message) after Jesus left. Jesus promised He would not leave His disciples as orphans—helpless, defenseless, and comfortless (John 14:18).

(5) Masculine pronouns are used for the Holy Spirit. It seems that in a few passages Jesus deliberately emphasized the Spirit's personhood by using the masculine form of the demonstrative pronoun[3] when referring to him. In John 14:26 he could have omitted the word without injury to the

[3]*Ekeinos* rather than the neuter *ekeino. Ekeinos,* strictly translated, means "that one," but it occurs often in place of the masculine personal pronoun *autos,* "he." Students of Scripture understand, of course, that Jesus would have spoken Aramaic to his disciples. Nevertheless, the only record we have is the inspired Gk. version which, we may assume, correctly conveys Jesus' thoughts.

grammar. The NASB reads, "'The Helper, the Holy Spirit, whom the Father will send in My name, He *[ekeinos]* will teach you all things.'" In John 16:13–14 Jesus twice used the masculine form of the pronoun even though, in Greek, no pronoun was necessary.[4] He said, "'But when he *[ekeinos]*, the Spirit of truth, comes, he will guide you into all truth. . . . He *[ekeinos]* will bring glory to me.'"

The Deity of the Holy Spirit

The Holy Spirit is a member of the Trinity, which means He is fully divine like the Father and the Son. He is often referred to as the Third Person of the Godhead.

Scriptural Evidences for His Deity

Many lines of evidence point to the absolute deity of the Holy Spirit. The following are the most important:

(1) He is mentioned coordinately with the Father and the Son. The following examples demonstrate that all three are equal to one another; otherwise it would be a case of mixing the proverbial apples and oranges: Jesus commanded the disciples to baptize "'in the name of the Father and of the Son and of the Holy Spirit'" (Matt. 28:19). Paul, in three parallel phrases, speaks of "the grace of the Lord Jesus Christ, and the love of God, and the fellowship of the Holy Spirit" (2 Cor. 13:14). In Ephesians 4:4–6 he makes reference to one Lord (Jesus Christ), one Spirit, and one God and Father. In 1 Corinthians 12:4–6, he speaks in parallel fashion of the Spirit, the Lord (Jesus Christ), and God (the Father).

(2) He is clearly distinguished from the Father and the Son. In a prophetic passage, Isaiah quotes the Messiah as saying, "'And now the Lord God has sent Me, and His Spirit'" (Isa. 48:16, NASB).[5] This distinction of identities is

[4]Students of Gk. understand that pronominal subjects are not necessary since the appropriate verb ending has the subject "built-in." When a pronoun is used, it is often for emphasis.

[5]Translations will vary. See treatment in chap. 3, "The Spirit and the Messiah."

also evident at the baptism of Jesus. The Son of God was standing in the Jordan River, the Holy Spirit came upon Him in the form of a dove, and the Father spoke from heaven (Luke 3:21–22).

Throughout Scripture, the Holy Spirit is often called the Spirit of God or the Spirit of the Lord. Because of this, some have concluded that He does not have independent existence, and that He must be regarded simply as a manifestation of God. But these titles emphasize that this Spirit is divine and not evil. Many satanic, evil spirits are at work in the world, but there is only one divine Holy Spirit. The concept of three persons in the Godhead must be maintained; otherwise it is impossible to come to a satisfactory understanding of some passages of Scripture (such as those in the previous paragraph).

(3) He has divine attributes. For our purposes, the expression "divine attributes" refers to characteristics or qualities which God alone possesses. Among the most important are these:

Eternality. God alone has neither beginning nor ending. Hebrews 9:14 speaks thus of the Holy Spirit when it describes Him as "the eternal Spirit."

Omnipotence. The Holy Spirit is all-powerful. This is evidenced in Scripture by the mighty signs and wonders He performs (Rom. 15:19; Heb. 2:4). For example, He participated in the creation of our world (Gen. 1:2); He effects the new creation, or the new birth (John 3:5; Titus 3:5); He raises the dead (Rom. 1:3–4; 8:11).

Omnipresence. He is everywhere present. David said, "Where can I go from your Spirit? Where can I flee from your presence?" (Ps. 139:7). The answer is obvious (see vv. 8–10). Difficult as it is for the finite human mind to grasp, the Spirit of God is simultaneously present everywhere. How else would it be possible for Christians everywhere to be engaged in worship at the same time, for Christians are those who "worship by the Spirit of God" (Phil. 3:3; see also John 4:23–24)?

Omniscience. The Holy Spirit is all-knowing. Nothing is

hidden from Him (1 Cor. 2:10–11). As the One who inspired Holy Scripture, He revealed to Moses details of the creation story which otherwise would be humanly unknowable. By the operation of spiritual gifts such as prophecy and a word of knowledge, He may disclose inner secrets and sins of the human heart (1 Cor. 14:24–25). He guides God's people into all truth (John 16:13), and gives them spiritual insight (1 Cor. 2:9–10).

The Holy Spirit is omniscient not only in matters pertaining to the eternal past and the present; He also knows all about the future. He moved upon the biblical writers to record events of the last days, for Jesus said that the Spirit would show His disciples "'what is yet to come'" (John 16:13). And Paul records, "The Spirit clearly says that in later times some will abandon the faith and follow deceiving spirits and things taught by demons" (1 Tim. 4:1).

Absolute Holiness. The designation "Holy Spirit" occurs more than ninety times in Scripture; all but three references are in the New Testament. He is specifically called *the* Holy Spirit, indicating his unique holiness and also his separation from all other spirit-beings whether Satan, evil spirits, or angels. Paul goes so far as to call Him "the Spirit of holiness" (Rom. 1:4), which is the way "Holy Spirit" is expressed in the Hebrew language (Ps. 51:11; Isa. 63:10–11).

(4) He performs the works of Deity. God alone created and sustains our universe. He alone can regenerate and spiritually resurrect souls that are dead in trespasses and sin. He alone has power to raise the dead. And as previously noted, the Holy Spirit either participated/participates in or is the sole agent of these works.

(5) He is expressly called God. The apostle Peter accepted without question the full deity of the Holy Spirit. This is especially evident in the story of his encounter with Ananias and Sapphira (Acts 5:1–11). Peter said to Ananias, "'How is it that Satan has so filled your heart that you have lied to the Holy Spirit?'" (v. 3). He went on the say, "'You have not lied to men but to God'" (v. 4). Sinning against the Holy Spirit, says Peter, is the same as sinning against God.

Prayer and Praise to the Holy Spirit

Is it proper to pray to the Holy Spirit, or to ascribe praise to Him? This is a natural question to raise in view of the Spirit's personhood and deity. We have seen that He is coequal with the Father and the Son. But there is no clear indication in Scripture that He may be addressed in prayer or in worship. Prayer is normally addressed to the Father through Jesus our Mediator; it is done in or by the Holy Spirit (John 4:23–24; 16:23; Eph. 2:18; Phil. 3:3).

In the New Testament, two prayers indirectly invoke the Holy Spirit. At the conclusion of 2 Corinthians, Paul asks that the communion or fellowship of the Holy Spirit may be with the Corinthian Christians (13:14).[6] John, in the Book of Revelation, asks that grace and peace may come to his readers "from the seven spirits" (1:4). These seven Spirits are elsewhere called "the seven Spirits of God" (Rev. 3:1; 4:5; 5:6). This is an obvious reference to the Holy Spirit. The Book of Revelation is full of symbolism, and numbers in this book are often symbolic. Seven is the number of completeness; therefore "seven Spirits" refers to the Spirit of God in His fullness or His complete activity.[7] Isaiah 11:2 is sometimes taken as a commentary on this, since it contains seven descriptive terms relating to the Holy Spirit: "The Spirit *of the* Lord will rest on him [the Messiah]—the Spirit *of wisdom* and *of understanding,* the Spirit *of counsel* and *of power,* the Spirit *of knowledge* and *of the fear of the* Lord."

In the Book of Revelation, the four living creatures around the throne of God say, "'Holy, holy, holy is the Lord God Almighty'" (4:8). This recalls the seraphs in Isaiah's vision who also say, "'Holy, holy, holy is the Lord Almighty'" (Isa. 6:3). Biblical scholars sometimes take this triple repetition of

[6]The thought may be: grace which comes from Christ, love which comes from the Father, and fellowship/communion which comes from the Holy Spirit (the Gk. genitive/ablative of source, or the subjective genitive).

[7]The NIV footnote to Rev. 1:4 suggests the alternative reading "sevenfold Spirit."

"holy"[8] to be an ascription of praise to the Triune God.

If there is no clear example in Scripture of prayer or praise addressed to the Spirit, there is also nothing in Scripture which prohibits it. It is perfectly understandable that one who believes the Holy Spirit to be God will pray to Him occasionally. This is reflected especially in hymns and choruses in which Christians sing not only *about* the Holy Spirit, but also *to* Him.[9]

The Creeds of the Early Church

A creed is a statement of faith containing articles needful for salvation or the theological integrity of the Church. One may think of a creed more simply as a doctrinal statement drawn up to contain the beliefs of the Church to help in distinguishing truth from error.

During the first century, no formal creed was adopted by the Church. But because false teachings increasingly made their appearance, three great creeds arose to articulate what the Church deemed to be sound doctrine. Our concern is to see what each of them says about the Holy Spirit.

The Apostles' Creed

Contrary to what its name suggests, the Apostles' Creed was not drawn up by the apostles. It received this title because it was believed to reflect the teachings of the apostles. The exact date for its formulation cannot be fixed with certainty, but very possibly it emerged during the second century.

This creed contains only two brief references to the Spirit. In the section about Jesus Christ, it says that He "was conceived by the Holy Spirit." Following that section, it simply says, "I believe . . . in the Holy Spirit." It was not until controversy arose about the personhood and deity of

[8]Called technically the Trisagion or the Tersanctus—Greek and Latin terms meaning "thrice-holy."

[9]For example, hymns like "Holy Ghost, with Light Divine" and "Breathe on Me, Breath of God" and choruses like "Come, Holy Spirit" and "Spirit of the Living God."

the Holy Spirit that additional statements about Him appear in later creeds.

The Nicene Creed

The Council of Nicea[10] (A.D. 325) drew up a creed which amplified the Apostles' Creed but added nothing concerning the Holy Spirit. Its main concern was with the Arian heresy, which denied the full deity of Christ.

In A.D. 381 the Council of Constantinople[11] expanded the Nicene Creed and because of controversy over the Holy Spirit, included some details about His nature and work. Arianism denied the deity of both the Son and the Holy Spirit. Arius taught that the Son was the first being created by the Father and that the Holy Spirit was the first creature brought forth by the Son.

Macedonius, bishop of Constantinople from A.D. 341–60, was especially prominent among those denying the Spirit's deity. He taught that the Holy Spirit was inferior and subordinate to both the Father and the Son and spoke of Him as a messenger or minister. He said, in effect, that the Spirit was on the same level as angels, who are God's messengers. The Spirit was thus reduced to the status of a created being. The followers of Macedonius, who were often called Macedonians or Pneumatomachians (lit. "Spirit-fighters"), generally taught, like Arius, that the Father created the Son and that the Son in turn created the Holy Spirit.[12] Therefore, a created being—a creature—could not be God.[13]

[10]Present-day Iznik in northwest Turkey.

[11]Present-day Istanbul.

[12]The Tropici, a local sect in Egypt which predated the Macedonians/ Pneumatomachians, also taught that the Spirit was a creature brought into existence out of nothingness and that he was an angel superior to all other angels in rank but, like angels, to be included among the "ministering spirits [angels]" of Heb. 1:14.

[13]It would be unfair to impugn the motives of men like Arius, Macedonius, and Sabellius. They sought to preserve the doctrine of one God; consequently they could not conceive of either the Son or the Holy Spirit as persons coequal with and of the same nature as the Father which, in their thinking, constituted tritheism. They felt that their theology safeguarded the doctrine of monotheism.

The Nicene Creed, which more properly should be called the Niceno-Constantinopolitan Creed, clearly stated the personhood and deity of the Spirit in the following article:

"And [I believe] in the Holy Spirit, the Lord and Giver of Life, who proceeds from the Father, who with the Father and the Son is worshiped and glorified together; who spoke by the prophets."

In A.D. 451, at the Council of Chalcedon,[14] the Church in the western part of the Roman Empire adopted this creed as well.

THE ATHANASIAN CREED

The origin of this creed is unknown, but the name of the church father Augustine (A.D. 354–430) is associated with it. It came into existence prior to the fifth century. It is so called because it reflects the theology of another important church father, Athanasius (c. A.D. 293–373), who argued successfully against Arius (c. A.D. 250–336) at the Council of Nicea. Even though not composed by Athanasius, it sets forth much of his argumentation in favor of the doctrine of the Trinity.

This creed states that there is one Godhead consisting of the Father, the Son, and the Holy Spirit, and that the three are equal in glory and coequal in majesty. Some of the language in the creed may seem unnecessarily repetitious to us, but in an era when the heresy of Arianism threatened to displace the doctrine of the Trinity, it was necessary to be explicit. The creed goes on to make propositional statements to reinforce the idea of the three members of the Godhead being equal in every respect. It says that each of them is uncreated, unlimited, eternal, almighty, and God, but that they are not three Gods but one God.

The Athanasian Creed was not an ecumenical creed, being adopted only by the Church in the West.

[14]Asian city near Constantinople. Modern-day Kadikoy, a district of Istanbul.

THE *FILIOQUE* CONTROVERSY

The Synod of Aachen[15] (A.D. 809) inserted the *filioque* clause ("and the Son") into the Nicene Creed to make it say that the Holy Spirit proceeds from both the Father and the Son. Augustine taught this "double procession" of the Spirit, but the concept had not worked its way into the ecumenical creeds. It seems that, prior to the Synod of Aachen, the Nicene Creed with this addition had been recited at a council in Toledo (Spain) in A.D. 589. However, "it was doubtless the name of Pope Gregory [A.D. 590–604] . . . which secured the final adhesion of the Latin [Western] Church to Augustine's doctrine of the Procession."[16] But "it was probably not until the final rupture with Constantinople [A.D. 1054] that Rome accepted the . . . addition to the Eastern Creed."[17]

The understanding and agreement of both the Eastern and the Western segments of the Church had previously been that the Spirit proceeds *"out of* the Father *through* the Son."[18] The Church in the East condemned the *filioque* addition to the creed. The addition remains one of the theological differences between Eastern Orthodoxy and the Roman Catholic Church.[19]

MODALISTIC MONARCHIANISM

Modalistic monarchianism was an attempt to preserve the doctrine of one God. It was explicated by Sabellius, who taught his doctrine in Rome in A.D. 215 and was subsequently condemned. His teaching was that God, who is

[15]In present-day Germany near the Belgian border, and known also by its French name Aix-la-Chapelle.

[16]Henry Barclay Swete, *The Holy Spirit in the Ancient Church* (1912; reprint, Grand Rapids: Baker Book House, 1966), 347.

[17]Ibid., 349.

[18]J. N. D. Kelly, *Early Christian Doctrines* (New York: Harper & Row, 1958), 263, Kelly's emphasis.

[19]See Gerald Bray, "The Double Procession of the Holy Spirit in Evangelical Theology Today: Do We Still Need it?" *Journal of the Evangelical Theological Society* 41, no. 3 (September 1998): 415–26.

One, reveals himself successively in three different modes or forms, which are three roles, or parts, played by the one Person. There is only one Person, who has three names: Father, Son, and Holy Spirit.[20]

[20]Otto W. Heick, *A History of Christian Thought* (Philadelphia: Fortress Press, 1965), 1:150–51. The teaching of Oneness Pentecostals on the Godhead is strikingly similar to that of Sabellius.

Chapter 2

The Spirit in the Old Testament Period

The Holy Spirit is not a stranger to the Old Testament. He is mentioned in both its first book (Gen. 1:2) and its last book (Mal. 2:15, NASB).[1] In the Hebrew Scriptures, where the book order differs from the English Scriptures, He is also mentioned in the last book (2 Chron. 24:20, for example). All told, He appears in almost two-thirds of the Old Testament books. Obviously, then, his work prior to the New Testament era was most important.

Two things stand out in the Old Testament's teaching on the Holy Spirit:

(1) The accent is on what He *does,* not on what He *is.* There is no emphasis on His personhood or deity. It is the work, rather than the nature, of the Spirit that the Old Testament emphasizes. Consequently, He may be referred to as "God-in-action." The same is true of the New Testament, but with some important exceptions, as noted in chapter 1.

(2) Old Testament pneumatology foreshadows much of what appears in the New Testament. Indeed, it would be difficult to understand some New Testament passages if it were not for the light the Old Testament sheds on them.

[1]See NKJV; NRSV footnote.

We proceed, then, to consider some of the main teachings of the Old Testament on the Holy Spirit.[2]

Creation

The Spirit of God was actively involved in the creation of the earth. When the earth was without form, and void, with darkness upon the face of the deep, the Spirit of God "was hovering over the waters" (Gen. 1:2),[3] bringing order out of chaos. He is presented under the imagery of a hovering bird. He participated with both the Father and the Son in the work of creation.

The creation of human beings is also associated with the Holy Spirit. God said, "'Let us make man in our image, in our likeness'" (Gen. 1:26). The writer then says that "the LORD God formed the man from the dust of the ground and breathed into his nostrils the breath of life, and the man became a living being" (Gen. 2:7). The breath of God is a metaphor for the Holy Spirit. Even though the word "breath" in this verse is not the same as *ruach,* which is used for the Spirit of God, the idea is the same. This is evident from other passages which link the creation of man with the activity of the Spirit (Job 33:4; Ps. 104:30).

[2]See monographs such as Stanley M. Horton, *What the Bible Says About the Holy Spirit* (Springfield, Mo.: Gospel Publishing House, 1976); Wilf Hildebrandt, *An Old Testament Theology of the Spirit of God* (Peabody, Mass.: Hendrickson Publishers, 1995); Leon J. Wood, *The Holy Spirit in the Old Testament* (Grand Rapids: Zondervan Publishing House, 1976). See also excellent and comprehensive articles like William Ross Schoemaker, "The Use of *Ruach* in the Old Testament, and of *Pneuma* in the New Testament: A Lexicographical Study," *Journal of Biblical Literature* 23 (1904): 13–67; M. R. Westall, "The Scope of the Term 'Spirit of God' in the Old Testament," *The Indian Journal of Theology* 26 (January–March 1977): 29–41; Carl Armerding, "The Holy Spirit in the Old Testament: Part I," *Bibliotheca Sacra* 92 (1935): 277–91 and "Part III," 92 (1935): 433–41; R. S. Cripps, "The Holy Spirit in the Old Testament," *Theology* 24 (1932): 272–80; G. Henton Davies, "The Holy Spirit in the Old Testament," *Review and Expositor* 63 (1966): 129–34.

[3]Some versions and commentators prefer the translation "a wind from God" (for example, NRSV; and Westall, "Scope"). While this is lexically possible, other passages clearly associate the Spirit with creation—and its NT counterpart, the new creation.

Finally, the Spirit of God was not only an agent in the creation of all things (Job 26:13);[4] He is also the Sustainer of life (Job 34:14–15). All this brings to mind the words of the Nicene Creed which call him the Lord and Giver of Life.

Sinful Men

The Old Testament suggests that the Spirit of God will withdraw himself from people who persist in sin. He indeed strives with sinners, trying to bring them to repentance. "'My Spirit will not contend with man forever'" (Gen. 6:3). The verb translated "contend" may also be rendered "remain, dwell, or abide in." The fearsome consequences of the Flood followed this removal of God's Spirit from the midst of sinful humankind.

First Samuel 16:14 says that "the Spirit of the LORD had departed from Saul" because of his disobedience to God's command. Samson, upon whom the Spirit of God had come mightily numerous times (Judg. 13:25; 14:6,19; 15:14–16), similarly experienced the withdrawal of God's presence (16:20).

David's experience is worth noting. He prayed, "Do not cast me from your presence or take your Holy Spirit from me" (Ps. 51:11).[5] He feared that he would lose the indwelling of the Holy Spirit because of his sin with Bathsheba. This is the first Old Testament occurrence of the designation "Holy Spirit." The emphasis is upon the adjective "holy," in contrast to David's sin. Unconfessed and unrepented sin may result in the loss of the Holy Spirit; only after offering prayer for a clean heart and a right spirit can a person be assured of not forfeiting the presence of God.

[4]NKJV reads "Spirit"; some translations read "breath," which is a metaphor for "spirit."

[5]Some understand "Holy Spirit" to mean a person's breath which, coming from God, is holy. David's prayer then would mean, "Do not take my life." In light of other passages which speak clearly about the Lord's withdrawal of His Spirit from a person, this interpretation is inadequate.

The Natural Realm

The Spirit operated in the physical, or natural, realm with respect to individuals. This can be seen in a number of different ways.

Superhuman Strength

The Spirit came upon Samson in such a mighty way that he was able to tear up a lion (Judg. 14:6), kill thirty men of Ashkelon (14:19), and break the ropes that bound him and slay one thousand men with the jawbone of a donkey (15:14–15). When the Spirit came upon some others, they were imbued with unnatural, extraordinary power and were able to lead their people to victory—men like Othniel (Judg. 3:10), Gideon (6:34), and Jephthah (11:29).

Ability in Relation to God's House

The Spirit came upon certain people to equip them for the tasks of building the tabernacle and making the garments for the High Priest (Exod. 28:2–3;[6] 35:30–35). Bezalel and Oholiab were among those chosen for these apparently mundane, "nonspiritual" assignments. But even in these cases it was necessary for them to be endowed with divine wisdom in order to perform their duties acceptably.

The physical task of rebuilding the temple after the seventy-year Babylonian captivity was overwhelming. Opposition without and dissension within threatened to abort the project. But words of encouragement and assurance came to Zerubbabel, saying, "'"Not by might nor by power, but by my Spirit," says the LORD Almighty'" (Zech. 4:6). What they had not been able to do with their own physical resources, God would make possible by his Spirit. The work of God could never progress simply on the basis of human power and human strength. The power of His Spirit was needed to give them the added resources necessary for the accomplishment of the task.

[6]In v. 3, NASB and NKJV read "the spirit of wisdom."

Physical Transportation

Miraculous transportation was provided for Elijah (2 Kings 2:11; note 1 Kings 18:12). Perhaps the whirlwind which transported him to heaven is symbolic of the Holy Spirit. Even the skeptics (2 Kings 2:16) conceded the possibility of such an occurrence. Philip the evangelist experienced a similar phenomenon of physical transportation. "The Spirit of the Lord suddenly took Philip away" from the Gaza Road and he "appeared at Azotus and traveled about" (Acts 8:39–40).

Ezekiel had comparable experiences, but it is not always easy to decide whether he is speaking of spiritual rapture or of physical transportation (Ezek. 3:12–14; 8:3; 11:1,24; 43:5). This could be akin to Paul's testimony about being "caught up to the third heaven" but not knowing whether it was "in the body or out of the body" (2 Cor. 12:2).

Leadership

A Variety of Terminology

Spiritual tasks can be accomplished only by the enabling power of the Holy Spirit. The Old Testament testifies amply to this. It contains a number of expressions for the way the Spirit contacted men.[7] The following are some of the most important, with a few representative passages:

(1) He "comes upon" individuals (Num. 24:2—Balaam; 1 Sam. 10:10—Saul; Isa. 61:1—the Messiah). This is the most frequently occurring expression.

(2) He comes "mightily" upon individuals (Judg. 14:19, NASB; 15:14, NASB—Samson).

(3) He "clothes" himself with people (lit. trans.; see Judg. 6:34—Gideon; 1 Chron. 12:18—Amasai; 2 Chron. 24:20—Zechariah, son of Jehoiada the priest). The translations do not usually bring this out, but the verb *(lavash)* is different from the one normally used for the Spirit coming upon individuals. It suggests that He has complete control of the person, that He "takes possession" of the individual.

[7]For an extended treatment, see Davies, "Holy Spirit in the Old Testament."

(4) He "fills" people with himself, or sometimes the expression "full of" is used (Exod. 31:3—Bezalel; Mic. 3:8—Micah).

(5) He is/will be "poured out" (Isa. 32:15, NASB; Ezek. 39:29; Joel 2:28–29).

(6) He is "in" individuals (Gen. 41:38—Joseph; Num. 27:18—Joshua; Ezek. 2:2—Ezekiel; Dan. 4:8–9; 5:11,14—Daniel).[8]

These expressions are remarkably similar to New Testament terminology, but it is important to note two significant differences between the Old and the New Testaments:

(1) In the Old Testament, the Spirit of God was experienced by only a select few. It is not until after the Day of Pentecost that He becomes the possession of all believers.

(2) Generally speaking, He was not the permanent possession of the Old Testament leaders. He acted upon them only when there was a specific work to do. In the New Testament, He is the permanent possession of all believers (Rom. 8:9,14–16).

Oil as a Symbol of the Holy Spirit

Old Testament leaders, especially kings and priests, were anointed with oil as a sign that they had been chosen by God for their task and that he would equip them with His Spirit. This link between oil and the Spirit becomes clear in Samuel's anointing of David to be king (1 Sam. 16:13; see also 10:1,6).

Moses and the Seventy Elders (Num. 11:16–29)

The Lord told Moses, because of Moses' advancing years and the complex demands of leading God's people, that the burden of the work was to be distributed among the seventy elders. The same Spirit who had been on Moses enabling him to fulfill his task would now also be placed upon these men. This incident teaches unquestionably that God's work can be administered properly only by the enablement of His Spirit.

[8]With respect to Joseph and Daniel, pagan rulers say that "the spirit of the gods" is in them.

A few additional lessons can be elicited from this narrative. One is that the Spirit of the Lord cannot be restricted to any one locale. Since He is omnipresent, He can move upon different people in different places at the same time. It is also noteworthy that even though the Lord himself indicated that the ceremony was to take place at the tabernacle, His appointed holy place, He nevertheless was not bound to restrict all His work to that one location. The Spirit is not only omnipresent; He is also sovereign. It may also be noted that when the Spirit of God is active among His people, there will sometimes be critics who insist that God's workings must conform to their own preconceived notions (see Num. 11:26–29).

Prophecy

When the Spirit came upon the elders and Eldad and Medad, the record says that they prophesied (Num. 11:25–26). Prophesying under the inspiration of the Holy Spirit is such a common phenomenon in the Old Testament that it deserves special attention.

The Nature of Prophecy

In common usage, the word "prophecy" often means foretelling, or prediction. This, however, is not the primary, or root, meaning of the word. Prophets at times did indeed foretell certain events, but a study of the prophetic books shows that much of their writings did not relate to the future; often they were concerned with contemporary problems.

A prophet, by definition, is a spokesperson—someone who speaks for someone else. A biblical prophet is one who conveys God's message to people. True prophecy is always given under the inspiration of the Holy Spirit; it is not simply the thoughts of the prophet given whenever the prophet pleases. A recurring theme in the Old Testament is that when the Spirit comes upon people, they prophesy. Prophecy was therefore one of the signs in the Old Testament that the Spirit of God had come upon an individual.

The Early Period of Prophecy

The account in Numbers 11 is the first instance of prophetic utterance being linked with the Holy Spirit. The record does not give the content of the prophecies of those men. The important point is that they prophesied, and this indicated to the people that they had been chosen by God to be their leaders.

First Samuel describes a group of prophets who traveled together. Samuel had just anointed Saul as king of Israel and told him that when he encountered these prophets the Spirit would come upon him and he too would prophesy (1 Sam. 10:5–10). In connection with this, Saul also experienced an inner change (v. 6).

On a later occasion Saul again found himself in the company of these prophets, prophesying along with them (1 Sam. 19:20–24). In this instance, however, Saul was living in a state of disobedience. He was seeking to kill David and sent messengers to apprehend him. But the messengers met the prophets and they prophesied along with them. The question needs to be asked, "How can the Spirit of God come upon people who are planning evil?" The answer may lie in the sovereignty of God. The Lord will do whatever He wishes with whomever He wishes whenever He wishes!

Prophesying was a sign that the Spirit had come upon an individual; it was not necessarily an endorsement of the recipient's lifestyle. On one occasion, the Lord even chose to speak through a donkey (Num. 22:28–30). In Saul's case, the Lord could very well have been showing him that even though he (Saul) was the king of Israel, he was subject to the King of the universe.[9]

[9]A clarifying note is in order on 1 Sam. 19:24, which says that Saul "also stripped off his clothes, and he too prophesied before Samuel and lay down naked all that day and all that night" (NASB). The word "naked" means "without outward garments" (NASB marginal note), a meaning borne out by the following passages: Isa. 20:2; Mic. 1:8; see also John 21:7. We note also that Saul was under the overpowering influence of the Spirit for an entire day and night. Very likely, this was a delaying tactic by God, to give David a chance to escape.

Other notable prophets during this early period include Samuel, Elijah, and Elisha—each of whom played a vital role in the history of God's people.

THE LATER PROPHETS

The eighth century B.C. began a period in which God spoke to His people primarily through prophets. As noted, one curious element during the earlier period of prophecy is that the contents of the prophecies are seldom given. The emphasis was more on the *fact* that people prophesied than on *what* they prophesied.

Because many of their messages were committed to writing, the prophets of this later period are sometimes called the literary prophets. The books of Isaiah through Malachi record their prophecies. Some of their prophecies were directed against the sins of Israel and the surrounding nations, with warnings of impending doom. Other prophecies contained messages of hope for the godly who were suffering. Some attacked the social evils of their day; others made remarkable predictions of the coming Messiah and the Messianic Age.

Ezekiel is an outstanding example of a prophet whose life and message were dominated by the Spirit of God. He states that the Spirit

- entered him (Ezek. 2:2; 3:24);
- caused him to stand (2:2; 3:24);
- fell upon him (11:5);
- lifted him up (3:12,14);
- took him away (3:14);
- brought him, whether physically or spiritually, to the temple (11:1; 43:5), to Jerusalem (8:3), to Babylonia (11:24), and into a valley (37:1). He indicates that some of these experiences were like visions.

Throughout the book of Ezekiel, the prophet says, "The word of the LORD came to me saying . . . " (see Ezek. 7:1, NASB). This expression is equivalent to saying that the Spirit came upon him, spoke personally to him, and gave him a message for God's people. It is by His Spirit that the Lord communicates with His people; it is by His Spirit that His Word is transmitted.[10]

Other Manifestations

In addition to prophecy, a number of other gifts or manifestations are directly attributed to the Holy Spirit. The following are some of the most prominent:

- bestowal of spiritual power (Mic. 3:8)
- wisdom, understanding, and good judgment (Dan. 4:8–9,18; 5:14; Mic. 3:8)
- teaching ability (Exod. 35:31,34–35)
- ability to interpret a divine message given in another language (Dan. 5:12)

Added to this list would be items discussed earlier in this chapter under the headings "The Natural Realm" and "Leadership."

The Twofold Promise of the Spirit

Relatively few people in Old Testament times experienced the indwelling and the power of the Holy Spirit. But a radical change was to take place under the new covenant promised through the prophets Ezekiel and Joel.[11]

The Intertestamental Period

What was the concept of the Holy Spirit among the Jews during the four centuries from Malachi to Matthew? The religious writings of this period are not part of Holy Scripture; therefore their teaching cannot be regarded as divinely inspired and authoritative. They do help, nevertheless, to form a bridge between the two Testaments and to provide some background for the New Testament teaching on the Holy Spirit.

[10]See part 1, chap. 6.

[11]See part 2, chap. 7, pp. 96–98.

Mainstream Judaism

The chief literary sources are the noncanonical books (the Apocrypha and the Pseudepigrapha) and the writings of the rabbis. The following is a composite of the main ideas about the Holy Spirit that are found in these writings.[12]

(1) "Holy Spirit" is an occasional title for the *Ruach* in the noncanonical books and a common term in the rabbinic literature.

(2) All the Old Testament writings are inspired by the Holy Spirit. The Spirit is, above all else, the Spirit of prophecy. There is no more inspired revelation comparable to the Old Testament, for prophetic revelation ceased with the closing of the canon with the last prophets (Haggai, Zechariah, Malachi).

(3) The Holy Spirit is given to those who live a life of obedience to God's will. But when a devout man sins, the Spirit leaves him.

(4) All the great figures of the Old Testament period were inspired by the Holy Spirit, not just the prophets.

(5) In the age to come, the Messiah will possess the Spirit. So will all the redeemed people of the Messianic Age. This will result in the moral renewal of God's people (Ezek. 36:26–27), and all God's people will be prophets (Joel 2:28–29).

(6) The Spirit is spoken of in personal terms and as separate from God. He is portrayed as speaking, warning, weeping, rejoicing, consoling, and so on. But these writings do not portray him as a member of the Godhead. The Spirit is personified, but he/it is not a person.

The Qumran Community

The now famous Dead Sea Scrolls were written and preserved by the Qumran community, a monastic-like Jewish

[12]Extracanonical and rabbinic sources for the points that follow are given in Erik Sjoberg, "*Ruach* in Palestinian Judaism" in *Theological Dictionary of the New Testament,* ed. Gerhard Kittel and Gerhard Friedrich, trans. Geoffrey W. Bromiley, 9 vols. (Grand Rapids: Wm. B. Eerdmans, 1964–74), 6:375–89. Hereafter referred to as *TDNT.*

group that withdrew to the Judean desert and settled near the Dead Sea in intertestamental times. The following summarizes the community's concept of the Holy Spirit as found in the scrolls:[13]

(1) Even though the term "Holy Spirit" occurs only three times in the Old Testament, it occurs much more frequently in these scrolls.

(2) He is not regarded as a person, much less as a member of the Godhead.[14]

(3) He is called the spirit of truth, of light, and of holiness.

(4) He is associated with the prophets, called "anointed ones," who make known God's purposes.

(5) He is the fount of knowledge. He enables the community to understand God's purposes revealed through the prophets.

(6) He is a guide and protector of faithful members of the community.

(7) He purifies from sin.

(8) He is defiled when God's people sin.

(9) He indwells the holy community of God's people.[15]

[13]These points are extracted from F. F. Bruce, "Holy Spirit in the Qumran Texts," in *Dead Sea Scrolls Studies* (Leiden, Netherlands: E. J. Brill, 1969), 49–55. Bruce gives appropriate documentation for points 3–9. For a more detailed study, see Alex R. G. Deasley, "The Holy Spirit in the Dead Sea Scrolls," *Wesleyan Theological Journal* 21(spring–fall 1986): 45–73.

[14]In this listing, I have used the masculine pronoun when referring to the Holy Spirit, even though the Qumranians did not think of Him in personal terms. In fact, from their standpoint it would even be improper to capitalize the words "holy spirit."

[15]For the interested reader, in this article Bruce points out parallels between the scrolls and the NT, as well as differences between the two.

Chapter 3

The Spirit and the Messiah

In the Old Testament, the Holy Spirit was often called "the Spirit of God" or "the Spirit of the LORD." In the New Testament, several titles indicate an intimate connection between Him and the Lord Jesus Christ. He is called "the Spirit of Jesus" (Acts 16:7), "the Spirit of Christ" (Rom. 8:9), and the Spirit of God's Son (Gal. 4:6). This close connection between the Holy Spirit and Jesus Christ, the Messiah, is worthy of examination.

The Prophecies in Isaiah

In addition to Old Testament promises of the Spirit for all believers, the Book of Isaiah contains four predictions which specifically link the Holy Spirit with the earthly ministry of the Messiah.

(1) "The Spirit of the LORD will rest on him—the Spirit of wisdom and of understanding, the Spirit of counsel and of power, the Spirit of knowledge and of the fear of the LORD" (11:2). The seven "of" phrases are often linked with John's references to "the seven spirits of God" (Rev. 3:1; 4:5; 5:6; see also 1:4). The Messiah will thus be enabled to render righteous judgments in His dealings with people (Isa. 11:3–5). This passage applies specifically to the millennial reign of Jesus but is applicable as well to His first-century appearance on earth, for the Holy Spirit rested on Him at

the time of His baptism (Matt. 3:16; John 1:32).

(2) In 42:1–4, the Messiah is called God's "servant" and God's "chosen one" upon whom God puts His Spirit (cf. Luke 3:22). It emphasizes the compassion of the Messiah for those in distress. Matthew quotes this passage in connection with the healing of the man with the withered hand and the resultant opposition from the Pharisees (Matt. 12:17–21).

(3) Isaiah 48:16 predicts that when the Messiah is sent to accomplish His work, both the Father and the Spirit are involved in that ministry. The translations vary, because of the ambivalence of the Hebrew grammar. For example:

"The Sovereign LORD has sent me, with his Spirit" (NIV). The meaning is unclear because of the comma. Does "with his Spirit" modify "the Sovereign LORD," or does it modify "me"? Very possibly the latter.

"The Lord GOD has sent [both] me and his spirit" (NRSV). Both the Messiah and the Spirit are sent by the Father.

"'The Lord GOD and His Spirit have sent Me'" (NKJV). Both the Father and the Spirit send the Son.

"'The Lord GOD has sent Me, and His Spirit [has sent me]'" (NASB). The comma suggests that both the Father and the Spirit send the Son.

(4) In the most comprehensive of these prophecies, the Messiah says in 61:1–2: "The Spirit of the Sovereign LORD is on me, because the LORD has anointed me to preach good news to the poor. He has sent me to bind up the brokenhearted, to proclaim freedom for the captives and release from darkness for the prisoners, to proclaim the year of the LORD's favor." At the outset of His public ministry in Luke 4:16–22, Jesus read this passage at a synagogue service in Nazareth and then declared, "'Today this scripture is fulfilled in your hearing'" (v. 21).

The Earthly Jesus

The Holy Spirit was mightily at work in the Lord Jesus Christ from the time of His conception in the womb of

Mary to His resurrection from the dead.[1] During the years of His earthly life, Jesus was both fully God and fully man; this section of the chapter will look at Jesus as a man.

His Virginal Conception

The conception of Jesus is often called the Virgin Birth, but my purpose here is to emphasize the activity of the Spirit upon Mary at the time she conceived the Messiah. The angel said to her, "'The Holy Spirit will come upon you, and the power of the Most High will overshadow you. So the holy one to be born will be called the Son of God'" (Luke 1:35). Matthew states that Mary "was found to be with child through the Holy Spirit" (Matt. 1:18) and that the angel said to Joseph, "'What is conceived in her is from the Holy Spirit'" (1:20).

The Holy Spirit was at work in the Man Jesus from the moment He was conceived. He had no human father, a fulfillment of the prophecy given by Isaiah that "'the virgin will be with child and will give birth to a son, and will call him Immanuel'" (7:14). This miraculous event, according to the prophecy, was a sign the Lord would give to His people.

His Baptism

Jesus was anointed by the Holy Spirit at the time of His baptism by John. The Spirit descended on Him in the bodily form of a dove (Luke 3:22). This calls to mind the activity of the Spirit in creation (Gen. 1:2), where He is likened to a hovering bird. There is added significance in likening the Holy Spirit to a dove. The dove was a symbol of innocence and harmlessness (Matt. 10:16); this would be most appropriate on the occasion of Jesus' baptism because John the Baptist referred to him twice as the "'Lamb of God'" (John 1:29,36). The sinless, spotless Lamb was visited by the innocent, harmless Dove!

[1]See the excellent article by John O'Donnell,"In Him and Over Him: The Holy Spirit in the Life of Jesus," *Gregorianum* 70, no. 1 (1989): 25–45.

Anointing was a common practice among the Jews. It marked the beginning of a person's service to God, indicating that God had set him aside for a special work and would provide the necessary power to fulfill his mission. Jesus is here at the outset of His public ministry, and His Father indicates His approval by saying, "'You are my Son, whom I love; with you I am well pleased'" (Luke 3:22).

"Messiah" is the transliteration of the Hebrew word *mashiach,* which means "anointed one." Likewise, the designation "Christ" is a title, more than a name, for the Son of God. It comes from the Greek *Christos,* which also means "anointed one." The two titles may be used interchangeably (John 1:41). The angel had indicated that the Babe of Bethlehem was "'Christ the Lord'" (Luke 2:11), but not until His baptism could Jesus properly be called Christ. Thereafter, the Spirit remained on Him (John 1:33), and furthermore He experienced the Spirit in unrestricted measure (John 3:34).

Did the Son of God need the anointing of the Holy Spirit in order to fulfill His mission? Could He not, by His own inherent deity, perform all the works necessary to accomplish His purpose? The eternal Son of God never relinquished His deity, even when He united himself with a human nature.[2] The apostle Paul helps our understanding of this problem when he says that Christ Jesus, "being in very nature God, did not consider equality with God something to be grasped, but made himself nothing, taking the very nature of a servant, being made in human likeness" (Phil. 2:6–7). Different opinions exist on the exact interpretation of this passage, but the basic idea is that the Son of God willingly and deliberately chose to limit himself while here on earth. He did not cease to be God, but He elected to live as a man relying on the power of the Spirit to sustain Him and help Him in His work for God.

[2]A discussion of the "hypostatic union"—that the God-man Jesus Christ has two natures, fully divine and fully human, but that He is one person—is beyond the scope of this chapter.

His Temptation in the Wilderness

Immediately following His baptism, Jesus was led by the Spirit into the Judean wilderness (Matt. 4:1; Luke 4:1). Mark says more forcefully that the Spirit "impelled Him to go out into the wilderness" (Mark 1:12, NASB). Jesus was a man completely dominated and guided by the Holy Spirit, even when it meant forty days of hunger, loneliness, and temptation. It was there that Jesus, "full of the Holy Spirit" (Luke 4:1), encountered the arch evil spirit, Satan.

It is often emphasized, and rightly, that Jesus overcame Satan's temptations by quoting the Word of God. But it is important to see that this had to be done in the power of the Spirit. Undoubtedly, the Spirit helped Jesus to recall the appropriate Scripture passages to effectively silence the tempter. As Paul teaches, spiritual warfare must be fought with spiritual weapons (Eph. 6:11–18). Among these weapons are "the sword of the Spirit, which is the word of God" and praying "in the Spirit on all occasions with all kinds of prayers and requests" (vv. 17–18).

Christians are also God's anointed ones (2 Cor. 1:21–22). John, in his first epistle, emphasizes that Christians have an anointing, or unction, from God that will enable them to combat erroneous teaching, because the Spirit himself will enlighten their understanding (1 John 2:20). He says that this anointing "teaches you about all things" and that it is "real, not counterfeit" (v. 27).

As in the case of Jesus, God by His Spirit may lead believers into a time of severe testing. But like Jesus, they can emerge triumphant by relying for help on His Spirit and His Word.

His Mighty Works

The Gospels record a succession of miracles performed by Jesus—healings, demon expulsions, raisings from the dead. While the Gospel writers do not always attribute these works directly to the power of the Spirit, we have already seen how both the Isaianic prophecies and Jesus himself made general statements to that effect.[3]

Following the wilderness temptation, Jesus "returned to Galilee in the power of the Spirit" (Luke 4:14). He then launched into His public ministry. Peter, in his message to the household of Cornelius, said that "'God anointed Jesus of Nazareth with the Holy Spirit and power'" and that He "'went around doing good and healing all who were under the power of the devil, because God was with him'" (Acts 10:38; see also 4:27).

One outstanding example of this ministry of deliverance from the power of the devil is the casting out of a demon from a blind, mute man (Matt. 12:22–30). The Pharisees insisted that Jesus had performed this and similar miracles by the power of Satan. But Jesus responded that Satan does not cast out Satan, and went on to insist that He cast out demons "'by the Spirit of God'" (v. 28).

The Book of Acts records many instances of miracles wrought by the hands of the disciples. Jesus had promised, "'Anyone who has faith in me will do what I have been doing. He will do even greater things than these, because I am going to the Father'" (John 14:12). Immediately after that statement He spoke of the coming of the Holy Spirit. Just prior to His ascension to the Father, He again promised, "'You will receive power when the Holy Spirit comes on you; and you will be my witnesses'" (Acts 1:8). The means by which the disciples witnessed included the "greater" works that validated the verbal claims they made about Jesus. Hebrews 2:3–4 makes a clear connection between the preaching of the gospel and the accompanying manifestations of the power of God: "How shall we escape if we ignore such a great salvation? This salvation, which was first announced by the Lord, was confirmed to us by those who heard him. God also testified to it by signs,

[3]Yet it is an extreme position to maintain that Jesus, while on earth, performed every one of His works only as a man enabled by the Holy Spirit. Certainly His forgiving of sins (Mark 2:5–7) was the result of His own inherent deity, without the mediation of the Holy Spirit. The same could be said of "nature" miracles such as the stilling of the tempest and the feeding of the five thousand.

wonders and various miracles, and gifts of the Holy Spirit distributed according to His will."

His Death

Christ "through [*dia,* "by means of"] the eternal Spirit offered himself unblemished to God" (Heb. 9:14). It was through the power of the Spirit that Jesus accomplished every phase of His ministry. Now His crowning work—His atoning death on the Cross—is also associated with the enabling power of the Spirit.[4]

His Resurrection

The Holy Spirit participated in the stupendous miracle of the resurrection of Jesus from the dead. Paul declares that Jesus "through the Spirit of holiness was declared with power to be the Son of God by his resurrection from the dead" (Rom. 1:4;[5] see also 8:11). He says elsewhere that Jesus was "vindicated by the Spirit" (1 Tim. 3:16). The claims of Jesus to be the Son of God were vindicated, or justified, by the mighty operation of the Spirit of God in raising Him from the dead. Had Jesus remained in the grave, His claims to deity would have been negated. In addition, Peter says that Christ "was put to death in the body but made alive by the Spirit" (1 Pet. 3:18).

The Spirit not only quickened the lifeless body of Jesus; He also transformed it from a natural, physical body to a spiritual body (1 Cor. 15:44–45). It was because of this

[4]O'Donnell, "In Him" (36), argues that when Jesus on the cross "bowed his head and gave up his spirit" (John 19:30), the correct understanding is that Jesus gave up the Holy Spirit, with whom He had been endued. A strict translation does allow for the rendering "gave up the S/spirit." The meaning would then be that Jesus surrendered, or returned, the Holy Spirit to the Father, because He no longer needed the Spirit's enabling. Luke, however, records Jesus as saying, "'Father, into your hands I commit my spirit'" (23:46). The possessive pronoun *mou* (my) is in the Gk. text. The simplest and surely correct interpretation is that the death of Jesus meant the separation of His body from His human spirit, which He was returning to God.

[5]The phrase "Spirit of holiness" is the Heb. way of saying "Holy Spirit."

change that the risen Lord could appear to the disciples even though they were behind locked doors (John 20:19).

The Risen Lord

During His earthly life, Jesus' relation to the Holy Spirit was one of dependence; in order to fulfill His mission, He needed to be anointed by the Spirit. But following His resurrection, a change occurred in the roles of these two Persons of the Godhead. As the risen Lord, Jesus is the one who sends the Spirit to His waiting disciples.

From the beginning of His public ministry, the Gospels indicate that such a change was to take place. At His baptism, the Spirit came upon Jesus empowering Him for His work. The Father himself told John the Baptist that this One upon whom the Spirit descended was also the One who would baptize in the Holy Spirit (John 1:32–33). He to whom the Spirit was sent would become the Sender of the Spirit!

There is an inversion of roles in the relationship of the Son to the Holy Spirit. The Son is no longer passive to the Spirit's impulses but actively pours out the Spirit upon the Church.[6] The Gospel of John records the promises of Jesus to send the Spirit. Jesus said, "'It is for your good that I am going away. Unless I go away, the Counselor will not come to you; but if I go, I will send him to you'" (John 16:7). The coming of the Spirit on the Day of Pentecost was evidence that Jesus had indeed ascended to the Father. Peter, when defending his Lord, said of Him: "'Exalted to the right hand of God, he has received from the Father the promised Holy Spirit and has poured out what you now see and hear'" (Acts 2:33).

Jesus had promised to send the Paraclete (John 15:26) to be His earthly representative. The Holy Spirit is separate from the Lord Jesus Christ, but He always works together with Him. He does nothing on His own authority (John 16:13–14). John tells of three activities of the Holy Spirit as they relate specifically to Christ:

[6]O'Donnell, "In Him," 38.

(1) He will remind the disciples of everything Jesus said (John 14:26).

(2) He will testify concerning Jesus (15:26). When Peter preached Christ before the Sanhedrin, he concluded by saying, "'We are witnesses of these things, and so is the Holy Spirit, whom God has given to those who obey him'" (Acts 5:32). The three primary means by which the Holy Spirit bears witness to Christ are (a) verbal communication of the Word, whether by preaching, teaching, or informal conversation; (b) signs and wonders; and (c) the godly lives of believers.

(3) He will glorify Jesus (John 16:13–14). In other words, He will direct attention to Jesus. The test of any true work of the Spirit is whether it draws attention to the Lord. The King James rendering of verse 13 ("He shall not speak of himself") is often misunderstood to mean that the Holy Spirit will not speak *concerning* himself. This cannot be the true meaning, since we know that the Scriptures, which the Spirit himself inspired, say much about the Spirit. The NIV gives a correct understanding of the Greek text: "'He will not speak on his own.'" The NASB adds the word "initiative." A strict translation would read, "He will not speak from himself." Jesus was talking about the *source,* not the *content,* of what the Spirit would say.[7]

One further matter belongs to this section: the incident of the resurrected Jesus breathing on the disciples (John 20:19–23), and especially the meaning of His words, "'Receive the Holy Spirit'" (v. 22).[8]

Subordination of the Spirit

Some statements in Scripture about the Holy Spirit may give the impression that He is not equal to the Father or the Son. We have already noted some of the statements made by Jesus himself, such as: "'whom the Father will send in

[7]The Gk. phrase is *aph' heautou,* the preposition being a genitive/ablative of source.

[8]Discussion of this passage is given in part 2 of this book, chap. 8, pp. 112–15.

my name'" (John 14:26); "'whom I will send to you from the Father, the Spirit of truth who goes out from the Father'" (15:26); "'I will send him to you'" (16:7); "'he will not speak on his own'" (John 16:13).

It is important to distinguish between the ideas of subordination and inferiority. The Spirit is not inferior to the Father or the Son. All three Persons are equally God; there is no difference as to their *essence* or *nature*. But there are differences in their *functions*. All three work together harmoniously, but each also has separate functions. The Spirit is sometimes called the Executive of the Godhead because through Him God's blessings and presence are mediated to people.

An analogy will help to clarify this point, though we must remember that an analogy cannot be applied in every particular. All persons are created in the image of God; therefore, as far as the innermost nature is concerned, no one is inferior to anyone else, even though one person may be subordinate to another in a given situation. So it is in the relationship between the Spirit on the one hand and the Father and the Son on the other.

Chapter 4

The Spirit and the Church

The Holy Spirit and the Church are inseparable. Wherever the true Church is, there is also the Holy Spirit at work. In its fullest sense, the Church did not come into existence until the Day of Pentecost, because it was on that occasion that the Spirit came upon the assembled body of believers.[1]

The New Testament employs two figures of speech which depict this connection between the Spirit and the Church: a temple and a body. The temple metaphor stresses the relationship between the Church and God, and the body metaphor the relationship of the Church to fellow believers and unbelievers.

The Temple of the Holy Spirit

The Church is likened to a building—and more specifically, a temple. As 1 Corinthians 3:16–17 shows, the terms "temple of the Holy Spirit" and "temple of God" are interchangeable. Paul's writings contain several direct references to this imagery.

The New Testament Evidence

Perhaps the most familiar passage is 1 Corinthians 6:19, in which Paul is talking about the individual Christian, not

[1]The purpose of this chap. is to explore the relationship between the Holy Spirit and the Church. It cannot, for obvious reasons, be a comprehensive discussion of the Church.

the entire Church, when he says, "Do you not know that your body [singular] is a temple of the Holy Spirit, who is in you, whom you have received from God?" His appeal is to personal purity of life, as the context indicates.

But three other Pauline passages speak of all Christians collectively forming one temple:

(1) "Don't you know that you yourselves are God's temple and that God's Spirit lives in you? If anyone destroys God's temple, God will destroy him; for God's temple is sacred, and you are that temple" (1 Cor. 3:16–17). The warning is directed at any individual who does harm, or attempts to do harm, to the Church, as the first part of the chapter shows.[2]

(2) Paul, in calling God's people to be separate from all that is evil, says: "What agreement is there between the temple of God and idols? For we are[3] the temple of the living God. As God has said, 'I will live with them and walk among them'" (2 Cor. 6:16).

(3) In another passage, he says that in Christ "the whole building is joined together and rises to become a holy temple in the Lord. And in him you too are being built together to become a dwelling in which God lives by his Spirit" (Eph. 2:21–22).

Peter also uses this symbolism, but does not use the word "temple." He says, "You also, like living stones, are being built into a spiritual house to be a holy priesthood, offering spiritual sacrifices acceptable to God through Jesus Christ" (1 Pet. 2:5).

The Old Testament Background

The Church as the temple of the Holy Spirit is the fulfillment of what God instituted in the Old Testament in both the tabernacle and the temple. When the tabernacle was first set up, we are told:

> Then the cloud covered the Tent of Meeting, and the glory of the LORD filled the tabernacle. Moses could not enter the

[2]Note that v. 9 says, "You [pl.] are . . . God's building."

[3]The variant reading "you [pl.] are" is unimportant for this discussion.

> Tent of Meeting because the cloud had settled upon it, and the glory of the LORD filled the tabernacle (Exod. 40:34–35).

Similarly, when Solomon's temple was dedicated, we read:

> When the priests withdrew from the Holy Place, the cloud filled the temple of the LORD. And the priests could not perform their service because of the cloud, for the glory of the LORD filled his temple (1 Kings 8:10–11; see also 2 Chron. 5:13–14; 7:1–2).

Even though God is everywhere present, He chooses at times to manifest His presence in one place in a very special way. We may refer to the tabernacle and the temple as places of the localization, or focalization, of God's presence. He elected to dwell there in this special manner. This particular manifestation of himself is sometimes called the "Shekinah"[4]—a Hebrew word meaning "dwelling place," which is sometimes used as a synonym for this demonstration of God's glory.

I have already mentioned that the Holy Spirit is the means by which God makes His presence known. Two passages in the Psalms clearly bring this out. In Hebrew poetry the writer often states the same truth in two different ways, a poetic device called parallelism. The following passages show that "Holy Spirit" and "God's presence" may be used interchangeably:

> Do not cast me from your presence or take your Holy Spirit from me (Ps. 51:11). Where can I go from your Spirit? Where can I flee from your presence (Ps. 139:7)?

When the Lord Jesus Christ was on earth, He was the special manifestation and focalization of God's presence among humankind. "The Word became flesh and made his dwelling ["tabernacled"][5] among us. We have seen his glory, the glory of the One and Only, who came from the Father, full of grace and truth" (John 1:14). Jesus himself

[4]This is not a biblical term, though the concept is.

[5]The Gk. verb *eskēnōsen (skēnoō)* is the verbal form of the nouns *skēnē/skēnos/skēnōma* ("tent, booth, lodging"). In most NT passages, *skēnē* refers to the OT tabernacle or Tent of Meeting (Acts 7:44; Heb. 8:2,5; 9:2–3,6,8,11,21; 13:10; Rev. 15:5).

referred to His body as "'this temple'" (2:19). He had come to fulfill the Law; therefore His coming superseded the Old Testament temple and tabernacle.

This recalls the words of Paul and Peter previously quoted. The Church is now the true temple of God, indwelt by the Holy Spirit. God's presence is not bound to a physical building. Stephen reminded his persecutors of this when he said, "'The Most High does not live in houses made by men'" (Acts 7:48). And Paul in idolatry-ridden Athens declared, "'The God who made the world and everything in it . . . does not live in temples built by hands'" (17:24). Even the prophet Isaiah was given this message for God's people, centuries before the coming of Jesus (Isa. 66:1–2).

We return to the important thought that it is a spiritual temple, the Church, which is now the special dwelling place of God on earth. When did this change from the literal tabernacle and temple to the spiritual temple, the Church, as God's dwelling place on earth take place? It was on the Day of Pentecost. Luke does not tell where the disciples were when the Spirit was poured out; he simply says they were "in one place" (Acts 2:1). Many infer from 1:13 that this place was the Upper Room.[6]

But it is also possible that they were in the temple area. Luke ends his Gospel by saying that after the disciples returned to Jerusalem following Jesus' ascension, "they stayed continually at the temple, praising God" (Luke 24:53). We know from other passages in Acts that even after Pentecost the disciples went to the temple to pray (2:46; 3:1). It would be very appropriate indeed if the Lord chose the site of the physical temple as the place where His spiritual temple would be actualized![7]

[6]The question must be raised, "How could the hearers below distinguish different languages that were being spoken in the Upper Room?"

[7]This viewpoint is not without its difficulties, however. The record says that they were sitting (*kathēmai*—Acts 2:2). This verb may in a very limited number of places mean "stay, be, live, reside, settle" (Matt. 4:16; Luke 1:79; 21:35; Rev. 14:6), but in the preponderance of occurrences it has the basic meaning of "sit." The same may be said of this verb's synonym (*kathizō*), which has the meaning of "settle, stay, live" in two passages (Luke 24:49;

PRIESTHOOD OF BELIEVERS

The temple was staffed with priests, a select corps of men who represented the people before God. Much of their work involved the offering of sacrifices on behalf of the people.

"The universal priesthood of all believers" was a watchword of the Protestant Reformation in the sixteenth century. Martin Luther taught, as the Scriptures teach, that every Christian has direct access to God. The Lord Jesus Christ is the only Mediator (1 Tim. 2:5). Paul says that through Christ both Jews and Gentiles "have access to the Father by one Spirit" (Eph. 2:18). This verse is especially interesting because immediately after it, Paul talks about the spiritual temple. So the Spirit establishes direct contact between God and believers. And because this is a work of the Holy Spirit, Peter can refer to all believers as "a holy priesthood" (1 Pet. 2:5). He goes on in verse 9 to speak of Christians as "a royal priesthood"—a thought echoed in the Book of Revelation where the idea of priesthood is linked with that of reigning with Christ (1:6; 5:10; 20:6).

The spiritual priesthood of the spiritual temple must therefore offer spiritual sacrifices acceptable to God (1 Pet. 2:5). The New Testament clearly mentions three[8] such sacrifices:

(1) Our Bodies. The one supreme Sacrifice was crucified on the cross, so that God no longer wishes dead sacrifices to be offered to Him; he now seeks living sacrifices. Paul speaks of this when he says, "I urge you, brothers, in view of God's mercy, to offer your bodies as living sacrifices, holy and pleasing to God—this is your spiritual act of worship" (Rom. 12:1).

(2) Our Praise. Animal sacrifices were made daily in the temple, so that there was a continual burning of their bodies with the resultant smoke and aroma ascending to God.

Acts 18:11), with the meaning "sit"predominating elsewhere. However, the word "house" is sometimes used as a synonym for the temple (for example, 2 Sam. 7:5,13; 1 Chron. 22:6; Acts 7:47).

[8]The apostle Paul mentioned a fourth spiritual sacrifice, resulting from the ministry God had given him: The Gentiles who came to Christ through his ministry would become "an offering acceptable to God, sanctified by the Holy Spirit" (Rom. 15:16).

Against this backdrop, Christians are told to "continually offer to God a sacrifice of praise—the fruit of lips that confess his name" (Heb. 13:15).

(3) Our Good Works. "And do not forget to do good and to share with others, for with such sacrifices God is pleased" (Heb. 13:16). Paul commends the Philippians for sending him things that helped to ease the hardships of prison life, characterizing them as "a fragrant offering, an acceptable sacrifice, pleasing to God" (Phil. 4:18).

A Body Animated by the Spirit

Unlike the idea of the temple, the metaphor of the Church as a body, and in particular the body of Christ, is not based on anything in the Old Testament. Furthermore, Paul is the only New Testament writer who employs this analogy. It is one of the most meaningful ways of speaking about the Church. The key passages are Romans 12:3–8; 1 Corinthians 12:12–27; and Ephesians 4:4–13. Each of them links the idea of the Church as a body with the work of the Holy Spirit.[9] Just as a human body can exist only when there is breath to sustain its life, so Christ's body, the Church, can exist only when there is the energizing of the Holy Spirit.

The Spirit Constitutes the Church

"For we were all baptized by[10] one Spirit into one body" (1 Cor. 12:13; see also Rom. 6:3; 12:5; Gal. 3:27). At the moment of conversion, one becomes a member of this body. The person is saved as an individual but is immediately incorporated into the body of Christ by the operation of the Holy Spirit.

[9]Other passages, of course, use the Body image for the Church (especially in Col. and elsewhere in Eph.), but our concern here is the link between the Body and the Holy Spirit.

[10]For a discussion of the appropriateness of the translation "by" rather than "in," see part 2, chap. 7, pp. 100–105.

HE ADDS TO THE CHURCH

Not only is the Spirit the inner life of the Church, He also adds new members continually to the Body. He accomplishes this by working through God's people. The apostle John records, "The Spirit and the bride [another metaphor for the Church] say, 'Come!' . . . and whoever wishes, let him take the free gift of the water of life" (Rev. 22:17).

The Book of Acts is a running commentary on this point. Only by the power of the Holy Spirit were the disciples able to witness effectively (Acts 1:8). As a result of the Spirit-inspired preaching of Peter (2:14),[11] his listeners were "cut to the heart [convicted by the Holy Spirit]" (2:37), resulting in the addition of three thousand souls to the Church that day (2:41). Luke states further that "the Lord added to their number daily those who were being saved" (2:47).

Human instrumentality in the furtherance of God's work cannot be overemphasized. God could have ordained it otherwise, sovereignly deciding that people would be saved by the direct, unmediated work of the Holy Spirit. But He has chosen to use believers, as they yield to the Spirit, to be instrumental in adding other members to the body of Christ. Just as the Lord Jesus Christ needed a physical body to fulfill God's redemptive plan for humankind, so now the implementation of that plan takes place through His spiritual Body, the Church.

HE UNITES THE BODY

The Holy Spirit is the only true Agent in achieving genuine unity among Christians. Paul told the Christians at Ephesus to "make every effort to keep the unity of the Spirit through the bond of peace." He then added the significant statement, "There is one body and one Spirit" (Eph. 4:3–4). The church at Corinth was guilty of fragmenting itself because of several competing elements in the con-

[11]For a discussion of the term *apophthengomai,* see part 2, chap. 9, p. 141.

gregation, each claiming allegiance to a specific individual. Paul is compelled to ask them, "Is Christ divided?" (1 Cor. 1:13). Because of this divisive spirit in the congregation, he tells them that they are carnal[12] (3:1–4). Anything that is opposed to the work of the Spirit is carnal; that is, Christians who do not permit the Spirit of God to control them in their relationships with other Christians are dominated by their lower, unsanctified nature—which the Scriptures often call "the flesh" (see Rom. 8:5–9,13; and Gal. 5:16–26, NASB).

All who have been born again by the Spirit are members of the one Body, even though this may not always be outwardly evident. God's Word appeals to Christians to demonstrate among themselves and to the world that this unity is indeed a reality. This is achieved only when Christians are "completely humble and gentle" and are "patient, bearing with one another in love" (Eph. 4:2). One important factor in the success of the Apostolic Church is found in the Greek word *homothumadon,* which means "with one mind, or purpose, or impulse"[13] (Acts 1:14; 2:46; 4:24; 15:25; see also 2:1 for a related word). Without this unity among themselves, the early Christians would not have experienced the presence and power of God in their midst and in their witnessing.

He Appoints Members of the Body for Specific Functions

All of 1 Corinthians 12 is a commentary on members of the Body being appointed for specific functions by the

[12]NIV has "worldly" for the adjectives *sarkinoi* (1 Cor. 3:1) and *sarkikoi* (v. 3). NASB reads "men of flesh" (v. 1) and "fleshly" (v. 3). The meaning of both words in these verses is "fleshly, belonging to the realm of the flesh," according to Walter Bauer, *A Greek-English Lexicon of the New Testament and Other Early Christian Literature,* translated by William F. Arndt and F. Wilbur Gingrich; 2d ed. of translation revised and augmented by F. Wilbur Gingrich and Frederick W. Danker (Chicago: University of Chicago Press, 1979), 742–43. Hereafter referred to as BAGD.

[13]BAGD, 566.

Spirit. The following are some important lessons to be drawn from it.[14]

(1) There is wide diversity in the gifts and functions that the Spirit assigns to individual members. The operations that are often called "the gifts of the Spirit" range from a word of wisdom to the interpretation of tongues (1 Cor. 12:8–10). Paul also includes as gifts ministries associated with leadership: apostles, prophets, evangelists, pastors, teachers (vv. 28–30; Eph. 4:8,10–12). In Romans, he lists additional gifts, such as service, exhortation, liberality, and mercifulness (12:7–8).[15]

(2) All members of the Body possess some gift. "To each one the manifestation of the Spirit is given" (1 Cor. 12:7). No Christian can say, "I have no function in the Body of Christ." Just as every member of our physical bodies has an appointed task, so every member of Christ's Body has some vital function for the well-being of the Body. No useful purpose is served by one person wishing for someone else's gift or talent. All members must determine for themselves, prayerfully, what function the Lord wants them to serve in the Body.

(3) The Spirit distributes the gifts sovereignly; "He gives them to each one, just as he determines" (1 Cor. 12:11). Paul says further, "God has arranged the parts in the body, every one of them, just as he wanted them to be" (v. 18). He repeats the same idea when he says in Romans that "we have different gifts, according to the grace given us" (Rom. 12:6). Christians must place themselves in a position to be used by the Holy Spirit and to receive spiritual gifts, but the bestowal of specific gifts is the prerogative of the Spirit. God, in his wisdom and for reasons not always disclosed to us, grants to others gifts which we ourselves might like to manifest.

(4) All members of the Body are interdependent. "The eye cannot say to the hand, 'I don't need you!' And the head cannot say to the feet, 'I don't need you!'" (1 Cor. 12:21). No member may consider itself superior to other

[14]For a further discussion of the body of Christ and spiritual gifts, see part 3.

[15]See part 3 for a treatment of the individual spiritual gifts.

members. There are two main reasons for this: (a) Such a "superior" member cannot exist in isolation from the other members (even the "inferior" members) any more than one's "superior" head can exist in isolation from one's "inferior" hands, which supply food for one's "inferior" stomach, which provides nourishment for the entire body, including the head. (b) The gifts are not distributed on the basis of personal merit; they are distributed sovereignly by God. This immediately rules out any grounds for boasting.

(5) All the members share in the joys or sorrows of any one member. "If one part suffers, every part suffers with it; if one part is honored, every part rejoices with it" (1 Cor. 12:26). When a person's ear aches, the entire body suffers. When beautiful music falls on one's ears, it is not only the ears that are delighted; the entire body enjoys it. So it is, ideally, in the body of Christ. Someone has expressed it well: "Our sorrows are divided and our joys are multiplied."

(6) The overarching purpose for the divine bestowal of the different gifts on the members of the Body is the edification or building up of the Church. "To each one the manifestation of the Spirit is given for the common good" (1 Cor. 12:7). Even though at times the gifts, talents, and ministries that God by His Spirit grants may edify the individual manifesting them, they are primarily for the strengthening and edification of the Church. In addition, they may minister to the needs of unbelievers (for example: evangelists, healings, miracles).

The Fellowship of the Spirit

Paul uses the expression "the fellowship *[koinōnia]* of the Holy Spirit" (2 Cor. 13:14; cf. Phil. 2:1). This concept is inseparable from that of the Church as the body of Christ. *Koinōnia* may also be translated "communion" or "participation." There are two basic, but not mutually exclusive, interpretations of the phrase "the fellowship of the Holy Spirit." One is that it means the partaking of the Holy Spirit by Christians.[16] The other refers to the work of the Spirit

[16]The partitive genitive.

that forms Christians into a community or a fellowship.[17]

Both interpretations have a firm basis in Scripture, and one is impossible without the other. It is because repentant sinners have partaken of the Holy Spirit (1 Cor. 12:13; Heb. 6:4) that they are privileged to enter the fellowship created by Him—the Church. This idea of the fellowship of the Spirit is not found in the Old Testament, however, because only selected individuals partook of the Spirit prior to the outpouring on the Day of Pentecost.

[17]A genitive/ablative of source, or the subjective genitive.

Chapter 5

The Spirit and the Believer

Jesus in His earthly state was a Man completely controlled by the Holy Spirit. From the time of His miraculous conception to His resurrection from the dead and exaltation at the right hand of the Father, the Spirit of God was mightily at work in Him. So it ought to be with a Christian; from beginning to end the Christian life is possible only by the power of the indwelling Holy Spirit.

This chapter will trace the activity of the Spirit in a believer's experience from new birth to resurrection from the dead.

The Spirit and the Sinner

Unregenerate people are spiritually dead in their trespasses and sins (Eph. 2:1), and consequently insensitive to spiritual things. Only when the Holy Spirit moves upon them can they become aware of their spiritual need. They must then decide whether to continue in their sinful state or to respond positively to the voice of the Spirit. The Book of Acts throughout gives a very graphic picture of this. Some, like Stephen's opponents, resist the Holy Spirit (Acts 7:51); others, like the three thousand on the Day of Pentecost, accept Peter's Spirit-anointed message (2:41).

The Conviction of the Spirit

Jesus told His disciples that when the Holy Spirit came, He would "'convict the world of guilt in regard to sin and righteousness and judgment'" (John 16:8). The word "convict" might better be translated "convince."

The Spirit convinces sinful persons of their spiritual need; mere logic or rhetoric cannot persuade them. The basic sin of humankind is rejection of Jesus Christ (John 16:9); this rejection is due to a failure to admit one's sinful state and to believe in Him who alone can effect the needed change.

The Spirit will further convince of righteousness (John 16:10). This is related to Jesus' resurrection and His ascension to the Father—events demonstrating that He was indeed the Son of God and that His claims were righteous, or justified (Rom. 1:4; 1 Tim. 3:16). This concept of righteousness also involves the idea of the "rightness" of God in punishing unrepentant sinners (Rom. 1:18). But it also includes the justification of sinners—their "right-standing" before God when they repent and believe (Rom. 4:25).[1]

Finally, the Spirit will convince of judgment (John 16:11). The prince of this world, Satan, suffered a series of crushing defeats at the hands of Jesus, which culminated in Jesus' resurrection from the dead. Jesus defeated Satan in the wilderness (Matt. 4:1–11; Mark 1:12–13; Luke 4:1–13). He defeated him further in demon expulsions and in healings (Acts 10:38). Satan has already been judged, and every sinner who truly believes in Jesus Christ serves as a continuing evidence of this defeat of Satan.

The Means of Conviction

Conviction of sin comes only by the Holy Spirit. But only rarely does He bypass human instrumentality in speaking to the hearts of sinful people. The means He uses is the message of the gospel delivered by faithful witnesses, for which Paul stresses a need in Romans 10:9–17.

The Book of Acts chronicles the message of the Early

[1]An unusual interpretation of the Spirit convincing men "'of righteousness'" is that it is their self-righteousness of which He convinces them, just as in the preceding phrase the words "'of sin'" mean their own sin and in the following phrase the words "'of judgment'" mean their own condemnation (see John 16:9–11, NKJV).

Church. It consisted basically of the message of Jesus Christ as the Savior and the need to believe in Him on the basis of His death and resurrection, lest the judgment of God come upon the hearers if they reject Him. The result of this kind of Spirit-inspired witnessing was that people were "cut to the heart" and asked, "'What shall we do?'" (Acts 2:37).

The Holy Spirit alone can convict and convince people of their need for salvation. The believers' responsibility is to declare and share the message of salvation, and to leave the results in the Lord's hands as He speaks to hearts by His Spirit. Paul's words on this point are so appropriate that he needs to be heard at length:

> When I came to you, brothers, I did not come with eloquence or superior wisdom as I proclaimed to you the testimony about God. For I resolved to know nothing while I was with you except Jesus Christ and him crucified. I came to you in weakness and fear, and with much trembling. My message and my preaching were not with wise and persuasive words, but with a demonstration of the Spirit's power, so that your faith might not rest on men's wisdom, but on God's power (1 Cor. 2:1–5).

On occasion God may choose to speak to a sinner's heart by the manifestation of some spiritual gift, very often a prophetic utterance. Paul says that through prophecy a sinner may be "convinced" and "judged" by all and thus "the secrets of his heart will be laid bare. So he will fall down and worship God, exclaiming, 'God is really among you!'" (1 Cor. 14:24–25).

Salvation

Terminology

The work of salvation is so comprehensive that the New Testament writers present it in a number of different ways, each way highlighting a special facet. A number of these are specifically related to the work of the Spirit.

Regeneration

Jesus told Nicodemus, "'No one can enter the kingdom of God unless he is born of water and the Spirit. Flesh gives birth to flesh, but the Spirit gives birth to spirit'" (John 3:5–6). Peter says that believers are partakers of, or participate in, the divine nature (2 Pet. 1:4); and Hebrews 6:4 says that believers are partakers of, or have a share in, the Holy Spirit.

One can see some similarity[2] to the conception and birth of Jesus. He was conceived by the Holy Spirit; it was a miraculous work. It was impossible for the Virgin Birth to occur through human effort. So it is with the new birth; it can be explained only in terms of a miracle. It is a mystery that can be experienced, but the precise manner in which it takes place defies explanation. Jesus indicated this when He said, "'The wind blows wherever it pleases. You hear its sound, but you cannot tell where it comes from or where it is going. So it is with everyone born of the Spirit'" (John 3:8).

Paul's speaking of "the washing of rebirth and renewal by the Holy Spirit" (Titus 3:5) parallels Jesus' statement about being "'born of water and the Spirit'" (John 3:5). There are a number of interpretations concerning what Jesus meant by "'water,'" but it is very possible that He used water as a symbol for the Holy Spirit, just as He did when speaking of rivers of living water (John 7:37–39). The word "and" (Gk. *kai*) in the phrase "'water and the Spirit'" in John 3:5 can be translated, alternatively, as "even," "namely," "that is," so that Jesus could be saying, "unless he is born of water—that is, the Spirit."[3]

[2]I hesitate to use a stronger word such as "analogy" or "paradigm."

[3]Other significant interpretations understand the water to be (1) baptism; (2) a symbol for the Word of God; (3) the amniotic fluid which surrounds a fetus. My very brief response to each of these alternatives: (1) Given the importance the NT assigns to baptism, one should not dismiss this interpretation out of hand. But neither can one insist on the absolute necessity of baptism for salvation. (2) The Word of God is indispensable for salvation. Yet it is difficult to see why in the words "'water and the Spirit'" Jesus would use the first word symbolically and the second literally. He could more easily have said "the Word and the Spirit." (3) The amniotic fluid does not produce the birth of the child. Furthermore, Jesus contrasts the Spirit with the flesh, not with water (John 3:6).

Another alternative is to regard "'water and the Spirit'" as a hendiadys—"spiritual water."

Spiritual Resurrection and the New Creation

Closely related to the term "regeneration" are the terms "spiritual resurrection" and "new creation." All three emphasize the idea of new life. I have already noted the Holy Spirit in His work of creation and the raising of Jesus from the dead. The sinner is spiritually dead and needs to be spiritually resurrected (Eph. 2:1–2; Col. 3:1–2). Viewed from another angle, the sinner must be created anew (2 Cor. 5:17; Gal. 6:15).

Along the same lines, Paul says that the unregenerate have been spiritually blinded by Satan but that "God, who said, 'Let light shine out of darkness,' made his light shine in our hearts to give us the light of the knowledge of the glory of God in the face of Christ" (2 Cor. 4:6). When Jesus said that an unregenerate person cannot see the kingdom of God (John 3:5), He was talking about spiritual vision. An unregenerate person cannot perceive spiritual things (1 Cor. 2:14); such insight is available only to the regenerated (vv. 9–11).

Adoption

Viewed from another perspective, Christians have been adopted into God's family through the working of the Holy Spirit. They have received "the Spirit of adoption by whom we cry out, 'Abba, Father'" (Rom. 8:15, NKJV; see also Gal. 4:6). Adoption in New Testament times meant basically what it means today. The adopted child was entitled to all the privileges that the parents' biological children would receive. So it is with Christians. They were once children of Satan (John 8:44; Eph. 2:2), but have now been adopted by God.

The Indwelling of the Holy Spirit

All Christians are indwelt by the Holy Spirit. "If anyone does not have the Spirit of Christ, he does not belong to Christ" (Rom. 8:9; see also 1 Cor. 6:19). The Spirit of God enters a person's heart at the time of repentance and faith, causing regeneration. The Spirit remains with God's children as long as they walk in obedience to His will. He is ever present to guide and assist those who have committed themselves to the Lord.

This indwelling of the Spirit must be distinguished from the infilling of the Spirit.[4] The indwelling Holy Spirit is necessary for fellowship with God and for worship (John 4:23–24; Phil. 3:3). In addition, it is the Spirit who daily sustains the Christian, because He is the source of one's spiritual life. This indwelling of the Spirit was foretold through the prophet Ezekiel (Ezek. 36:25–27).

There is further indication of this wonderful truth in the imagery of the temple. Every Christian is a temple of the Spirit (1 Cor. 6:19); consequently, Christians are to glorify God in their bodies, since they are indwelt by the Spirit.

The Witness of the Spirit

How can people know that they have been truly born again? One obvious way is by realizing that a spiritual change has taken place. By repenting of sins and believing in Christ as personal Savior (Acts 20:21), old things pass away and one becomes a new creation in Christ (2 Cor. 5:17; Gal. 6:15). But there may be times of uncertainty concerning this new relationship with God. Ultimately, new believers must rest upon God's promises—that if they have truly met His conditions, then they are saved regardless of whether there is any accompanying emotion.

Yet, God has made an additional provision. "The Spirit himself testifies with our spirit that we are God's children" (Rom. 8:16; see also 1 John 3:24). An internal witness of assurance that one is indeed God's child is available to all Christians. In some quiet, inexplicable way, God's Spirit communicates with our spirit that there is no barrier between God and us, for it is by the Spirit that we have access to the Father (Eph. 2:18).

Sanctification

Sanctification is among the most important works of the Holy Spirit (Rom. 15:16; 1 Cor. 6:11–12; 2 Thess. 2:13–14;

[4]See part 2, chap. 8.

1 Pet. 1:2). It is the will of God for all believers (1 Thess. 4:3).

The Meaning of the Term

The word "sanctification" (Gk. *hagiasmos/hagiōsunē*) comes from the same root as the Greek word for "holy" *(hagios)*. In the New Testament, the words "sanctification" and "holiness" translate the same Greek word and are used interchangeably. The basic idea of the Greek word is that of separation. When Christians are called upon to be holy (or sanctified), they are being told to separate themselves from all that is unholy and to dedicate themselves to God. The words "dedication" and "consecration" may also be used to translate the Greek word.

Misconceptions About Sanctification

Three extreme views about sanctification must be avoided:

Legalism

Legalism teaches that a person can be sanctified only by living in complete obedience to the Law. For such people, sanctification consists of the observance of prescribed regulations. In effect, they teach that salvation and the retention of salvation depend on works, rather than faith. Often such teaching takes the form of extended lists of "do's" and "don'ts." Paul dealt with this problem in his letter to the Galatians. He asks, "Are you so foolish? After beginning with the Spirit, are you now trying to attain your goal by human effort?" (Gal. 3:3). This legalistic approach fails to account for the serious words Paul quotes from Deuteronomy 27:26, "'Cursed is everyone who does not continue to do everything written in the Book of the Law'" (Gal. 3:10).

From beginning to end, the Christian life is lived by faith, not works, by means of the indwelling Spirit. True faith will indeed produce genuine Christian works (Eph. 2:8–10), but it is wrong to hold that the performance of good works in itself guarantees salvation.

Antinomianism

Antinomianism is the opposite view, teaching that it makes no difference how a believer lives. It has an erroneous view of Christian liberty, saying that because Christians have been freed by Christ, they may do anything they please. But Paul counters with the statement, "Do not turn your freedom into an opportunity for the flesh" (Gal. 5:13, NASB).[5] Once again, those who have been truly regenerated by the Spirit of God will demonstrate love by their actions toward God and others.

Perfectionism

Some teach that regenerated persons may have a crisis experience that constitutes them sinlessly perfect. It is sometimes called "entire sanctification," and is based on the premise that sanctification must necessarily include the concept of sin. But the Greek word, as I have noted, means separation. Sin is not necessarily involved, for the sinless Son of God himself said, "'I sanctify myself'" (John 17:19). Furthermore, there is no example in Scripture of any person having an experience of being rendered sinlessly perfect.[6]

SANCTIFICATION AS A PROGRESSIVE EXPERIENCE

"Saints" (lit. "holy ones") is a recurring designation for Christians in the New Testament (for example, 1 Cor. 14:33; Eph. 1:1,18; Phil. 1:1; Col. 1:2, NASB). It is not reserved for a special category of believers, dead or alive. Rather, every Christian is a saint. This presents no difficulty if we remember that "saints" means "separated ones." Christians are people who are set aside for service to God.

This is why the Scriptures sometimes speak of sanctification as a past experience (1 Cor. 6:11), which happened at

[5]The entirety of Gal. 5 highlights the antipathy between the flesh and the Spirit.

[6]This is not to deny that some may have a crisis experience which will have a profound, even cleansing, effect on them. But the Scriptures nowhere suggest that such experiences make one sinlessly perfect.

the time of salvation (1 Cor. 1:30). But there is also the aspect of continuous sanctification. Christians are called upon to be "perfect" (Gk. *teleios*)—a word which is better understood to mean "whole" or "mature."[7] They must grow in grace (2 Pet. 3:18), not being satisfied with any degree of progress or level of maturity they have already attained. Paul himself says that he is not perfect (totally mature) and that he presses on toward that goal (Phil. 3:10–14).

But sanctification is not a do-it-yourself project. Christians mature spiritually only as they yield increasingly to the Holy Spirit. The call is to "purify ourselves from everything that contaminates body and spirit, perfecting holiness out of reverence for God" (2 Cor. 7:1), but it is only through the Spirit that one can put to death the misdeeds of the body (Rom. 8:13).

Paul says further that Christians are to experience a continuing transformation of their mind, or attitude (Rom. 12:2), and that this comes by the working of the Spirit of the Lord (2 Cor. 3:18).[8]

Entire sanctification (or total spiritual maturity or wholeness) is an ideal toward which all must strive with the aid of the Holy Spirit. But Christians must not allow themselves to come under condemnation for not having attained it. The important measure of one's sanctification is that of *progress* toward the goal.

The Fruit of the Spirit

Scripture makes an important contrast between the flesh and the Spirit (Rom. 8:5–9; Gal. 5:16 to 6:10). As Paul uses the term "flesh" in these passages, it means anything which militates against the Spirit of God. The works of the flesh (Gal. 5:19–21) are the opposite of what the Spirit produces, such as the fruit of the Spirit (vv. 22–23).

[7]See, for example, Matt. 5:48; 19:21; 1 Cor. 14:20; Eph. 4:13; Col. 4:12; James 1:4; 3:2.

[8]The word *metamorphoō* (transform) found in both vv. is in the present tense, which indicates a continuing action—"keep on being transformed," "we are being transformed."

A Christian may honestly and legitimately ask the question, "How can I know I am making spiritual progress? How do I know I am truly walking in the Spirit [Gal. 5:16,25]?" One very meaningful measurement is the degree to which one manifests the fruit of the Spirit. Is one's lifestyle characterized more and more by "love, joy, peace, patience, kindness, goodness, faithfulness, gentleness and self-control" (Gal. 5:22–23)? One measurement of such progress is a person's willingness to help restore a sinning fellow believer by seeking to restore that person in a spirit of gentleness (Gal. 6:1)—which is a fruit of the Spirit. The spiritual person sows to the Spirit, pursuing conduct which brings honor to God. This often takes the form of doing good to as many people as possible (Gal. 6:1–10). All this is in complete contrast to the carnal (fleshly) person who seeks only personal gratification.

Daily Walk

The Spirit helps the Christian in day-by-day living. He is:

The Christian's Teacher

Jesus told His disciples that the Holy Spirit would teach them all things (John 14:26). Sometimes this is done through human instrumentality, since the Spirit has set pastors and teachers in the Church (1 Cor. 12:28; Eph. 4:11). But there is also the direct ministry of the Spirit as the divine Teacher.

The Spirit will lead God's people into all truth (John 16:13). When the time comes for a critical decision to be made affecting doctrinal aspects of the work of God, the Spirit is there to instruct. To illustrate: The Early Church needed to make an important decision regarding the status of Gentiles in the Church (Acts 15). When the leaders of the church reached a decision, they were able to say, "'It seemed good to the Holy Spirit and to us'" (v. 28).

Jesus also told the disciples that the Spirit would show them things to come (John 16:13). The entire Book of

Revelation is a testimony to this. In it the Spirit is called the Spirit of prophecy (19:10), and the book was written as a result of John's being "in the Spirit" (1:10). Paul also attributes knowledge of future events to the Spirit when he says, "The Spirit clearly says that in later times some will abandon the faith" (1 Tim. 4:1).

The Christian's Guide

Truly spiritual persons allow themselves to be guided by the Spirit at all times. "Those who are led by the Spirit of God are sons of God" (Rom. 8:14). Like Jesus, believers may undergo times when the Spirit's leading takes them into severe testing (Matt. 4:1). But when the Spirit so leads, we may rest assured He is also alongside us—as our Paraclete—so that we too may emerge "in the power of the Spirit" (Luke 4:14).

The Spirit also guides God's people as to places of service. On Paul's second missionary journey, he wanted to preach the gospel in the province of Asia, but he was "forbidden by the Holy Spirit" to do so (Acts 16:6, NASB); it was not yet the Lord's will. (Later, he would be privileged to preach in that region [see Acts 19, especially vv. 8,22].) Then Luke says that Paul and his party wished to go into Bithynia, "but the Spirit of Jesus would not allow them to" (16:7). Sensitivity to the leading of the Holy Spirit was one of Paul's marks as a mature Christian.

The Spirit is present, as well, to direct Christians in what they will say in a delicate situation. Jesus taught His disciples not to worry beforehand what they would say when they were brought up before the authorities: "'Just say whatever is given you at the time, for it is not you speaking, but the Holy Spirit'" (Mark 13:11). This promise was fulfilled in Peter's life when he and John were brought before the religious authorities. On that occasion Peter experienced a special infilling of the Spirit (Acts 4:8) which enabled him to speak boldly even though he and John were "unschooled, ordinary men" (v. 13).[9]

[9]Additional ways in which the Spirit moves upon individuals to speak in a special way are treated in part 3.

The Christian's Co-Intercessor

There are times when a Christian finds it difficult to articulate a special burden in prayer. "We do not know what we ought to pray for, but the Spirit himself intercedes for us with groans that words cannot express" (Rom. 8:26). This is undoubtedly included in what the New Testament calls praying "in the Spirit" (Eph. 6:18; Jude 20), and is very likely related to praying in tongues (1 Cor. 14:2,14–15).[10]

Glorification

Christians' present experience of the Holy Spirit is only a foretaste of the glory awaiting them when they finally enter the presence of the Lord. The Holy Spirit's indwelling of Christians is God's guarantee of the consummation of their redemption (Rom. 8:22–23; 2 Cor. 1:21–22; 5:5; Eph. 1:13–14; 4:30). These passages contain several important points:

(1) The Spirit is the "earnest" (Gk. *arrabōn*) of our spiritual inheritance (Eph. 1:14). The Greek term refers to a "down payment" that is made on a purchase as a pledge by the buyer that payment will be made in full. Paul also refers to this idea as "the firstfruits [Gk. *archē*] of the Spirit" (Rom. 8:23).

(2) The same Spirit who raised the sinner from spiritual death to spiritual life will ultimately raise the mortal and corruptible body of the Christian so that it will be a "spiritual body" (1 Cor. 15:44). The Christian's body will be raised by the power of the Spirit. "He who raised Christ from the dead will also give life to your mortal bodies through his Spirit, who lives in you" (Rom. 8:11). This is the meaning of the phrase "the redemption of our bodies" (v. 23).

(3) The Christian's resurrection body will be like that of the Lord's. When the Lord shall appear, "we shall be like him" even though "what we will be has not yet been made known" (1 John 3:2). The Lord himself "will transform our lowly bodies so that they will be like his glorious body" (Phil. 3:21). At that time the redemption of Christians will

[10]See part 3, chap. 14, pp. 244–45.

be complete in all respects. Not only their spiritual nature but also their physical nature will be transformed by the power of the Spirit.

W. H. Griffith Thomas summarizes the work of the Spirit in the believer by dividing it into three periods of time: (1) In our past or initial experience, He becomes the Spirit of sonship (Rom. 8:15) and liberty (2 Cor. 3:17). (2) In our present experience He is the spirit of holiness whose presence guarantees spiritual fruit (Gal. 5:22).[11] (3) In the future He is the Spirit of heirship as the earnest of our inheritance (Rom. 8:23; Eph. 1:14) and the guarantee of our resurrection (Rom. 8:11).[12]

[11]I would add other matters such as guidance, empowerment for witness, etc.

[12]W. H. Griffith Thomas, *The Holy Spirit of God,* 4th ed. (Grand Rapids: Wm. B. Eerdmans, 1963), 28–29.

Chapter 6

The Spirit and the Word

God has given both His Word and His Spirit to the Church and to individual believers for their guidance and edification. The Spirit and the Word work harmoniously for the furtherance of God's purposes. In fact, at times the Scriptures use the two terms interchangeably. For instance, we read in some places that "the Spirit of the Lord came" upon certain people and they prophesied; in other places we read that "the word of the Lord came" and the person prophesied (see 2 Sam.23:2; Ezek. 11:5; and 2 Sam. 24:11–12; 2 Kings 7:1).

The Holy Spirit and the Scriptures are always in agreement. Throughout its history, the Christian Church has suffered because some elements emphasized one to the virtual exclusion of the other. Where the Spirit alone is emphasized, the consequences often will be fanaticism and a subjective approach based on the individual's own feelings or experiences. Where the Bible alone is emphasized, the result will be what is sometimes called "dead orthodoxy," in which there may be strict adherence to correct doctrinal belief but no vibrant, spiritual life to accompany it.

An intimate and complementing relationship exists between the Spirit and the Word. This relationship merits exploring.

Revelation

Human beings, because of their fallen, sinful state, are unable to come to a knowledge of God on their own initiative (1 Cor. 1:18–21). It was therefore necessary for God to reveal himself (1 Cor. 2:11). Revelation is the act by which God makes himself known to people.

God has revealed himself and His will to humankind in a number of ways. There is a revelation of God in nature (Ps. 19:1; Rom. 1:19–21), even though this is not sufficient for salvation. There is also a revelation of God in conscience (Rom. 2:14–16), since humanity has been endowed with the ability to discriminate between good and evil. Creation and conscience belong to "general" revelation. But God has also granted "special" revelation—the specific unveiling of His redemptive purpose in Jesus Christ. He chose to do this by means of His Word, the Scriptures. The divine Agent in this work of revelation is the Holy Spirit.

Inspiration

Inspiration is the Spirit's influence which enabled writers of Scripture to record God's message in such a way as to insure its infallibility.

2 Timothy 3:16–17

"All Scripture is God-breathed *[theopneustos]*" (2 Tim. 3:16). Since the breath of God is a symbol of the Holy Spirit, Paul here states that the Third Person of the Godhead was active in the transmission of the Word of God to people. In this connection, note also Peter's statement that "prophecy never had its origin in the will of man, but men spoke from God as they were carried along by the Holy Spirit" (2 Pet. 1:21). In the light of these passages, one may say that God is the *source* of Scripture, the Holy Spirit is the *agent* by whom the Scriptures were given, and people are the *instruments* who, under the guidance of the Spirit, wrote the Scriptures.

Paul said that *all* Scripture is God-breathed. There are no uninspired parts of Scripture; all are equally inspired. This view is often called "verbal, plenary inspiration." The phrase is an attempt to convey the idea that the Scriptures in their entirety, as well as every word, were written by men who were so guided in their choice of subject matter and words that what they wrote are God's words in the literary style of the writer.

THE INSPIRATION OF THE OLD TESTAMENT

In addition to these important general assertions by Paul and Peter (which apply specifically to the Old Testament), the New Testament writers make other statements about the inspiration of the Old Testament Scriptures.

Peter, in the Book of Acts, says that the Holy Spirit prophesied in Scripture by means of the mouth of David (1:16; 4:25). In a similar way, Paul says that the Spirit spoke through Isaiah the prophet (28:25). The Book of Hebrews contains references to the Old Testament expressed in terms like "the Holy Spirit says" (3:7); "the Holy Spirit was showing by this" (9:8); "the Holy Spirit also testifies to us about this" (10:15). Peter, in his first epistle, says that the Old Testament prophets "searched intently and with the greatest care, trying to find out the time and circumstances to which the Spirit of Christ in them was pointing when he predicted the sufferings of Christ and the glories that would follow" (1 Pet. 1:10–11). These passages are very clear about the active role of the Holy Spirit in the giving of the Old Testament Scriptures.

THE INSPIRATION OF THE NEW TESTAMENT

The New Testament bears internal witness to its own divine inspiration. Peter makes mention of Paul's letters and then goes on to refer to "the *other* Scriptures" (2 Pet. 3:15–16).[1] There is no question in Paul's mind concerning the authority with which he wrote his letters and conveyed his message (for example, 1 Cor. 2:13,16; 2 Cor. 2:17; 4:2; Gal. 1:8–9; 1 Thess. 2:3–4,13). Furthermore, he quotes Luke

[1]NASB reads, "the rest of the Scriptures" (v. 16).

10:7 (in 1 Cor. 9:14)[2] along with Deuteronomy 25:4 (in 1 Cor. 9:9; 1 Tim. 5:18) as being of equal authority.[3]

The Human Role in Inspiration

God chose to transmit His Word by human instruments, delighting to use human means whenever possible to accomplish His purposes. This same principle is evident regarding the preaching of the gospel, which He has committed to people and not to angels or other agents.

The human instrumentality in giving us the Scriptures raises a few important questions:

(1) Were the biblical writers always aware of the meaning of what they wrote? It is not necessary to answer the question in the affirmative. Generally speaking, they understood what it was that they spoke and wrote; but on occasion they recorded messages under the direct inspiration of the Spirit without grasping the full import of the message. This would be especially true of some predictive prophecies.

(2) Because the human factor is involved, does this not mean that the Scriptures are subject to error? This would be true if they were a purely human product. But statements like "'The Holy Spirit spoke long ago through the mouth of David'" (Acts 1:16; see also 4:25) indicate that the Holy

[2]It is understood that 1 Cor. predates the writing of Luke's Gospel, but Paul nevertheless cites the saying of Jesus that is recorded in Luke's Gospel.

[3]Of interest is René Pache's statement that before Jesus left his disciples, "he did not fail to promise them all the supernatural help they would need for the composition of the New Testament." He says that in John 14:26; 15:26–27; and 16:12–15, Jesus specified the different parts of the NT:

The Gospels: " 'The Holy Spirit . . . will remind you of everything I have said to you' " (14:26).

The Book of Acts: "'The Spirit of truth . . . will testify about me. And you also must testify'" (15:26–27).

The Epistles: "'The Spirit of truth . . . will guide you into all truth. . . . He will bring glory to me by taking from what is mine and making it known to you'" (16:13–14). "'The Holy Spirit . . . will teach you all things'" (14:26).

Revelation: "'He will tell you what is yet to come'" (16:13).

(René Pache, *The Inspiration and Authority of Scripture* [Chicago: Moody Press, 1969], 90). Not all, of course, will agree with Pache's assertion.

Spirit is the ultimate Author of Scripture. He so guided the biblical writers in their selection of material and choice of words that they were free from recording anything erroneous.

(3) Does the foregoing not strip the biblical writers of their free will and individuality? This would be true if God had dictated the Scriptures and the writers merely recorded them word for word. But there is considerable variety of literary style and vocabulary among the biblical writers. This indicates that they were free to express themselves in their own distinctive style. But if at any point there was the possibility of error, the Holy Spirit was present and active to correct their thinking.

(4) Why is it so important to have an errorless Bible? René Pache writes: "Full inspiration is necessary because of the fall of man. Were the Bible a mixture of truth and error, we would have to try to decide by ourselves what should be acknowledged as of divine origin or rejected as containing the alloy of human error. If man has not received from on high an exact standard, how can he distinguish between what is divine and what is human?"[4]

The Old Testament writers claimed they were transmitting the very words of God. Hundreds of times in the Old Testament the writers say they are conveying God's message (for example, Deut. 4:2; 6:1–2,6–9; 12:32; Pss. 19:7; 119:42,96,140,142,151,160,172). Throughout, one finds expressions like "thus says the Lord" and "the word of the Lord came, saying" (see Isa 7:7; Jer. 1:13). This indicates that since these messages came directly from God, they were free from error.

The Lord Jesus Christ also attested to the complete accuracy and inerrancy of Scripture in passages like Matthew 5:18, "'Until heaven and earth disappear, not the smallest letter, not the least stroke of a pen, will by any means disappear from the Law until everything is accomplished'"; and John 10:35, "'The Scripture cannot be broken.'"

[4]Ibid., 78.

Illumination

Illumination must be distinguished from inspiration. It is the activity of the Holy Spirit on a person's mind and spirit enabling an understanding of spiritual truth. I have noted that the Holy Spirit is the Author and Agent of Scripture. He is also the Interpreter of Scripture.

The Need for the Divine Interpreter

People, apart from God's saving grace, are spiritually blind (2 Cor. 4:4); they cannot see, or understand, the kingdom of God or spiritual realities (John 3:3). Only after regeneration are a person's spiritual eyes opened to the truths of God's Word. Paul expresses this same idea when he says, "A natural man does not accept the things of the Spirit of God; for they are foolishness to him, and he cannot understand them, because they are spiritually appraised" (1 Cor. 2:14, NASB). When a person comes to Jesus Christ in faith, the Holy Spirit removes from the heart the veil of unbelief and lack of understanding (2 Cor. 3:14–18). The Bible can be studied by unregenerate persons in the same manner that they study other literature, but its deepest truths are available only to spiritually receptive persons.

The Work of the Divine Interpreter

The Holy Spirit leads believers into all truth (John 16:13). The Author of the Book is its best Interpreter; but for the Christian as well as for the sinner, an understanding of the Scriptures comes only to one with a receptive heart. Believers who "live according to the sinful nature" rather than "according to the Spirit" (Rom. 8:4) are unable to come to a mature understanding of God's Word. They can digest only spiritual milk, whereas God wishes them to partake of solid food (1 Cor. 3:1–2; Heb. 5:11–14).

The Divine Teacher and Human Teachers

The Holy Spirit will teach us all things (John 14:26). With this in mind, the apostle John says, "The anointing you received from him remains in you, and you do not need anyone to teach you. But as his anointing teaches you about all things and as that anointing is real, not counterfeit—just as it has taught you, remain in him" (1 John 2:27). A Christian must therefore approach the study of Scripture in complete dependence on the Holy Spirit. At the same time, this dependence on the Spirit does not make serious study of the Bible unnecessary; God has given believers His Spirit not to make Bible study superfluous, but to make it meaningful and effective.

Total dependence on the Spirit for an understanding of the Scriptures does not preclude the ministry of God-appointed pastors and teachers. There is a divinely ordained teaching ministry in the Church; pastors and teachers are a gift to the Church (1 Cor. 12:28; Eph. 4:11). Consequently, they are an additional source of help in coming to a fuller understanding of God's Word.

Degrees of Illumination

All parts of Scripture are equally inspired. Ideally, all spiritually enlightened Christians should have the same interpretation of any given passage of Scripture. But not all Scripture is equally illuminated to Christians. This helps to explain the various opinions and interpretations on some relatively minor points. But it is reassuring to know that Christians are in agreement on the essentials of the Christian faith—such as the complete deity of the Lord Jesus Christ, His atoning death on the cross, His resurrection, and His coming again, as well as the need for repentance and faith for salvation.

Preaching and Teaching the Word

The truths of Scripture may be proclaimed in a cold, sterile manner, or they may be proclaimed in the power of the Holy Spirit. The promise given by Jesus was that His disciples would first receive the power of the Spirit, and then they would be effective witnesses (Acts 1:8). This is behind the success of the apostolic preaching of the gospel.

This combination of the power of the Spirit and the proclamation of the gospel accounts for the missionary success of the apostle Paul. He says to the Thessalonian Christians, "Our gospel came to you not simply with words, but also with power, with the Holy Spirit and with deep conviction" (1 Thess. 1:5). In similar language, he says to the Corinthians, "My message and my preaching were not with wise and persuasive words, but with a demonstration of the Spirit's power" (1 Cor. 2:4). Such is the benefit of the Spirit *and* the Word.

Part 2

Baptism in the Holy Spirit

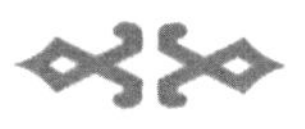

Chapter 7

Introductory Matters

This part of the book explores aspects of the Pentecostal teaching on the baptism in the Holy Spirit. It will necessarily deal with the two related issues of the experience as subsequent to salvation and also its accompaniment by speaking in tongues. The purpose of Spirit baptism[1] will also receive attention. The focus will be on the biblical basis for the experience.[2]

This chapter covers basic hermeneutical considerations, the Old Testament promise of the Spirit, and alternate terminology for Spirit baptism.

Hermeneutical Considerations

Serious attention must be given to hermeneutical matters as they relate to the doctrine of Spirit baptism, for two reasons: (1) The burgeoning movement that comprises Pentecostal, charismatic, and "third wave" elements is not unified in its understanding of Spirit baptism. (2) Serious challenges from three sources have been directed at the doctrine from a hermeneutical standpoint: (a) cessationists,

[1]The term "Spirit baptism" is shorthand for baptism in the Spirit, and is so used in this work.

[2]The history of the doctrine of Spirit baptism, especially in the nineteenth and twentieth centuries, is important and enlightening but its study would take us beyond the purpose of this work.

who argue for the discontinuation of extraordinary gifts after the first century; (b) noncessationists (continuationists), who allow for the continuation of extraordinary gifts, but who are not part of the broad movement and who reject the Pentecostal understanding of Spirit baptism; and (c) some exegetes within the movement who question the hermeneutical validity of the doctrine.

The following presuppositions and key hermeneutical points have guided the writing of this work. They are given briefly to provide a background and framework for understanding the treatment that follows.[3] Allusions to some of these matters will be made at appropriate points in the chapters that follow. These points are not listed necessarily in order of importance or in a strictly logical order, and there is some overlapping and shading of one into another.

1. All Scripture is divinely inspired. The Holy Spirit, the divine Author, will not contradict himself in Scripture. Therefore one biblical writing or writer will not conflict with another.

2. A proper understanding of the discipline of biblical theology must control the exegesis of Scripture. Definitions of biblical theology vary, but its essence is that teachings must emerge from the biblical text and not be read into it.

3. A specific biblical writer must be understood on his own terms. A Pauline grid must not be superimposed on Luke, nor Luke's on Paul. Since the Bible is not a work on dogmatic or systematic theology, different biblical writers may sometimes use similar terminology but with varying meanings. For example, the expression "to receive the Spirit" may have different nuances in Luke, Paul, John, etc. What does each writer mean by *his* use of the term?

4. Different biblical writers often have different emphases. John's Gospel, for example, highlights the deity of Christ; Paul emphasizes justification by faith; Luke (in both his

[3]Scholars within the classical Pentecostal tradition have written well and at length in the area of hermeneutics. Among them are French L. Arrington, Donald A. Johns, Robert P. Menzies, William W. Menzies, Douglas A. Oss, and Roger Stronstad.

Gospel and the Book of Acts) concentrates on the dynamic aspect of the Holy Spirit's ministry. Since Luke focuses on this aspect of the Spirit's work, it is important to understand what *he* says about it.

5. After a biblical writer is first understood on his own terms, then his teachings should be related to those of other writers and the whole of Scripture.

6. Complementariness, not competition or contradiction, usually characterizes seemingly irreconcilable differences. What is the perspective of the particular writer? For instance, does James really contradict Paul on the relationship between faith and works? Or are his statements guided by his reason for writing on the matter, and so need to be interpreted in that light? Do Paul and Luke really contradict each other on the Spirit's ministry?

7. Luke's writings belong to the literary genre of history. But the Book of Acts is more than a history of the primitive Church. Recent scholarship, especially, credits Luke with being a theologian in his own right, as well as a historian. He uses history as the medium for presenting his theology.

8. Within the framework of the historical-critical method of interpreting Scripture, the discipline called "redaction criticism" has gained wide acceptance in recent years. Its basic premise is that the biblical writer is an editor, and that his writing reflects his theology. He may take the material he has at hand and shape it in a way that will present his predetermined theological agenda. In its basic thrust, redaction criticism is a legitimate and necessary undertaking. But in its more radical form, it allows for the author to alter and distort facts, even to create and present a story as factual, in order to advance his theological purposes. To illustrate how a radical redactionist might reason: Paul could not have asked the Ephesian men, "Having believed, did you receive the Holy Spirit?" (Acts 19:2, my translation), because he teaches in his letters that the person who believes does indeed receive the Spirit at that time. Luke therefore either created the incident, or else altered the meaning of Paul's actual words, in order for the narrative

to reflect Luke's own understanding of the Spirit's work. This radical form of redaction criticism is unacceptable to those who hold a high view of biblical inspiration. The superintending Holy Spirit would not permit a biblical writer to present as fact something that did not actually happen.

9. Related to the preceding point is the fact that by nature the writing of history is selective and subjective, being influenced by the viewpoint and predilections of the writer. It is so with the Book of Acts, but with the proviso that Luke's historiography is ultimately not his own but that of the Holy Spirit.

10. Narrative theology is a relatively recent approach to hermeneutics. One aspect of it is called "narrative analogy."[4] This "analogy" aspect of narrative theology has affinities with the traditional Pentecostal approach of understanding Spirit baptism on the basis of the Acts narratives.

11. One objection to the Pentecostal understanding of Spirit baptism is that it is based on "historical precedent" which, it is said, cannot be used to establish doctrine. According to this view, it may be true that Luke recorded an experience of the Spirit subsequent to His work in regeneration, and even that the experience included glossolalia, but it is improper to formulate doctrine from this record. In other words, the narratives are descriptive, not prescriptive, since there is no propositional statement that says either that the disciples' experiences are for all believers or that tongues will accompany the experience of Spirit baptism. Induction, however, is a legitimate form of logic. It is the forming of a general conclusion from the study of particular incidents or statements. How else can one justify the doctrine of the Trinity or of the hypostatic union—

[4]For further discussion of narrative theology, see Douglas A. Oss, "A Pentecostal/Charismatic View," in *Are Miraculous Gifts for Today?* ed. Wayne A. Grudem (Grand Rapids: Zondervan Publishing House, 1996), 260–62; and Donald A. Johns, "Some New Dimensions in the Hermeneutics of Classical Pentecostalism's Doctrine of Initial Evidence," in *Initial Evidence: Historical and Biblical Perspectives on the Pentecostal Doctrine of Spirit Baptism,* ed. Gary B. McGee (Peabody, Mass.: Hendrickson Publishers, 1991), 153–56.

that Christ is both fully human and fully God, yet one person? The New Testament has no propositional statement about either of these doctrines.

One objection often raised by critics is that if Pentecostals insist on historical precedent for a postconversion experience of the Spirit, they should consistently follow historical precedent by, for example, pooling all their financial resources or casting lots to make decisions. But nowhere was the Early Church told by God or actuated by Him to do these things, nor is there even a recurring pattern of them. They were activities people thought up and did on their own initiative. But being filled with the Spirit is a divinely initiated activity and is furthermore commanded by God.

12. Another objection to the Pentecostal position is based on "authorial intent." The question is raised, What was Luke's purpose or intent in writing Acts? The answer given is that it is to record the spread of the gospel throughout the Roman world, not to teach Spirit baptism. Yet how can the spread of the gospel be understood apart from the impetus behind it—the power of the Holy Spirit? Acts 1:8 is often regarded as the key verse, an encapsulation, of the Book of Acts. The two main clauses in the verse are closely interrelated and cannot be divorced from each other: "'You will receive power'" and "'You will be my witnesses.'" If the mandate to go into all the world still holds true, then the enablement to do so should be the same as what Jesus promised the disciples.

13. Related to the previous objection is the idea that only representative groups in Acts had a special initiatory experience of the Spirit, to show the spread and inclusiveness of the gospel: Jews in Jerusalem (chap. 2), Samaritans (chap. 8), Gentiles (chap. 10), disciples of John the Baptist (chap. 19). But there are several objections to this position: (1) Very often Saul's postconversion, *personal* experience of being filled with the Spirit (9:17) is ignored or overlooked. It was not part of a group experience. (2) Did the early preachers not encounter any of John the Baptist's disciples during the

twenty-five years between Acts 2 and Acts 19? (3) Furthermore, were those men really disciples of John? Or were they disciples of Jesus needing further instruction?

The Old Testament Promise of the Spirit

The Old Testament is an indispensable prelude to a discussion of the baptism in the Holy Spirit. The events of the Day of Pentecost (Acts 2) were the climax of God's promises made centuries before about the institution of the new covenant and the inauguration of the Age of the Spirit. Two passages are especially important: Ezekiel 36:25–27 and Joel 2:28–29.

The Ezekiel passage speaks about being sprinkled with clean water, and so being cleansed from all spiritual filthiness. It goes on to say the Lord will remove the heart of stone from His people and give them "'a new heart'" and "'a heart of flesh,'" and will also put within them "'a new spirit'" (36:26). The indwelling of the Holy Spirit is the means by which this change will take place: "'I will put my Spirit in you.'" As a result, the Lord says, "'I will . . . move you to follow my decrees and be careful to keep my laws'" (v. 27).

The promise is clearly related to the New Testament concept of regeneration. Paul speaks about "the washing of rebirth and renewal by the Holy Spirit" (Titus 3:5), echoing Jesus' statement about the need to be "'born of water and the Spirit'" (John 3:5). The transformation that takes place with the new birth results in an altered lifestyle, made possible by the indwelling Holy Spirit. The Spirit dwells within all believers (Rom. 8:9,14–16; 1 Cor. 6:19); therefore the idea of a believer without the Holy Spirit is a contradiction in terms.

Joel's prophecy is quite different from Ezekiel's. It does not talk about inner transformation, a changed lifestyle, or the indwelling of the Holy Spirit. Instead, the Lord says, "'I will pour out my Spirit on all people'" (2:28). The result will be very dramatic—the recipients will prophesy, dream, and see visions. This prophecy recalls Moses' very intense desire: "'I wish that all the LORD's people were prophets and that the LORD would put His Spirit on them!'" (Num. 11:29). The narrative highlights, and foreshadows, the emphasis in Joel and the New Testament that the outpouring of the Spirit is not restricted to selected individuals or to a particular locale. The parallels between Joel's prophecy and Moses' wish are unmistakable.

In Joel the results of the Spirit's activity are quite different from those in Ezekiel; they are dramatic and "charismatic" in nature. The term "charismatic" has come to mean special activity of the Spirit of a dynamic nature, and will be so used in this work. It is understood, however, that the Greek word *charisma* has a wider range of meanings in the New Testament. Nevertheless, current usage determines current meaning. In Joel's prophecy, the Spirit comes upon God's people primarily to empower them to prophesy. This is evident in Peter's quotation of Joel in his Pentecost address (Acts 2:16–21). On the Day of Pentecost, the disciples were "filled with the Holy Spirit" (Acts 2:4); they were not regenerated by that experience.

Must we conclude, then, given the substantial differences between Ezekiel's and Joel's prophecies, that there were to be two separate historical comings of the Holy Spirit? The answer must be no. It is better to speak of one overall promise of the Spirit that includes both His indwelling and His filling or empowering of God's people. They are two aspects of the promised Holy Spirit's work in the new age. (See chart below, "The Twofold Promise of the Father.")

The promise of the Spirit was not completely fulfilled until the Day of Pentecost (Acts 2). The Spirit's activity is very prominent in the birth narratives of John the Baptist and Jesus (Luke 1 and 2); these events marked the beginning of the fulfillment. The descent of the Spirit upon Jesus at His baptism, together with the Spirit's activity through Him throughout His earthly ministry, serves as a model, or paradigm, for all believers, to whom the Lord in the Old Testament promised the indwelling and empowering of the Holy Spirit.

The Twofold Promise of the Father

Old Testament Prophecies

Ezekiel	*Joel/Moses*
Cleansing	Enduement
New heart, new spirit	Prophesying, dreams, visions
Spirit within	Spirit poured out/upon
Moral change	No mention of conduct
Inner work of Spirit	Observable work of Spirit
Nature—Indwelling	Nature—Charismatic

New Testament Counterparts

John 3:3–6; 14:17; Titus 3:5; 1 Cor. 6:19	Luke 24:49; Acts 1:8; 2:4
Baptized *by* the Spirit	Baptized *in* the Spirit
Incorporation into the Body	Empowerment

Terminology for Spirit Baptism

The Book of Acts contains more than seventy references to the Holy Spirit. Since it records the coming of the Spirit and gives examples of the Spirit's encounters with people, it is natural to turn to this book for specific terminology for Spirit baptism.[5] The following expressions are used interchangeably:

Baptized in the Holy Spirit (Acts 1:5; 11:16). As a metaphor, the point of correspondence is that this is an immersion in the Spirit. One writer incorrectly interprets this baptism in the light of the "pouring out" metaphor, saying it does not mean immersion in a liquid but rather being "deluged" or "sprinkled with a liquid that is poured out from above."[6]

[5]I recommend for further reading the following articles: M. Max B. Turner, "Spirit Endowment in Luke-Acts: Some Linguistic Considerations," *Vox Evangelica* 12 (1981): 45–63; and Tak-Ming Cheung, "Understandings of Spirit Baptism," *Journal of Pentecostal Theology* 8 (1996): 115–28.

[6]I. Howard Marshall, "Significance of Pentecost," *Scottish Journal of Theology* 8 (April 1996): 115–28. He proceeds to transfer the meaning of this applied metaphor to water baptism, opting for affusion (pouring) as the mode for water baptism. His methodology is questionable. One should not

Spirit coming, or falling, upon (1:8; 8:16; 10:44; 11:15; 19:6; see also Luke 1:35; 3:22). "Coming upon" is spatial imagery; it is "a vivid way of saying that something begins (perhaps suddenly) to happen, by picturing it (locally) as 'arriving.'"[7]

Spirit poured out (2:17–18; 10:45). This is certainly the terminology employed in Joel 2:28–29 and Zechariah 12:10. The same idea, though not the same word, occurs in Isaiah 32:15 and 44:3.

Promise of the Father (1:4). The Father gave the promise (Gk. subjective genitive) or is the source of the promise (Gk. ablative of source)

Promise of the Spirit (2:33,39). The Spirit *is* the promise (Gk. genitive of apposition). He is "the promised Holy Spirit" (Eph. 1:13).

Gift of the Spirit (2:38; 10:45; 11:17). The Spirit *is* the gift (Gk. genitive of apposition).

Gift of God (8:20). The gift is from God (Gk. ablative of source)

Receiving the Spirit (8:15–20; 10:47; 19:2; see also 11:17; 15:8). With 1:8, this is the only term that occurs in all the major accounts, excluding that of Saul. "This continuity in terminology corresponds to the continuity in manifestation between Pentecost and the three subsequent Spirit-receptions."[8] Max Turner is correct in saying it is "a relatively ambiguous metaphor," its precise meaning depending on an examination of the context in each instance, especially when it is used by different writers or even by the same writer in different contexts.[9]

---

try to explain a metaphor by another metaphor; much less should one transfer the result to something else (water baptism, in this case). The NT never uses the expression "pour out" (Gk. *ekcheō* or *ekchunnomai*) in connection with water baptism. See also his "The Meaning of the Verb 'To Baptize'," *The Evangelical Quarterly* 45 (1973): 140.

[7]Turner, "Spirit Endowment," 49.

[8]Walt Russell, "The Anointing with the Holy Spirit in Luke-Acts," *Trinity Journal*, n.s., 7, no. 1 (spring 1986): 61.

[9]See Turner's enlightening comments in his "The Concept of Receiving the Spirit in John's Gospel," *Vox Evangelica* 10 (1977): 26; and "Spirit Endowment," 59–60.

Filled with the Spirit (2:4; 9:17; see also Luke 1:15,41,67). Together with "full of the Spirit," "filled with the Spirit" has a wider application in Luke's writings; in Paul's writing (Eph. 5:18) it does not refer to the initial fullness of the Spirit.[10]

"Baptized in the Holy Spirit" occurs most frequently, when we include the Gospels (Matt. 3:11; Mark 1:8; Luke 3:16; John 1:33). The expression "baptism in the Holy Spirit," the noun equivalent of the verbal "baptized in the Holy Spirit," does not occur in the New Testament, but for ease of expression and identification it is often used in place of it. The term "Spirit baptism" also serves a useful purpose.

The wide variety of terms indicates that no one term fully conveys all that is involved in the experience. The terms should not be pressed literally, since the biblical writers employ a number of them as metaphors to help readers understand better the nature and meaning of the experience. Expressions like "baptized," "filled," and "poured out," for instance, should not be taken quantitatively or spatially, nor should one try to reconcile, for instance, being immersed in the Spirit (the Spirit being external) with being filled with the Spirit (the Spirit then being internal). Rather, these expressions emphasize that it is an experience in which the believer is thoroughly dominated or overwhelmed by the Holy Spirit. They suggest, not that the believer is previously devoid of any activity of the Holy Spirit, but that the experience heightens and intensifies the work of the already indwelling Spirit.

Baptized "By" and "In" the Holy Spirit

Does the New Testament distinguish between being baptized *by* the Holy Spirit and being baptized *in* the Holy Spirit? Seven passages contain the verb "baptize," the Greek preposition *en,* and the noun "Holy Spirit" or "Spirit." Do all these verses teach the same thing about the relationship between "baptize" and "(Holy) Spirit"?

[10]See chap. 10 for further discussion of these terms.

The New Testament writers never speak about a baptism *of* the Holy Spirit. The term is ambivalent, and could be used for either of two experiences of the Spirit: (1) baptism *by* the Spirit, which incorporates a person into the body of Christ (1 Cor. 12:13), and (2) baptism *in* the Spirit, which primarily empowers a person (Matt. 3:11; Mark 1:8; Luke 3:16; John 1:33; Acts 1:5; 11:16; see also Luke 24:49; Acts 1:8). Is this distinction valid?

The Pentecostal experience is properly spoken of as being "baptized *in* [Gk. *en*] the Holy Spirit." This rendering most clearly translates the Greek and most adequately conveys the meaning of the experience. The translation "in" is preferable for two reasons.

First, the Greek preposition *en* is the most versatile preposition in the New Testament and may be variously translated, depending on the context. "Most of the English prepositions, except such as *from* and *beside,* will have to be requisitioned at one time or another to translate it."[11]

Of all the translation options available, the most viable are "by," "with," and "in." We may eliminate "by" in the Gospels and Acts passages since John the Baptist said Jesus is the One who baptizes. It is a baptism *by* Jesus *in* the Holy Spirit.

Second, "in" is preferable to "with" because it properly conveys the imagery of baptism. The Greek verb *baptizō* means to immerse or to dip. It would be very awkward to say, "He shall immerse (or dip) you *with* the Holy Spirit"; the more natural rendering is "*in* the Holy Spirit." The preference for "*in* the Holy Spirit" is strengthened by John the Baptist's analogy of the experience with the baptism he administered, which took place *in* water.

A preference for "in" as the correct translation of the Gospels and Acts passages involves more than semantic hairsplitting. It reflects a correct understanding of the nature of the baptism in the Holy Spirit, emphasizing that

[11]C. F. D. Moule, *An Idiom-Book of New Testament Greek,* 2d ed. (Cambridge, England: University Press, 1959), 75.

it is an experience in which a believer is totally immersed in the Spirit.

Being baptized *in* the Holy Spirit should be distinguished from being baptized *by* the Spirit *into* the body of Christ (1 Cor. 12:13). The same preposition, *en*, occurs in this verse, the first part of which reads, "For we were all baptized by *[en]* one Spirit into one body." "By" designates the Holy Spirit as the means or the instrument by which this baptism takes place. The experience Paul speaks of is different from the experience mentioned by John the Baptist, Jesus, and Peter in the other six passages.

The two groups of passages under discussion (the six in the Gospels and Acts, the one in 1 Corinthians) do indeed have a few similar terms. But it is questionable to insist that because certain combinations of words occur in different passages, their translation and meaning must be the same in all. Apart from the similarities, some differences and disparities exist between the two groups of passages.[12] For instance, in 1 Corinthians 12 Paul mentions the "one" Spirit; he does not use the full two-word designation "Holy Spirit"; and he talks about being baptized "into one body" (v. 13). Furthermore, in the Greek text the prepositional phrase "*en* the one Spirit" precedes the verb "baptize"; in all the other passages it follows the verb. The one exception is Acts 1:5 where, curious to some, the verb comes between "Spirit" and "Holy."

Context often determines one's choice in translating a word or expression. Therefore we need to see how Paul himself uses expressions similar or identical to "*en* the one Spirit." The immediate context in 1 Corinthians 12, which contains four such phrases, is determinative.

Verse 3 reads, "No one speaking by *[en]* the Spirit of God says, 'Jesus is accursed'; and no one can say, 'Jesus is Lord,' except by *[en]* the Holy Spirit" (NASB). Verse 9, which con-

[12]John R. W. Stott says, incorrectly, "The Greek expression is precisely the same in all its seven occurrences." *The Baptism and Fullness of the Holy Spirit*, 2d ed. (Downers Grove, Ill.: InterVarsity Press, 1976), 40.

tinues Paul's list of spiritual gifts, reads, "To another faith by *[en]* the same Spirit, and to another gifts of healing by *[en]* the one Spirit" (NASB). In the Greek text, this last phrase is identical to the one in verse 13, with the exception that it contains the word "the." In all these occurrences in the immediate context of 1 Corinthians 12:13 where *en* is linked with the Holy Spirit, the translation "by" comes much more easily and is more readily understood than any other translation. Furthermore, the entire chapter talks about the activity of the Holy Spirit. Therefore the reading "by one Spirit" is preferable.[13]

This concept of being baptized into the body of Christ is mentioned in a slightly different way in Romans 6:3, which speaks about being "baptized into Christ Jesus," and in Galatians 3:27, which speaks about being "baptized into Christ." This baptism is therefore different from the baptism mentioned by John the Baptist, Jesus, and Peter in the Gospels and in Acts. According to John the Baptist, it is Jesus who baptizes in the Holy Spirit. According to Paul, it is the Holy Spirit who baptizes into Christ, or into the body of Christ. If this distinction is not maintained, we have the strange idea that Christ baptizes into Christ!

Following are the main translation options for 1 Corinthians 12:13 offered by various persons:

- Baptized by the Spirit into the body (the view of most Pentecostals and many non-Pentecostals)
- Baptized by the Spirit for[14] the body
- Baptized in (the sphere of) the Spirit into the body[15]
- Baptized in (the sphere of) the Spirit for the body

[13]E. Michael Green, *I Believe in the Holy Spirit* (Grand Rapids: Wm. B. Eerdmans, 1975), 141; and David Petts, "Baptism of the Spirit in Pauline Thought: A Pentecostal Perspective," *European Pentecostal Theological Association Bulletin* 7, no. 3 (1988): 93.

[14]Gk. *eis*, "for the purpose of/with a view to"; "with respect to." Petts, "Baptism of the Spirit," 93–94.

[15]Turner, "Spirit Endowment," 52.

- Baptized (charismatically) in the Spirit for (the purpose of) the body[16]

The precise meaning of the phrase "in/by the one Spirit" continues to be debated. Even if Paul meant "in" (sphere), the phrase would not necessarily mean what it does in the other six passages. Paul and Luke could use similar terms but with different nuances of meaning. But in no event should Paul's meaning determine Luke's meaning.[17]

The distinction between being baptized "by" the Spirit and being baptized "in" the Spirit is not attributable to a Pentecostal hermeneutical or doctrinal bias. A comparison of the translation of *en* in 1 Corinthians 12:13 in major versions of the Bible shows a decided preference even by non-Pentecostal scholars for the rendering "by." That translation appears in the following major versions: King James Version, New King James Version, *New American Standard Bible,* New International Version, Revised Standard Version, *The Living Bible,* Today's English Version, *The New Testament in Modern English.*

How do the two clauses in 1 Corinthians 12:13—"We were all baptized by one Spirit into one body" and "We were all given the one Spirit to drink"—relate to each other?[18]

The main interpretations are these:

1. The first clause refers to baptism in water, and the second clause to the Lord's Supper. But "were given to drink"

[16]Donald A. Johns explains: "To be baptized in the Spirit is the initiation into charismatic ministry that is directed toward the body, the local church, promoting healthy function and unity." "Some New Dimensions," 161.

[17]Oss, "Pentecostal/Charismatic View," 259. Some, however, insist that Paul's meaning is primary because it is "didactic." Stott, *Baptism and Fullness,* 15; Anthony A. Hoekema, *Holy Spirit Baptism* (Grand Rapids: Wm B. Eerdmans, 1972), 23–24.

[18]"We were given to drink" is one word in the Gk. text—*epotisthēmen,* the aorist indicative of *potizō.* For a discussion of whether the word in 1 Cor. 12:13 means "drink" or "water/irrigate," see E. R. Rogers, "EPOTISTHEMEN Again," *New Testament Studies* 29 (1983): 141 (prefers "drink"); and G. J. Cuming, "EPOTISTHEMEN (1 Corinthians 12.13)," *New Testament Studies* 27 (1981): 285 (prefers "water/irrigate").

is in the aorist (simple past) tense, indicating a completed action, and thus eliminates an allusion to the Lord's Supper.

2. Both clauses refer to conversion and are in the literary form of Hebrew synonymous parallelism; that is, the same thought is expressed in two different ways. The baptism is the baptism predicted by John the Baptist. This seems to be the view of many scholars. It is rejected by most Pentecostals.

3. The clauses refer to conversion and are an example of Hebrew synonymous parallelism, but they do not refer to the baptism predicted by John the Baptist. This is the position of many, perhaps most, Pentecostals. In my judgment, it is the most tenable.

4. The first clause refers to conversion, and the second to a subsequent work of the Spirit. It is the position of some Pentecostals and charismatics.[19]

5. Both clauses refer to a postconversion work of the Spirit. This is the position of some Pentecostals.

[19]See Howard M. Ervin, *Conversion-Initiation and the Baptism in the Holy Spirit* (Peabody, Mass.: Hendrickson Publishers, 1984), 98–102.

Chapter 8

Subsequence and Separability

Is there, for the believer, a distinct and identifiable charismatic type of experience of the Spirit separable from His work in regeneration? Many will answer in the negative.[1]

The following quotations are samples of the typical "nonsubsequence" view: "To early believers, getting saved, which included repentance and forgiveness obviously, meant specially to be filled with the Spirit."[2] "The NT refers to many and various experiences of the Spirit and actions of the Spirit in the Christian life, but none which is a distinctively further or second experience which all new Christians should be encouraged to seek."[3]

At the same time, other scholars (apart from those who identify themselves as Pentecostal) make a distinction between conversion and Spirit baptism. Typical comments: "For Acts it is a commonplace that to be a believer and to

[1]A leading opponent of the subsequence/separability view is Gordon D. Fee, *Gospel and Spirit: Issues in New Testament Hermeneutics* (Peabody, Mass.: Hendrickson Publishers, 1991), 105–19. Robert P. Menzies' response to Fee is typical of the traditional Pentecostal view: "Coming to Terms with an Evangelical Heritage—Part 1: Pentecostals and the Issue of Subsequence," *Paraclete* 28, no. 3 (summer 1994): 18–28.

[2]Fee, *Gospel and Spirit,* 115.

[3]James D. G. Dunn, "Baptism in the Spirit: A Response to Pentecostal Scholarship on Luke-Acts," *Journal of Pentecostal Theology* 3 (1993): 5.

be seized by the Spirit are separate events."[4] Eduard Schweizer comments that in Acts "salvation . . . is never ascribed to the Spirit. According to Ac. 2:38 the Spirit is imparted to those who are already converted and baptised."[5]

The thesis presented here is twofold: (1) The New Testament teaches the existence, availability, and desirability of such an experience for all Christians. (2) This experience is logically and theologically separate from the conversion experience, though it may take place either immediately upon conversion or some time afterward. The focus will be on the *fact* of such an experience. Matters related to its purpose, accompanying evidence(s), etc., will be discussed in later chapters.

In biblical studies it is axiomatic that for any given area of theology, one must go primarily to the biblical authors and their passages that treat the subject most extensively. For instance, Paul's writings, especially Romans and Galatians, explicate the doctrine of justification by faith. The phrase does not even occur in most New Testament books. Jesus is called the *Logos* (Word) only in John's writings. The Holy Spirit is designated the *Paraclete* only in John's Gospel. So with respect to matters related to the baptism in the Spirit, Luke's writings by far contribute more than those of any other New Testament author. Consequently, the starting point for understanding Spirit baptism must be Acts and Luke's Gospel.

Luke's reputation as an accurate historian has been adequately established; therefore, incidents he has recorded must be viewed as genuine. Furthermore, he is also a theologian in his own right, using the medium of history to convey theological truth.[6] Underlying all this is the fact that his writings were inspired by the Holy Spirit. Therefore,

[4]Hermann Gunkel, *The Influence of the Holy Spirit,* trans. R. A. Harrisville and P. A. Quanbeck II (Philadelphia: Fortress Press, 1979), 17.

[5]Eduard Schweizer, "*pneuma,* et al.," in *TDNT,* 6:412.

[6]See I. Howard Marshall, *Luke: Historian and Theologian* (Grand Rapids: Zondervan Publishing House, 1971).

what Luke says and teaches must be placed alongside other biblical writings and must not be construed to be antithetical to them. The biblical writers complement rather than contradict one another. Proper procedure is first to determine what a particular writer or writing says and then to correlate it with other parts of Scripture.

Narrative Examples in Acts

The Book of Acts is more than an objective recording of Early Church history. Indeed, no historical writing can be purely objective. By its nature, the writing of history is both subjective and selective. The writer determines the purpose of his writing and then includes materials that will further that purpose. His purpose will determine the emphases that will appear in the writing. In a real sense, a historical work reflects the conscious or unconscious bias of an author. For example, will histories of the Protestant Reformation written by Protestant and Roman Catholic scholars agree on all matters? Hardly!

With regard to the Book of Acts, many of the events it records have a theological purpose—to show the spread of the gospel throughout the Mediterranean world by the enabling of the Holy Spirit (1:8). The two themes of evangelization and Spirit-empowerment are so intertwined that one cannot be understood apart from the other. "'You will receive power when the Holy Spirit comes on you; and you will be my witnesses . . .'" (1:8). Luke was surely aware of other aspects of the Spirit's work. His close association with Paul would have exposed him to much of the apostle's thoughts about the Holy Spirit. But in the Book of Acts he chose to focus on the dynamistic, some say "charismatic," aspect of the Spirit's ministry, yet not to the complete exclusion of other works of the Spirit.

The first instance of disciples receiving a charismatic experience occurred on the Day of Pentecost (Acts 2:1–4). Luke later relates four other instances in which converts have initial Spirit-experiences similar to that of the Pentecost disciples (8:14–20; 9:17; 10:44–48; 19:1–7). It will be instructive to review and investigate these five instances.

The Day of Pentecost (Acts 2:1–4)

The coming of the Holy Spirit upon the waiting disciples on the Day of Pentecost was unprecedented. In a very important sense, it was a unique, historic, unrepeatable event. This coming of the Spirit was prophesied especially by Joel (Joel 2:28–29) and was bestowed by the ascended Jesus (Acts 2:33). It was a historical-redemptive event. The term "historical-redemptive" (or "salvation-historical") is the adjectival form of "salvation history," an important concept in biblical theology. It emphasizes the activity of God in and through history in order to accomplish His redemptive purposes for humankind. Don A. Carson says, "Pentecost in Luke's perspective is first of all a climactic salvation-historical event."[7]

I. Howard Marshall cites Leonhard Goppelt as regarding Acts 2 as programmatic for the Book of Acts.[8] Max Turner concurs, saying that "Acts 2 which is programmatic for Acts in general, and for Lucan pneumatology in particular, hinges on the citation of Joel's promise" by Peter in Acts 2:16–21.[9] He says further that "Peter's explanation of the Pentecost event in Acts 2.14–29 has perhaps greater claim than Lk. 4.16–30 to be called 'the programmatic' text of Luke-Acts."[10] G. W. H. Lampe says that "at every turning-

[7]Don A. Carson, *Showing the Spirit: A Theological Exposition of 1 Corinthians 12–14* (Grand Rapids: Baker Book House, 1987), 140.

[8]The term "programmatic" is sometimes used in biblical studies for an event that sets the stage, so to speak, for ensuing events. Marshall's reference is to Leonhard Goppelt's *Apostolic and Post-Apostolic Times,* trans. Robert A. Guelich (New York: Harper & Row, 1970), 20–24, in Marshall's "Significance of Pentecost," *Scottish Journal of Theology* 30, no. 4 (1977): 365 n. 2.

[9]M. Max B. Turner, "Spirit Endowment in Luke-Acts: Some Linguistic Considerations," *Vox Evangelica* 12 (1981): 57.

[10]M. Max B. Turner, *Power from on High: The Spirit in Israel's Restoration and Witness in Luke-Acts* (Sheffield, England: Sheffield Academic Press, 1996), 261.

point in the missionary enterprise [in the Book of Acts] something in the nature of a Pentecostal manifestation of the Spirit recurs. The key to the interpretation of these episodes seems to lie here."[11]

A related understanding sees the Acts 2 event as paradigmatic, a concept closely related to "programmatic"; the two terms are sometimes used interchangeably. A paradigm is a pattern; the Pentecost narrative is the pattern to which later outpourings of the Spirit conform.[12]

Some regard the Day of Pentecost as the counterpart of the giving of the Law and therefore the institution of the new covenant. Others see it as the birthday of the Church. Still others see it as a reversal of the confusion of tongues at Babel (Gen. 11:6–9);[13] one writer especially points up the verbal affinities between the two events.[14] Our concern at this point is with the personal significance of the Day of Pentecost for the disciples upon whom the Spirit came.

Was the Pentecost experience of the disciples "subsequent" to their conversion? If those disciples had died prior to the outpouring of the Spirit, would they have gone to be with the Lord? The answer is obvious. Hardly anyone would argue otherwise. On one occasion Jesus told seventy-two[15] of his disciples, "'Rejoice that your names are written in heaven'" (Luke 10:20). But did followers of Jesus prior to the Day of Pentecost experience regeneration in the New Testament sense of that expression?[16]

[11]G. W. H. Lampe, *The Seal of the Spirit,* 2d ed. (London: SPCK, 1967), 72.

[12]Roger Stronstad, *The Charismatic Theology of St. Luke* (Peabody, Mass.: Hendrickson Publishers, 1984), 61.

[13]See, for example, F. F. Bruce,"Luke's Presentation of the Spirit in Acts," *Criswell Theological Review* 5 (fall 1990): 19.

[14]J. G. Davies,"Pentecost and Glossolalia," *Journal of Theological Studies,* n.s., 3 (1952): 228–29.

[15]Some ancient manuscripts have seventy.

[16]Stott does not hesitate to say that in their case, but in their case alone, "the 120 were regenerate already, and received the baptism of the Spirit only after waiting upon God for ten days."He would not argue for the programmatic or paradigmatic nature of the event. John R. W. Stott, *The Baptism and Fullness of the Holy Spirit,* 2d ed. (Downers Grove, Ill.: InterVarsity Press, 1976), 28–29.

JOHN 20:21–23

Pentecostals often interpret Jesus' act in John 20:22 as the time when the disciples experienced regeneration: He "breathed on them and said, 'Receive the Holy Spirit.'" The incident, however, has been open to several main interpretations:

1. This is the so-called Johannine Pentecost. It is John's version of the Day of Pentecost.[17] On this interpretation, either John or Luke is wrong, because the timing of the two is irreconcilable. Harold D. Hunter, in fact, comments that "reconciliation with Acts 2 is futile."[18] In my judgment, this interpretation is untenable for those who hold to the infallibility of Scripture. Luke and John cannot both be speaking of the same event, if only on the basis that the two events occurred seven weeks apart.

2. There were two separate bestowals of the Spirit. The one in John is usually interpreted in terms of the new birth. The common Pentecostal understanding of this incident finds an unexpected ally in James Dunn, who says that "the Pentecostal thesis at this point cannot entirely be rejected," even though he adds that it was a unique situation and cannot be considered normative.[19]

3. The incident is proleptic in nature; that is, it anticipates what happened on the Day of Pentecost. In other words, it is an acted parable, "promissory and anticipatory to the actual coming of the Spirit at Pentecost."[20] According to

[17]According to Lyon, who holds this view, it is also held by C. K. Barrett, C. H. Dodd, R. H. Fuller, C. F. D. Moule, and Adolph Schlatter. Robert W. Lyon, "John 20:22, Once More," *Asbury Theological Journal* 43 (spring 1988): 75. Bruner says that John 20:22 is equivalent to the Pentecostal experience reported in Acts. Frederick Dale Bruner, *A Theology of the Holy Spirit: The Pentecostal Experience and the New Testament Witness* (Grand Rapids: Wm. B. Eerdmans, 1970), 214.

[18]Harold D. Hunter, *Spirit-Baptism: A Pentecostal Alternative* (Lanham, Md.: University Press of America, 1983), 108–9.

[19]James D. G. Dunn, *Baptism in the Holy Spirit* (London: SCM Press, 1970), 178, 181–82.

[20]George E. Ladd, *A Theology of the New Testament,* rev. ed. (Grand Rapids: Wm. B. Eerdmans, 1993), 325.

this view, nothing really happened to the disciples in John 20:22.

It is questionable whether the event recorded in John 20:19–23 should be identified as the new birth. The following points are pertinent:

1. The unusual verb for "breathe" *(emphusaō)* occurs only here in the New Testament, but it is found in the Septuagint in connection with the creation of man: "The LORD God . . . breathed into his [man's] nostrils the breath of life" (Gen. 2:7). Some argue that just as God's breath gave life to Adam (see also Ezek. 37:9), so Jesus' breath gave spiritual life to those ten apostles. While there is a verbal parallel between the two passages, that in itself cannot sustain the position that the disciples were here "born again." New Testament writers often use Old Testament language almost unconsciously, just as we often use expressions found, for instance, in Shakespeare's writings without having their contexts in mind. Max Turner comments: "An event of such tremendous significance [the ten disciples' new birth] is hardly likely to have escaped John's pen with only the faintest echo of an OT passage to draw attention to its importance!"[21]

The Greek word *emphusaō* does not necessarily mean the imparting of life. As Robert W. Lyon points out, it may also have a destructive connotation (Job 4:21; Ezek. 21:26; 22:21).[22]

2. An alternate translation could read, "He breathed [exhaled] and said to them, 'Receive the Holy Spirit'" (my translation). The word order in the Greek text is: "He breathed and said to them.""To them" is *autois.* If placed immediately after "breathed," it could mean "on them"; but since it occurs immediately after "said," the more natural translation is "to them." Turner concedes that "the absolute *emphusēsen* may simply be 'he expired a deep

[21]M. Max B. Turner, "The Concept of Receiving the Spirit in John's Gospel," *Vox Evangelica* 10 (1977): 33.

[22]Lyon,"John 20:22, Once More,"80.

breath'" rather than "he insufflated [breathed into] them."[23] The phenomenon of "a noise like a violent rushing wind" (Acts 2:2, NASB) very likely reminded them of Jesus' act of breathing seven weeks earlier.

3. Only ten people would have been "born again" on that occasion. When would all the other believers be born again?

4. The context does not say anything happened to those disciples at that time. Proponents of the "new birth" view often insist that the aorist tense of the verb "receive" *(labete)* requires that something must happen immediately. This cannot be true, for at least two reasons: (1) Other commands or requests in John's Gospel in the aorist tense obviously are not meant to be, or cannot be, obeyed on the spot. For example, Jesus prayed: "'And now, Father, glorify me in your presence with the glory I had with you before the world began'" (17:5).[24] Clearly, that prayer was not answered until Jesus' resurrection and ascension.[25] (2) The immediate context, both before and after, relates Jesus' saying to service, not salvation. "'As the Father has sent me, I am sending you'" (John 20:21). "'If you forgive anyone his sins, they are forgiven; if you do not forgive them, they are not forgiven'" (v. 23). This is very similar to Jesus' later statement that "'you will receive power . . . and you will be my witnesses'" (Acts 1:8). Lyon comments: "It is remarkable how similar the context here is with that of Acts 2:4 [I would add Acts 1:8], where the fullness of the Spirit is linked with mission and the power to engage in mission."[26]

5. Jesus' promises of the coming of the Spirit (John 14 to 16), as well as John's statement that Jesus' disciples would

[23]Turner, "Concept of Receiving," 29.

[24]The Gk. tenses available for commands are the present and the aorist. If Jesus had used the present tense in John 20:22, it would mean, "Keep on receiving the Holy Spirit," as though they had already been receiving Him. The alternative had to be the aorist tense.

[25]I am aware that John's Gospel sometimes uses the concept of glory in a twofold sense, one of which relates to the passion of Jesus. But Jesus' prayer in 17:5 very unambiguously looks to future fulfillment.

[26]Lyon, "John 20:22, Once More," 79.

receive the Spirit after he was glorified (John 7:39), militate against the "born-again" view. The glorification of Jesus must relate to his ascension to the Father—another tie-in with Acts 1 (vv. 4–10).

An alternative I suggest is that we are not required to pinpoint the precise moment at which Jesus' disciples experienced the new birth in the New Testament sense of that expression. It is possible to hypothesize, in view of the unique historical situation at that time, that the descent of the Spirit on the Day of Pentecost included His regenerating work, typified by the wind (John 3:8), which *preceded* the experience of being filled with the Spirit. But we must note that the wind and the fire were not a part of their being filled with the Spirit.

THE TEN-DAY WAITING PERIOD

The question remains, however, why there was a ten-day interval between the ascension of Jesus and the descent of the Holy Spirit. Jesus had instructed the disciples to "'stay in the city until you have been clothed with power from on high'" (Luke 24:49). The most satisfying explanation is that the Feast of Pentecost had typological significance that was fulfilled on the Day of Pentecost, just as the Feast of Passover was fulfilled in the death of Jesus. In other words, both the death of Jesus and the descent of the Spirit were divinely timed to coincide with the Old Testament feasts that foreshadowed them. The Feast of Pentecost was a harvest festival, at which the firstfruits of the harvest were offered to the Lord. Acts 2 celebrates a harvest of three thousand persons who were gathered into the kingdom of God. And it is worth noting that pilgrims would have been in Jerusalem from all parts of the Roman Empire.

The Samaritan Pentecost (Acts 8:14–20)

A CLEAR EXAMPLE OF SUBSEQUENCE

If one must look for an incident that illustrates the doctrine of subsequence more than any other, none is more decisive than the experience of the Samaritan converts. This passage is the clearest of all for the Pentecostal, and the most troublesome for the non-Pentecostal. Marshall calls Acts 8:16 "perhaps the most extraordinary statement in Acts."[27] Verses 15 and 16 say that Peter and John prayed for the Samaritans "that they might receive the Holy Spirit, because the Holy Spirit had not yet come upon any of them; they had simply been baptized into the name of the Lord Jesus." Many exegetes find themselves faced with a problem here because they do not distinguish between Luke's terminology and Paul's on this matter. We have noted previously that for Luke, receiving the Spirit is a technical term referring to a charismatic experience, whereas for Paul it is usually identified with the salvation experience.

A further problem is engendered by the view of some that genuine faith and repentance, followed by water baptism, will automatically result in reception of the Spirit. Once again, we must remember that Luke nowhere denies the work of the Spirit in regeneration; he simply does not stress it. Furthermore, responsible Pentecostals have always taught that one is indwelt by the Spirit at the time of conversion (Rom. 8:9; 1 Cor. 6:19), but that the baptism in the Spirit is an experience of the Spirit distinct from His indwelling.

Nevertheless, one vigorous opponent goes so far as to say that this incident is the exception that proves the rule, the rule being that believers receive the Spirit at the time of conversion. His rather puzzling statement is that the giving of the Spirit is temporarily suspended from baptism in this instance so as "to teach the Church at its most prejudiced juncture [regarding the animosity between Jews and Samaritans], and in its strategic initial missionary move beyond Jerusalem, that suspension cannot occur."[28] Ernst Haenchen says similarly that "the few cases in Acts when

[27]I. Howard Marshall, *The Acts of the Apostles* (Grand Rapids: Wm. B. Eerdmans, 1980), 157.

[28]Bruner, *Theology of the Holy Spirit,* 178.

reception of the Spirit is separated from baptism are justified exceptions."[29] (Readers must understand that in the thinking of commentators such as these, water baptism results in reception of the Spirit.)

Some insist that the Samaritans upon whom Peter and John laid their hands to receive the Spirit had not been genuinely converted. One prominent advocate of this position maintains that the faith of the Samaritans was superficial because Luke says that "they believed Philip" (Acts 8:12) rather than believing in Jesus. But elsewhere, similar statements are in the context of the hearers becoming genuine converts, as with Lydia (Acts 16:14).[30]

James Dunn and Anthony Hoekema are typical of those who hold the view that the Samaritans were not converted until Peter and John arrived.[31] Howard Ervin and Harold Hunter speak for those who maintain that the Samaritans were genuinely converted before Peter and John arrived.[32]

Luke says that the apostles in Jerusalem heard that Samaria "had accepted the word of God" (*dechomai ton logon*—8:14). A study of that expression shows that it is synonymous with genuine conversion.[33] It occurs again in 11:1, which refers to the conversion of Cornelius and his household, and in 17:11, which speaks of the people of Berea, who "received the message with great eagerness." The next verse talks about the faith of these people. In addition, 2:41 tells about people who accepted Peter's message and were baptized. The expression in Greek has a compound form of

[29]Ernst Haenchen, *The Acts of the Apostles,* trans. Bernard Noble and Gerald Shinn, rev. ed. (Philadelphia: Westminster Press, 1971), 184.

[30]The Gk. construction *pisteuein en* ("believe in") is used elsewhere in Acts to describe genuine faith in God (16:34; 18:8). Robert P. Menzies, "The Distinctive Character of Luke's Pneumatology," *Paraclete* 25, no. 4 (fall 1991): 24.

[31]Dunn, *Baptism in the Holy Spirit,* 55–68; Anthony A. Hoekema, *Holy Spirit Baptism* (Grand Rapids: Wm. B. Eerdmans, 1972), 36–37.

[32]Howard M. Ervin, *Conversion-Initiation and the Baptism in the Holy Spirit* (Peabody, Mass.: Hendrickson Publishers, 1984), 25–28; Hunter, *Spirit Baptism,* 83–84.

[33]Turner, *Power from on High,* 365.

the verb: *apodechomai ton logon autou* ("they received his word/message").

Others teach that we must take a historical-redemptive approach in interpreting the passage. A special outpouring of the Spirit upon the Samaritans was necessary, it is held, in order for the Jerusalem leadership to show it endorsed the inclusion of the alienated Samaritans into the Church. It would be the means of healing the rift between Samaritans and Jews.[34] A purely salvation-historical approach, however, tends to relegate charismatic reception of the Spirit solely to the Book of Acts.

THE LAYING ON OF HANDS

"Then Peter and John placed their hands on them, and they received the Holy Spirit" (Acts 8:17). On two other occasions in the Book of Acts the laying on of hands is associated with the reception of the Spirit (Saul—9:17; the Ephesians—19:6). The practice is also found in 6:6 in connection with the appointing of the seven men to serve the Hellenistic widows and in 13:3 in connection with the sending off of Barnabas and Saul. (See also 1 Tim. 4:14 and 2 Tim. 1:6.) No one will quarrel seriously with the view that Peter and John represented the leadership in Jerusalem in welcoming the Samaritan converts into the fellowship of the Church—the salvation-historical view. But this incident also points to human instrumentality that God sometimes uses in imparting His blessings.[35]

Some hold that the laying on of hands in these three incidents (of the Samaritans, of Saul, and of the Ephesians) is

[34]Stott, *Baptism and Fullness,* 157–58; Lampe, *Seal of the Spirit,* 70; E. Michael Green, *I Believe in the Holy Spirit* (Grand Rapids: Wm. B. Eerdmans, 1975), 168.

[35]The Acts accounts do not justify the Roman Catholic view of confirmation, which is administered by a bishop by the laying on of hands, in order for the Holy Spirit to be imparted in some way. Ananias was not in the "apostolic succession," yet he laid hands on Saul that he might be filled with the Spirit. For the official Roman Catholic explanation of the rite/sacrament of confirmation, see *Catechism of the Catholic Church* (Liguori, Mo.: Liguori Publications, 1994), 325–33.

part of a commissioning or ordination ceremony.[36] While this may be true in the case of Paul (though he was commissioned directly by the Lord on the Damascus Road), there is nothing in the other two accounts to suggest commissioning. It is best to understand the three accounts in terms of the reception of a blessing—even, perhaps, as a transfer of power—which is mediated by a human instrument.[37] This is not to deny that in some New Testament instances the laying on of hands is in connection with a commissioning or ordination.

We summarize and make the following comments:

1. Philip's message to the Samaritans in Acts 8 was clear. He proclaimed Christ to them (v. 5); he preached the good news about the kingdom of God and the name of Jesus Christ (v. 12).

2. Philip's ministry was attested by "the miraculous signs he did" (v. 6), which included demon expulsions and healings.

3. The Samaritans who believed were baptized. It is unthinkable that Philip would have baptized them, or permitted them to be baptized, if they had not been genuinely converted.

4. The apostles in Jerusalem heard that Samaria had "accepted the word" (v. 14). This expression is synonymous with being converted (Acts 2:41; 11:1; 17:11–12).

5. The endorsement of the Jerusalem leadership was indeed desirable, almost imperative, in view of the long-standing antipathy between Jews and Samaritans. But whatever the reason or reasons, this incident clearly shows that neither conversion nor water baptism entails receiving the Spirit in the sense that Luke uses the expression.

[36]Robert P. Menzies, *Empowered for Witness: The Spirit in Luke-Acts* (Sheffield, England: Sheffield Academic Press, 1994), 212; Lampe, *Seal of the Spirit,* 69–77. M. Max B. Turner does not agree: "'Empowerment for Mission'? The Pneumatology of Luke-Acts: An Appreciation and Critique of James B. Shelton's *Mighty in Word and Deed* [1991]," *Vox Evangelica* 24 (1994): 116.

[37]Turner, "'Empowerment,'" 16.

6. The Scriptures nowhere teach or imply that *salvation* is received by the laying on of hands (Acts 8:17). The Book of Acts does show, however, that sometimes a *postconversion experience* of the Spirit is received following the imposition of hands (9:17; 19:6).

7. This experience of the Spirit by the Samaritans was not the internal change that comes at conversion. It had an external, observable aspect. (Recall our discussion of the difference between Ezekiel's and Joel's prophecies as they relate to the promised Holy Spirit.)

It is true that "one swallow does not make a summer." Yet the Samaritans' unusual and identifiable experience of the Spirit some time *after* their conversion and baptism is a strong argument in favor of the doctrine of subsequence.[38]

Saul of Tarsus (Acts 9:17)

Saul's initial encounter with the risen Jesus is recorded in Acts 9:1–8; 22:4–11; and 26:12–18. Three days later, he was visited in Damascus by the godly Ananias, who laid hands on him and said, "'Brother Saul, the Lord—Jesus, who appeared to you on the road as you were coming here—has sent me so that you may see again and be filled with the Holy Spirit'" (9:17). Some contend that this event marks the conversion experience of Saul; this position is held by those who say that the first filling of the Spirit is an element in the conversion experience.

Against the view that Saul was converted in Damascus and not on the road to Damascus, the following observations and comments are appropriate:

1. Ananias addressed him as "'Brother Saul.'" While admittedly this could simply be a way of addressing a fellow Jew without Christian implications, it is more natural to see it as one Christian addressing another.

2. Ananias did not call upon Saul to repent and believe in Jesus, but he did tell him to be baptized, which would sym-

[38]I suggest, as an area for further study, the connection with this passage of the accounts of the woman of Samaria (John 4) and the journey of Jesus through Samaria (Luke 9:51–56).

bolize the washing away of his sins (Acts 22:16).

3. The imposition of Ananias's hands was in order for Saul to be filled with the Spirit, not to be saved. Nowhere in Scripture is the laying on of hands presented as a means of imparting salvation.

4. The terminology of being filled with the Spirit occurs in the Book of Acts first in 2:4, and prior to that with regard to John the Baptist (Luke 1:15). The Scriptures nowhere use this terminology as a synonym for being saved.

5. Saul's Damascus Road experience included Jesus' appointment of him for his great missionary ministry (Acts 26:16–18). It is hardly likely that such a commission would be given to one not yet converted.

6. There was a time span of three days between Saul's conversion and his being filled with the Spirit.

7. An individual, not a group, is filled with the Spirit. Often those who emphasize the historical-redemptive approach focus only on groups (which, they say, are representative) upon whom God bestowed the Spirit in a special way when he incorporated them into the Church.

Cornelius and His Household (Acts 10:44–48)

The intriguing narrative about Cornelius reaches its climax with the outpouring of the Spirit upon him and his household. Cornelius was not a Christian prior to Peter's visit; he was a Gentile who had forsaken paganism and had embraced Judaism to the extent that he was a God-fearer. At the moment Peter spoke of Jesus as the one through whom "'everyone who believes in him receives forgiveness of sins'" (v. 43), Cornelius and his household apparently responded in faith.

Simultaneously, it seems, they experienced a special outpouring of the Spirit similar to that received by the disciples at Pentecost, as Peter later told the leadership in Jerusalem (11:17; 15:8–9).

The terminology Luke employs to describe their experience of the Spirit is not used elsewhere in the Book of Acts to describe one's conversion: "the Holy Spirit came on ["fell upon," NASB]" (10:44), "the gift of the Holy Spirit" (10:45; see also 11:17), "poured out on . . . " (10:45), "'"baptized with the Holy Spirit"'" (11:16, NASB). These expressions are interchangeable with terms like "filled with the Holy Spirit" found in connection with Pentecost and Saul (2:4; 9:17) and "receiving the Spirit" found in the Samaria narrative (8:15,17,19). In addition, the Samaria incident speaks of the Holy Spirit "falling upon" the believers (8:16, NASB), as well as the experience being a "gift" (8:20)—two additional terminological connections with the Caesarea account.

Harold Hunter, a Pentecostal, speaks of the Caesareans having "a unified experience."[39] I understand him to mean not that the two experiences are indistinguishable from each other, but that no time gap is discernible between them, because he goes on to say that Peter identified their experience with that of the Jewish believers in Jerusalem.

French Arrington, also a Pentecostal, presents a minority view, suggesting that these Gentiles were saved prior to Peter's visit.[40] He bases his position on the following: (1) Peter did not call them to repentance or conversion; (2) Philip the evangelist lived in Caesarea (8:40; 21:8), and he or some other evangelist might have introduced them to the gospel; (3) they already knew basics about Jesus' anointed ministry (Acts 10:37–38).

The majority interpretation of non-Pentecostals is that these Gentiles experienced conversion and reception of the Spirit simultaneously, Spirit reception being equated with the work of the Spirit in regeneration. Their position is predicated on the view that there can be no "reception" of the Spirit beyond what occurs at conversion.[41]

[39]Hunter, *Spirit-Baptism,* 86.

[40]French L. Arrington, *The Acts of the Apostles* (Peabody, Mass.: Hendrickson Publishers, 1988), 112–13. In a footnote, however, he does present in a fair way the generally accepted Pentecostal interpretation: that they were saved during or at the end of Peter's message and received the outpouring of the Spirit immediately after (113 n. 1).

[41]Dunn, *Baptism in the Holy Spirit,* 79; Bruner, *Theology of the Holy Spirit,* 192.

The Spirit experience of the new believers in Caesarea parallels that of their predecessors in Jerusalem, Damascus, and Samaria. But unlike the experiences of the Samaritans and Saul, its occurrence was virtually simultaneous with their salvation experience.

The Ephesian Men (Acts 19:1–7)

Two important and interrelated questions are crucial for a proper understanding of the Ephesian passage: (1) At the time Paul encountered these men, were they disciples of Jesus or disciples of John the Baptist? (2) What did Paul mean when he asked them, "'Did you receive the Holy Spirit?'" (v. 2). We must remind ourselves that Luke, writing under the inspiration of the Spirit, has accurately given the essence of Paul's question.

Whose Disciples Were They?

When Paul arrived at Ephesus, he found "some disciples" (v. 1). The word "disciple" (Gk. *mathētēs*) occurs thirty times in the Book of Acts. Both before and after this passage, it always means a disciple of Jesus. The only exception is in 9:25, where the word is qualified by "his," meaning they were Paul's disciples (the NIV translation is "his followers"). There is no reason why Luke, in 19:1, would have deviated from his consistent application of the word to Jesus' disciples.

Some argue that Luke's use of the word "some" (Gk. *tinas,* the masculine accusative pl. form of the indefinite pronoun *tis*) implies they were not Jesus' disciples. Unfortunately, some translations render the word as "certain," which can cause some confusion as to meaning. Luke uses the same word in the singular when he speaks about persons who are clearly disciples—Ananias, Dorcas, and Timothy (Acts 9:10,36; 16:1—NIV translates these simply as "a disciple"). Even Max Turner, who rejects the idea of subsequence, allows for the possibility of this interpretation when he says that "*tines mathētai* [some disciples] does not *necessarily* refer to Christians (as the absolute *mathētai* would), even if it may (as at 9.10; 16.1)."[42] The simplest explanation for Luke's use of "some" is found in 19:7, which says there were "about *[hōsei]* twelve men"; Luke was not sure of the exact number.[43] A valid paraphrase would say that at Ephesus Paul found "a small group of disciples."

Considerable disagreement exists concerning the spiritual status of these men. The following listing illustrates the diversity of interpretations:

1. They were merely disciples of John the Baptist, and not Christians in any sense of the word.[44] They were "sectarians with no real commitment to Jesus at all."[45] "These persons are not truly regenerate."[46] The circular reasoning of some is that they could not have been disciples because "they had not received the gift of the Spirit."[47] Dunn concurs, saying that "discipleship without the Spirit is self-evidently a contradiction in terms" and that "their complete ignorance of the Spirit puts a question mark against the status of their discipleship."[48] This is the position of many who identify "the gift of the Spirit" with the Spirit's work in regeneration.

2. They were followers of John the Baptist but also Christians in a limited sense. They were "people affected by Christianity and called disciples but who revealed

[42]Turner, *Power from on High,* 391 n. 133, Turner's emphasis.

[43]"More than two but fewer than many" is suggested in BAGD, 899. See 1:15 and 2:41 for other examples. Another authority says that before numerical expressions, the word means "approximately"; see Friedrich Blass and Albert Debrunner, *A Greek Grammar of the New Testament and Other Early Christian Literature,* trans. and rev. Robert W. Funk (Chicago: University of Chicago Press, 1961), 236. Hereafter referred to as BDF.

[44]Marshall, *Acts of the Apostles,* 305.

[45]Richard N. Longenecker, *The Acts of the Apostles* (Grand Rapids: Zondervan Publishing House, 1981), 493.

[46]William J. Larkin, Jr., *Acts* (Downers Grove, Ill.: InterVarsity Press, 1995), 272.

[47]Marshall, *Acts of the Apostles,* 305.

[48]James D. G. Dunn, *The Acts of the Apostles* (Valley Forge: Trinity Press International, 1996), 254–55. I will comment shortly on whether it was indeed "complete ignorance of the Spirit" on their part.

severe shortcomings with regard to their understanding of Christian doctrine."[49]

3. They are indeed Christians. "That they were indeed disciples of Jesus is implied in Paul's first question to them, 'Did you receive the Holy Spirit when you believed?'"[50] "Had Luke meant to indicate that they were disciples of John the Baptist . . . , he would have said so explicitly."[51] These men were Christians "of a pre-Pentecostal kind. They had been converted but not filled with the Spirit."[52]

4. Though the word "disciples" denotes Christians, E. Michael Green says that "Paul clearly mistook them for Christians. But he soon found out his mistake" and that it is "crystal clear that these disciples were in no sense Christians."[53] Marshall says, "Paul met some men who *appeared to him* to be disciples. . . . Luke is not saying that the men were disciples."[54]

The situation of these men is comparable to that of Apollos (Acts 18:24–28), a believer who "had been instructed in the way of the Lord, and . . . spoke with great fervor and taught about Jesus accurately, though he knew only the baptism of John" (v. 25). Priscilla and Aquila "invited him to their home and explained to him the way of God more adequately" (v. 26). He was a Christian in need of further instruction; so it was with the Ephesian men. Indeed, what Christian has ever outgrown the need for further instruction?

Did You Receive the Holy Spirit?

Considerable discussion revolves around Paul's question: "'Did you receive the Holy Spirit when you

[49]Johannes Munck, *The Acts of the Apostles,* rev. William F. Albright and C. S. Mann (Garden City, N.Y.: Doubleday, 1967), 188.

[50]Bruce, "Luke's Presentation," 25.

[51]F. F. Bruce, *The Acts of the Apostles: The Greek Text with Introduction and Commentary* (Grand Rapids: Wm. B. Eerdmans, 1983), 363.

[52]Arrington, *Acts of the Apostles,* 191. Carson likewise says they are like the pre-Pentecost disciples. *Showing the Spirit,* 148–49.

[53]Green, *I Believe,* 134–35.

[54]Marshall, *Acts of the Apostles,* 306.

believed?'" (Acts 19:2). Some translations read "since" or "after" instead of "when." A strict translation, and one which lessens theological bias, is: "Did you receive the Holy Spirit, having believed?" (my translation). In the Book of Acts, the terminology "receiving the Holy Spirit" is found in the Samaria and Caesarea accounts (8:15,17,19; 10:47; see also 2:38). Paul therefore is asking the Ephesian men if they have had an experience of the Spirit comparable to that of the Samaritan and Caesarean believers.

Paul was not playing a theological word game with these men, even though one writer says that Paul "for some reason doubted the reality of their faith or he would never have asked the question."[55] Paul acknowledged that they had indeed believed; if he had any doubts about the genuineness or adequacy of their faith, he was quite capable of expressing himself about it.

Much has been written about the tenses of the two verb forms (*elabete*, "received/did receive," and *pisteusantes*, "having believed") in Paul's question. *Elabete* is the main verb of the sentence; *pisteusantes* is an aorist participle whose action relates to that of the main verb. From a grammatical standpoint, should "did you receive" be understood as taking place at the time of "having believed" or, alternatively, at a time subsequent to the believing? To use grammatical terminology: Are the actions of believing and receiving *coincident* with each other, or is the believing *antecedent*, or prior to, receiving? Those who argue for coincidence prefer the translation "when you believed."[56] F. F. Bruce says that the idea of coincidence is "doctrinally important."[57] Others argue for antecedence and prefer the meaning, "after/since you believed."[58] Stanley M. Horton

[55]Stott, *Baptism and Fullness*, 35.

[56]For example: Dunn, *Acts of the Apostles*, 255; and *Baptism in the Holy Spirit*, 86, 158–59; Bruce, "Luke's Presentation," 25; M. Max B. Turner, "The Significance of Receiving the Spirit in Luke-Acts: A Survey of Modern Scholarship," *Trinity Journal*, n.s., 2 (fall 1981): 131 n. 1.

[57]Bruce, *Acts of the Apostles*, 353.

[58]Stanley M. Horton, *What the Bible Says About the Holy Spirit* (Springfield, Mo.: Gospel Publishing House, 1976), 160–61; Arrington, *Acts*

gives examples in Scripture where the aorist participle clearly indicates action prior to the action of the main verb.[59] Dunn, in later dialogue with Pentecostal fellow scholars, concedes that it is "technically possible . . . for the participle ['having believed'] to be translated 'after you believed.'"[60] I add that, on the basis of the Greek grammars, it is not only technically possible but entirely probable.

At one point, Dunn says that anyone who argues for antecedent action "betrays an inadequate grasp of Greek grammar."[61] I can only cite reliable authorities on Greek grammar who say that the principal idea behind the aorist participle is that it ordinarily indicates action prior to that of the main verb.[62] On the other hand, simultaneous action relative to the main verb is ordinarily expressed by the present tense.

A note of interest is that the same Greek grammatical construction occurs twice more in this account; in both instances it indicates an action that follows, not accompanies or is coincident with, the action of the participle. The men were baptized in Jesus' name *after* they heard (Acts 19:5). The Spirit came upon them *after* Paul laid his hands on them (v. 6).

The preceding extended treatment of the grammar of Paul's question in 19:2 is important, but ultimately the context decides the time relationship of the aorist participle to the main verb.[63] Robert Menzies correctly states that "the

---

of the Apostles, 191–92; see also Ervin, *Conversion-Initiation,* 52; James B. Shelton, *Mighty in Word and Deed* (Peabody, Mass.: Hendrickson Publishers, 1991), 132.

[59]Horton, *What the Bible Says,* 160–61.

[60]Dunn, "Baptism in the Spirit: A Response," 23.

[61]Dunn, *Baptism in the Holy Spirit,* 86–87.

[62]H. E. Dana and Julius R. Mantey, *A Manual Grammar of the Greek New Testament* (New York: Macmillan Co., 1957), 230; BDF, 174–75; H. P. V. Nunn, *A Short Syntax of New Testament Greek* (Cambridge: University Press, 1956), 124; Nigel Turner, *Syntax,* vol. 3 of *A Grammar of New Testament Greek,* ed. James Hope Moulton (Edinburgh, Scotland: T. & T. Clark, 1963), 79.

[63]See BDF, 174–75.

specific temporal nuance of the participle is ultimately irrelevant, for the potential separation of belief from reception of the Spirit is presupposed by the question itself."[64]

Max Turner concurs, even though he argues for the probability of a coincident, rather than antecedent, action of "having believed"; he says that "one does not ask Paul's question unless a separation between belief and Spirit-reception is conceivable."[65]

The context therefore provides the best answer. The experience of the Spirit about which Paul inquired is the charismatic experience recorded in verse 6, which in this instance came about by the imposition of his hands and was accompanied by external manifestations similar to those previously experienced by believers (2:4; 10:46). The Ephesians' experience recorded in 19:6 was not coincident with their salvation. Even if one is convinced that Paul, by his question, had reservations about the genuineness of their salvation, the fact remains that this experience of the Spirit *followed* both their baptism in the name of the Lord Jesus and the laying on of Paul's hands.

It is often maintained that Luke's portrayal of the Holy Spirit, especially with reference to being filled with the Spirit, differs from that of Paul in his letters. This incident, however, shows that Paul, like Luke, believed in an experience of the Spirit for believers that was distinguishable from the Spirit's work in salvation. The question is sometimes raised about whether the question in Acts 19:2 was actually expressed by Paul. Extreme redaction critics might say that Luke created the entire incident in order to buttress his presentation of the Spirit in charismatic terms. Other redactionists might say that there was such an incident but the words are really Luke's, not Paul's. However, if Luke is indeed a responsible historian and theologian, then the question must be understood as being framed by Paul. Students of Scripture generally understand that in biblical

[64]Robert P. Menzies, "Luke and the Spirit: A Reply to James Dunn," *Journal of Pentecostal Theology* 4 (1994): 122–23.

[65]Turner, "Significance of Receiving," 131 n. 1.

times quotations attributed to a person did not have to be recorded verbatim. But from a biblical point of view it is important to state that quotations which the Scriptures attribute to an individual must be understood as accurately reflecting what that person said, even if the quotation is not word-for-word. In other words, it was Paul, not Luke, who actually asked the question that, to most Pentecostals and some others, indicates a separation between conversion and Spirit baptism.

The charismatic work of the Spirit is found in many of Paul's epistles; it is certainly reasonable that if he did not see evidences of that work in these Ephesian men, he would ask if they had received the Spirit.

The very strong likelihood is that Paul recounted this incident to Luke when the two were together once again (Acts 20:5 to 21:18). It would be strange indeed if the two men did not discuss theology during the days Luke was in the company of Paul (16:10–17; 20:5 to 21:18; 27:1 to 28:16—the "we" passages in Acts; see also Col. 4:14; 2 Tim. 4:11; Philem. 24).

Some comments are in order on the Ephesian men's response, "'No, we have not even heard that there is a Holy Spirit'" (Acts 19:2). It cannot mean that they did not know about the Spirit's existence. Even granted, minimally, that they were only disciples of John the Baptist (not necessarily literally but followers identifying themselves with him), they would certainly know about the role of the Holy Spirit in the life and ministry of John, including John's declaration that Jesus would baptize in the Holy Spirit. Their response must be interpreted in the light of a similar statement found in the Gospel of John. When Jesus promised streams of living water, the author editorializes with the statement: "By this he meant the Spirit, whom those who believed in him were later to receive. Up to that time the Spirit had not been given, since Jesus had not yet been glorified" (John 7:39). The word "given" is not in the Greek text, but is supplied, justifiably, to give the sense of what Jesus said. Similarly, in Acts 19:2 the statement should be understood to mean, "We have not even heard that the Holy Spirit has been given."

It is significant that this incident occurred about twenty-five years after the Day of Pentecost. It teaches, among other things, that the Pentecostal experience was still available to believers well removed from that day both temporally and geographically.

Summary Statements

The postconversion experience of being baptized in the Spirit is a work of the Spirit distinct from that of regeneration, but it does not imply that salvation is a two-stage process.

In three of the five instances (Samaria, Damascus, and Ephesus), persons who had an identifiable experience of the Spirit were already believers. At Caesarea, that experience was virtually simultaneous with the saving faith of Cornelius and his household. In Jerusalem, the recipients were already believers in Christ, even though it is difficult (or even unnecessary) to determine with absolute precision the point at which they were born again in the New Testament sense.

A variety of interchangeable terminology is used for the experience, such as "baptized in the Spirit," "receiving the Spirit," "filled with the Spirit," "the Spirit coming upon," etc.

The experience is recorded for groups (Jerusalem, Samaria, Caesarea, and Ephesus) as well as for an individual (Paul, in Damascus).

The imposition of hands is mentioned in three instances (Samaria, Damascus, and Ephesus)—by apostles on two occasions (Samaria, Ephesus), by a nonapostle on one (Damascus).

In three instances there was a clear time lapse between conversion and being baptized in the Spirit (Samaria, Damascus, and Ephesus). The waiting interval for the Jerusalem outpouring was necessary in order for the typological significance of the Day of Pentecost to be fulfilled.

In the case of Cornelius, there was no time lapse.

This postconversion experience of the Spirit is called a "gift" (2:38; 8:20; 10:45; 11:17). Therefore it cannot be earned; neither is it a reward for, or a badge of, holiness.

It is a gift, but it is inappropriate to call it "a second work of grace." Such language implies that a believer can have no experience of God's grace between initial faith in Christ and the initial filling of the Spirit. Yet every blessing ever received comes from the Lord as a result of His grace.

This distinct postconversion work of the Spirit does not rule out other experiences of the Spirit that may precede or follow it.

A pattern has emerged from this inductive study pointing up the reality of a postconversion, identifiable work of the Spirit in a believer's life that is sometimes called the "baptism in the Holy Spirit."[66] Some see Jesus' birth by the power of the Spirit and His later anointing by the Spirit as the paradigm for New Testament believers, who are born of the Spirit and should subsequently be anointed by Him. In my judgment, this analogy is only partially correct. I have difficulty seeing the new birth of believers as analogous to the birth of Jesus. Gordon D. Fee argues against both events being analogies.[67]

Jesus' promise in Luke 11:13 is applicable, in which he says, "'How much more will your Father in heaven give the Holy Spirit to those who ask him!'" Bruce suggests: "Possibly Luke understands the future tense 'will give' of the post-Pentecostal situation."[68] Turner disagrees, under-

[66]Two non-Pentecostal/charismatic writers of some stature, among others, opt for a subsequent and separable experience of the Spirit, though they do not concede the necessary accompaniment of tongues. See D. Martyn Lloyd-Jones, *The Baptism and Gifts of the Spirit,* ed. Christopher Catherwood (Grand Rapids: Baker Books, 1984); and Hendrikus Berkhof, *The Doctrine of the Holy Spirit* (Richmond: John Knox Press, 1964), 84–87. In addition, Berkhof says that Karl Barth, in *Church Dogmatics,* 4:3, "is aware of a third dimension in pneumatology," which Barth refers to as "calling" (Berkhof, 90).

[67]Fee, *Gospel and Spirit,* 108–9.

[68]Bruce, "Luke's Presentation," 17.

standing Jesus "to be referring to a kind of receiving the Spirit which was available to the disciples during the [Jesus' earthly?] ministry."[69] We should note that "'giv[ing] the Holy Spirit'" (Luke 11:13) is the verbal counterpart of "the gift of the Spirit" Luke speaks about in the Book of Acts, which he identifies with the baptism in the Holy Spirit.

Ephesians 4:5 speaks of "one baptism." Pentecostals are often criticized for believing in three baptisms: baptism by the Spirit into the Body of Christ, water baptism, and baptism in the Spirit. It is important to understand the context of Paul's statement about the one baptism. He deals with the broad subject of unity (vv. 4–6) and is referring to the unique work of the Holy Spirit that brings repentant sinners into the Body of Christ. This baptism (1 Cor. 12:13) is the one indispensable baptism.[70]

Apart from the segments in Christianity that see water baptism as essential for inclusion in the body of Christ, virtually all other Christians believe in at least two baptisms—baptism into the Body of Christ, which is then followed by baptism in water.

The Pentecostal view, and I believe the biblically correct one, on this matter of subsequence or separability is encapsulated in the statement that "the 'ideal' paradigm for New Testament faith was for the new convert also to be baptized in the Holy Spirit at the very commencement of his or her Christian life."[71] I add that the emphasis of responsible Pentecostals has always been on theological separability, not temporal subsequence.

[69]Turner, "Spirit Endowment in Luke-Acts," 63 n. 68.

[70]See French L. Arrington, "The Indwelling, Baptism, and Infilling with the Holy Spirit: A Differentiation of Terms," *Pneuma* 3, no. 2 (fall 1981), 3 n. 1, 5 n. 1.

[71]Douglas A. Oss, "A Pentecostal/Charismatic View," in *Are Miraculous Gifts for Today?* ed. Wayne A. Grudem (Grand Rapids: Zondervan Publishing House, 1996), 255.

Chapter 9

Initial Physical Evidence

According to Old Testament prophecies, the coming of the Spirit in an unusual way would herald the dawn of the new age (for example, Isa. 32:15; Ezek 36:25–27; Joel 2:28–29). During the four-century intertestamental period, Israel had been without a significant prophetic voice; for all practical purposes, there was no overt activity of the Holy Spirit among God's people. But that situation changes dramatically when we observe the opening events of the New Testament era, which show the Holy Spirit once again at work among God's people.

Events connected with the birth of Jesus, both before and after his virginal conception by the Holy Spirit (Matt. 1:18,20; Luke 1:35), signaled that the new covenant was being inaugurated. The angel told Zechariah that the promised child (John the Baptist) would be filled with the Spirit "'while yet in his mother's womb'" (Luke 1:15, NASB). This very likely occurred at the time his mother, Elizabeth, was filled with the Spirit, at which time the baby leaped in her womb (Luke 1:41). In addition, New Testament scholarship regards Mary's song of praise as a Spirit-inspired utterance (Luke 1:46–55). Zechariah was filled with the Spirit after the birth of John (1:67). The Holy Spirit was also upon the righteous and devout Simeon, who was very much under the Spirit's guidance (2:25–27).

Luke also mentions that Anna was a prophetess (Luke 2:36). The new age—the Age of the Spirit—was being inaugurated.

It is not advisable to attempt to identify the precise moment when the Age of the Spirit was inaugurated. It is better to think of it as an inclusive period extending from the announcement of John's birth to the outpouring of the Spirit on the Day of Pentecost. The link throughout this period is Jesus Christ. John the Baptist was His forerunner. Jesus himself was anointed by the Spirit at His baptism for His messianic mission (Matt. 3:13–17; Mark 1:9–11; Luke 3:21–22). He conducted His ministry in the power of the Spirit (Luke 4:16–19; Acts 10:38). He himself poured out the Spirit on those who would continue and extend His anointed ministry (Luke 24:49; Acts 1:4–5,8; 2:33).

Spirit-Inspired Utterance Prior to Pentecost

In the Old Testament, the Holy Spirit manifested himself in a variety of ways. Indeed, virtually everything the New Testament says about His work and ministry is already found, in some way, in the Old Testament.[1] But in the Old Testament, the Spirit's most characteristic and most frequently occurring work is that of giving inspired utterance. The prophetic books, both major and minor, are predicated on the assumption that the Spirit inspired the writers: "Prophecy never had its origin in the will of man, but men spoke from God as they were carried along by the Holy Spirit" (2 Pet. 1:21). In addition, there were many instances when people prophesied orally at the Spirit's prompting. Repeatedly, we find accounts of people prophesying when the Spirit of the Lord came upon them (for example, Num. 11:25–26; 24:2–3; 1 Sam. 10:6,10; 19:20–21). This *oral* inspiration of the Spirit to prophesy is the link that connects Old Testament oracular utterances with (1) Joel's prediction

[1]For example, his role in creation (Gen. 1:2); in striving with men over sin (Gen. 6:3); in guiding workmen in construction of the tabernacle (Exod. 35:31); in physically transporting people (Ezek. 8:3; 11:1); in giving life (Job 33:4); and in what the NT identifies as spiritual gifts, such as prophecy, etc.

that one day *all* God's people would prophesy (Joel 2:28–29) and (2) Moses' intense desire—Moses himself being a prophet—that all God's people might prophesy (Num. 11:29).

In light of all this, we see a clear connection between Spirit-inspired utterances in the Old Testament and comparable experiences of people in the pre-Pentecost, New Testament incidents recorded in Luke 1 to 4. This is with the correct understanding that the concept of prophesying per se focuses on the source and means of an utterance and does not necessarily include a predictive element. But those accounts in Luke's Gospel anticipate the wider, more inclusive outpourings of the Spirit recorded in the Book of Acts. It will be instructive to see how the Spirit-experiences of believers in Acts relate to those of their predecessors. This returning to the Old Testament and Luke 1 to 4 for an understanding of the fulfillment of Joel's prophecy is indispensable, because it establishes a clear linkage between the experiences of New Testament believers and those of earlier times.

Methodology

Incidents recorded in Acts in which believers experience an initial filling with the Spirit have a direct bearing on the question of whether speaking in tongues is a necessary component of the baptism in the Spirit. The inductive method is a legitimate means of trying to reach a conclusion on the matter. This methodology was employed from the earliest days of the Pentecostal movement to demonstrate that, based on the Acts accounts, tongues will indeed accompany one's initial filling with the Spirit.

Yet we must also utilize any legitimate methodological approach that will enhance our understanding of matters related to the activity of the Holy Spirit in the Scriptures. This would include a pan-biblical approach, such as I have already discussed, and the utilization of disciplines like narrative theology and redaction criticism, rightly employed. After all, Luke specializes in narrative as a means of conveying theological truth and, in addition, is careful to utilize sources that will effectively portray what he, under the guidance of the Spirit, wishes to emphasize.

Following a discussion of the five relevant Acts incidents, I will close with appropriate observations and conclusions.

The Disciples at Pentecost (Acts 2:1–21)

THE PROMISE OF THE FATHER (LUKE 24:49; ACTS 1:4)

The expression "promise of the Father" can mean either the promise which originates with the Father (Gk. ablative of source) or the promise given by the Father (Gk. subjective genitive). The term has been variously interpreted. Paul refers to "the promise of the Spirit" (Gal. 3:14) and "the promised Holy Spirit" (Eph. 1:13). It is generally understood that he is speaking about the work of the Spirit in regeneration and that the promise aspect must include Old Testament passages like Isaiah 32:15; 44:3–5; Ezekiel 11:19–20; 36:26–27; 37:1–14; 39:29; and Zechariah 12:10. James Dunn notes that the language of the Spirit being poured out occurs in some of these passages; this would then tie them in with the Acts 2 outpouring. He would not deny that "the promise of the Father" also includes Joel 2:28–32.[2]

One interpretation says that "Jesus' remark ['which you have heard me speak about,' Acts 1:4] must refer to one of two prior statements regarding the Spirit . . . : Luke 11:13 or 12:12. Neither passage connects the promise of the Spirit to an Old Testament text."[3] In Luke 11:13, Jesus talks about the Father bestowing the Spirit upon those who ask Him. In 12:12, the promise is that the Holy Spirit will teach the disciples what they ought to say when they are brought up before the civil and religious authorities; the parallel pas-

[2]James D. G. Dunn, "Baptism in the Spirit: A Response to Pentecostal Scholarship on Luke-Acts," *Journal of Pentecostal Theology* 3 (1993): 22–23.

[3]Robert P. Menzies, *Empowered for Witness: The Spirit in Luke-Acts* (Sheffield, England: Sheffield Academic Press, 1994), 171.

sage in Matthew 10:20 specifically mentions the Father. However, we cannot overlook Jesus' statements about the promised Paraclete in John 14 to 16 as well, since some striking parallels exist between the Paraclete passages and the Book of Acts.[4]

No one questions that the expression "the promise of the Father" must include Joel's prediction of the outpouring of the Spirit (Joel 2:28–32). That is the primary interpretation for the Acts 2 narrative, for Peter identified the outpouring with Joel's prophecy (vv. 17–21).

We should note the variety of terms found in Acts 1 and 2 by which the disciples' experience on the Day of Pentecost is called: the promise of the Father (1:4; 2:33); baptized in the Holy Spirit (1:5); receiving of power (1:8); the Spirit coming upon (1:8); being filled with the Spirit (2:4); the Spirit being poured out (2:17); the gift of the Holy Spirit (2:38).

The Wind and the Fire

Three unusual phenomena occurred on this day: "a sound like the blowing of a violent wind," "what seemed to be tongues of fire," and speaking in tongues (Acts 2:1–4). (It is tempting to see in the threefold manifestation of the Holy Spirit indications of His agency in salvation [wind], sanctification [fire], and service [tongues].)

The wind and fire are sometimes called theophanies—visible manifestations of God. On historic occasions like the giving of the Law there were thunder, lightning flashes, a thick cloud, and a very loud trumpet sound (Exod. 19:16); so on this historic day the Lord manifested himself in a most unforgettable way with heaven-sent wind and fire. We should note, however, that the wind and fire *preceded* the infilling of the Spirit; they were not part of it. Furthermore, nowhere else in Acts are they mentioned again in conjunction with people being filled with the Spirit.

[4]I. Howard Marshall, "Significance of Pentecost," *Scottish Journal of Theology* 30, no. 4 (1977): 351.

They were one-time occurrences to mark the full inauguration of a new era in God's dealings with His people.

The audiovisual phenomena of wind and fire are reminiscent of the giving of the Law on Mount Sinai (Exod. 19:18; Deut. 5:4); wind is not mentioned in connection with that event, but with the crossing of the Red Sea (Exod. 14:21), as well as other Old Testament special manifestations of God's presence (2 Sam. 22:16; Job 37:10; Ezek. 13:13; 37:9–14).[5]

Wind is an emblem of the Holy Spirit (Ezek. 37:9; John 3:8); indeed, the Hebrew word *ruach* means both "wind" and "spirit," as does the comparable Greek word *pneuma*. The Greek word for wind used in Acts 2:2 *(pnoē)* is a form of the same Greek word. Fire is also associated with the Holy Spirit in the Old Testament (Judg. 15:14), in the promise that Jesus would baptize in the Holy Spirit and fire (Matt. 3:11; Luke 3:16), and in the identification of the "seven lamps of fire" with the Holy Spirit (Rev. 4:5, NASB). Notice the mention of the Holy Spirit in connection with Zechariah's vision of the seven lamps (Zech. 4:2–6). Max Turner maintains that the description of the Pentecost theophany is "full of Sinai allusions with which the reference to 'clouds of smoke' in the Joel citation [by Peter] will especially cohere."[6]

In addition, the wind and fire phenomena on the Day of Pentecost must be related to John the Baptist's prediction that Jesus would baptize in the Holy Spirit and fire; the winnowing metaphor with which John follows up his statement certainly contains the elements of wind, which separates the grain from the chaff, and fire, which consumes the chaff (Matt. 3:11–12; Luke 3:16–17). I. Howard Marshall comments, "The fire in Acts is surely to be linked

[5]"Storm and fire are motifs found in Old Testament theophany stories (cf. 1 Kings 19:11). Yahweh 'descended' upon Mount Sinai 'in fire' (Exod. 19:18) and Isaiah proclaimed, 'Behold the Lord shall come like fire . . . in the flame of fire. . . . I come to gather all nations and tongues' (Isa. 66:15, 18, LXX)." Gerhard A. Krodel, *Acts* (Minneapolis: Augsburg Publishing House, 1986), 75.

[6]M. Max B. Turner, *Power from on High: The Spirit in Israel's Restoration and Witness in Luke-Acts* (Sheffield, England: Sheffield Academic Press, 1996), 274.

primarily with the fire in John the Baptist's saying."[7]

The interpretations of John the Baptist's statement vary significantly. The following are among them:

1. John predicted only a baptism of fire, which would be one of judgment. The Greek should probably be translated "in the Holy Spirit, that is, fire." The Holy Spirit *is* the fire.

2. John predicted only a baptism for the righteous, which would be "in the Holy Spirit, that is, fire."

3. There are two baptisms, one in the Spirit for the righteous and one in fire for the unrighteous. The first is fulfilled in the Book of Acts, the second is eschatological. John, as with some Old Testament prophets, telescoped the two events; he failed to distinguish between the time of the Spirit baptism and the time of the fire baptism.[8]

4. There is a twofold aspect to the one baptism: Spirit for the righteous, fire for the unrighteous. It is a single baptism which, from John's perspective, would be experienced by all. The Spirit is "purgative and refining for those who had repented, destructive . . . for those who remained impenitent."[9] Robert Menzies dissents, saying, "We search in vain for a reference to a messianic bestowal of the Spirit which purifies and morally transforms the individual." In his view, the cleansing is national, not personal.[10] This position is sometimes argued on the basis of a single preposition for the two objects in the Greek text: not "in the Holy Spirit and in fire," but "in the Holy Spirit and fire."

[7]Marshall, "Significance of Pentecost," 366; see also F. F. Bruce, "Luke's Presentation of the Spirit in Acts," *Criswell Theological Review* 5 (fall 1990): 19.

[8]This is the basic view of Stanley M. Horton, *What the Bible Says About the Holy Spirit* (Springfield, Mo.: Gospel Publishing House, 1976), 85–86; and, apparently, of Roger Stronstad, who says, "John's harvest metaphor suggests that this will be both a baptism of blessing . . . and of judgment. . . . Jesus says, 'I have come to cast fire upon the earth' (Luke 12:49–50)." *The Charismatic Theology of St. Luke* (Peabody, Mass.: Hendrickson Publishers, 1984), 51.

[9]James D. G. Dunn, *Baptism in the Holy Spirit* (London: SCM Press, 1970), 9–10, 13. Turner appeals to Isaiah 4:2–6, which promises the cleansing of Jerusalem "by a spirit of judgment and a spirit of burning." *Power from on High*, 184.

[10]Menzies, *Empowered for Witness*, 128.

While the precise meaning of John the Baptist's statement continues to be debated, there is little doubt that Jesus invested it with new, or at least additional, meaning. The disciples, He said, would receive power which would be intimately connected with their evangelizing mission (Acts 1:8). Furthermore, the fire on the Day of Pentecost was not destructive in nature. It more closely resembles the fire in the burning bush (Exod. 3:2–5; Acts 7:30) and speaks of the presence and holiness of God. Significantly, the only other symbolic reference to fire in the Book of Acts relates to the burning bush incident, unless one interprets the fire in Joel's prophecy symbolically (Acts 2:19).[11]

Stanley M. Horton suggests that in view of its occurrence during the Feast of Pentecost, the fire signified God's acceptance of the Church body as the temple of the Holy Spirit (1 Cor. 3:16; Eph. 2:21,22) and, then, the acceptance of the individual believers as also being temples of the Holy Spirit (1 Cor. 6:19). He draws attention to Old Testament incidents where fire came down on an altar, as with Abraham, and at the dedication of both the tabernacle and Solomon's temple.[12]

Douglas A. Oss says that fire is associated in the Old Testament with God's sanction of prophetic activity such as prophetic speech (Jer. 5:14; 23:29; Ezek. 1:4 to 2:8) and judgment (Ezek. 15:4–8; 19:12–13). He concludes: "The 'tongues of fire' in Acts 2:3 may very well have symbolized God's own sanctioning of the church's prophetic activity."[13]

Speaking in Tongues (Glossolalia)

"Glossolalia" is a technical term often used for speaking in tongues; it is a combined form of the Greek words *lalia*

[11]See F. F. Bruce, *The Book of Acts,* rev. ed. (Grand Rapids: Wm. B. Eerdmans, 1988), 51.

[12]Stanley M. Horton, *What the Bible Says,* 141; *The Book of Acts* (Springfield, Mo.: Gospel Publishing House, 1981), 31.

[13]Douglas A. Oss, "A Pentecostal/Charismatic View," in *Are Miraculous Gifts for Today?* ed. Wayne A. Grudem (Grand Rapids: Zondervan Publishing House, 1996), 254 n. 25.

("speech," "speaking") and *glōssa* ("tongue," "language"). The phenomenon of speaking in tongues, unlike the wind and the fire, is integral to the disciples' being filled with the Spirit. "And all were filled with the Holy Spirit and began to speak in other tongues, as the Spirit was giving them inspired utterance" (Acts 2:4, my translation). The first important observation is that my phrase "inspired utterance" is a rendering of the Greek word *apophthengomai,* which is used in the Septuagint for supernaturally inspired speech, whether divine (1 Chron. 25:1) or demonic (Mic. 5:12). Especially important is the observation that this same unusual word, which occurs only three times in the New Testament, is used in Acts 2:14 to introduce Peter's address to the crowd (he "addressed" them). Peter's speech that day was actually a prophetic utterance. The third New Testament occurrence is in Acts 26:25. Paul says to Festus, "'I am not out of my mind [Gk. *mainomai*], most excellent Festus, but I utter [Gk. *apophthengomai*] words of sober truth'" (NASB). Festus had accused him of being out of his mind, possibly because Paul's manner of speech was quite animated. The likelihood is that Paul had spoken under the direct impetus of the Spirit.

The record says that the disciples "began *[archomai]* to speak in other tongues" (Acts 2:4). There is no indication that the disciples initiated, or that they themselves "began," the speaking in tongues. Appealing to this idea of "began," a not altogether uncommon teaching of some well-meaning Pentecostals says: "You start it, and then the Holy Spirit takes over." But *archomai* in this verse is a pleonasm—a grammatical peculiarity in Greek and in some other languages. It is sometimes called a "redundant auxiliary." In this grammatical construction, the translation of *archomai* can be eliminated and the infinitive "to speak" is converted to the indicative mood. The meaning of "They began to speak in tongues" is simply, "They spoke in tongues."[14]

[14]See C. F. D. Moule, *An Idiom-Book of New Testament Greek,* 2d ed. (Cambridge, England: Cambridge University Press, 1959), 181–82; Bruce, *Book of Acts,* 222 n. 13; Richard N. Longenecker, *The Acts of the Apostles* (Grand Rapids: Zondervan Publishing House, 1981), 395.

Examples of this grammatical construction are found elsewhere in Scripture. One particularly applicable example is Acts 11:15, where Peter says, in referring to his preaching to the household of Cornelius, "'As I began to speak, the Holy Spirit came on them.'" Obviously, the Spirit did not descend on those people at the start of Peter's message; he was well into it (Acts 10:34–44). The disciples at Pentecost spoke in tongues "as the Spirit was giving them inspired utterance" (my translation), not under their own impetus. The conjunction "as" *(kathōs)* may be rendered "to the degree that," "since," or "in so far as."[15]

The phenomenon of speaking in tongues is expressed in a number of ways in the New Testament:

- To speak in other tongues—Acts 2:4
- To speak in tongues—Acts 10:46; 19:6; 1 Cor. 12:30; 14:5–6,18,23
- To speak in a tongue—1 Cor. 14:2,4,13
- To speak in the tongues of men and of angels —1 Cor. 13:1
- To speak in new tongues—Mark 16:17
- Kinds of tongues—1 Cor. 12:10,28
- Tongues—1 Cor. 13:8; 14:22
- A tongue—1 Cor. 14:14,19,26

The specific terminology used in Acts ("to speak in tongues"; Gk. *glōssais lalein*) occurs in that precise form, along with some variations, in Paul's treatment of spiritual gifts in 1 Corinthians 12 to 14. The two-word Greek term does not appear anywhere else in canonical or noncanonical literature as a technical term for an unusual occurrence whereby a person, under the impulse of the Holy Spirit (or any spirit), speaks a language unknown to him or her. Consequently, the phenomenon that both Luke and Paul refer to is essentially the same.

Different interpretations have been given about the nature of biblical glossolalia. The more important views will be set forth; variations within individual viewpoints

[15]BAGD, 391.

have been kept to a minimum in order to arrive at a clearer understanding of the basic position of the exponents of these schools.

A Miracle of Hearing

This view relates primarily to the "other tongues" of Acts 2:4 and stresses, not the "speaking" of verse 4, but the "hearing" of verses 6, 8, and 11. "Luke seems to affirm that the miracle did not lie in the tongues of the speakers, but in the ears of the hearers."[16] The church historian Philip Schaff says that the glossolalia at Pentecost "was at once internally interpreted and applied by the Holy Spirit himself to those hearers who believed and were converted to each in his own vernacular dialect."[17]

Max Turner responds that the Pentecost event is God's activity "in the one hundred and twenty *believers*." He goes on to say that Luke does not suggest "that the apostolic band prattled incomprehensibly, while God worked the yet greater miracle of interpretation of tongues in the *un*believers." He echoes John Calvin's comment that if it was indeed a miracle of hearing, the Spirit would have been given not so much to the disciples as to nondisciples.[18]

Meaningless, Ecstatic Sounds

This view almost always relates New Testament glossolalia to similar phenomena in the non-Christian and pagan

[16]George Barton Cutten, *The Psychological Phenomena of Christianity* (New York: Charles Scribner's Sons, 1909), 50. See also F. Godet, *Commentary on St. Paul's First Epistle to the Corinthians*, trans. A. Cusin (Edinburgh, Scotland: T. & T. Clark, 1898), 2:320.

[17]Philip Schaff, *History of the Christian Church*, vol. 1 (New York: Charles Scribner's Sons, 1882), 241. See also Jenny Everts, "Tongues or Languages? Contextual Consistency in the Translation of Acts 2," *Journal of Pentecostal Theology* 4 (1994): 71–80.

[18]M. Max B. Turner, *The Holy Spirit and Spiritual Gifts: In the New Testament Church and Today*, rev. ed. (Peabody, Mass.: Hendrickson Publishers, 1998), 222, Turner's emphasis; John Calvin, *Commentary upon the Acts of the Apostles*, ed. Henry Beveridge (Edinburgh, Scotland: Edinburgh Printing Co., 1844), 1:77.

world. The speaker, it is maintained, is in a trancelike state and utters incoherent sounds.[19] Speaking in tongues, one advocate maintains, involves "the notion of the disconnected, unmeaning use of the tongue for the making of sounds."[20] James Dunn, interestingly, ascribes this type of "ecstatic utterance" to the Corinthian believers, but proceeds to say that the view Paul has is different in that he says glossolalia can be controlled.[21]

It is difficult to understand how, if this view is correct, the Scriptures should set forth speaking in tongues as a gift of the Holy Spirit, since babbling can hardly be identified as one of His works. However low some may wish to place this gift in the hierarchy of the charismata, it is still a gift of the Spirit and, as such, ought not to be spoken of lightly or disparagingly.

Some contend that the verb *lalein,* used consistently in connection with glossolalia, suggests the idea that the phenomenon is one of "lalling," that is, of babbling. But in Hellenistic times the verb did not ordinarily mean incoherent speech. Furthermore, Paul uses it also in connection with prophesying (1 Cor. 14:29) and with women asking questions (14:34–35). In addition, he does use the more common word for speak *(legein)* at least once in connection with glossolalia (14:16).[22]

[19]A lengthy discussion of this viewpoint would go beyond the purpose of the present work. The literature, both for and against, is considerable. For a work discounting the similarity between biblical glossolalia and seeming parallels in the Hellenistic world, see C. Forbes, *Prophecy and Inspired Speech in Early Christianity and Its Hellenistic Environment* (Peabody, Mass.: Hendrickson Publishers, 1997).

[20]Alexander Mackie, *The Gift of Tongues* (New York: George H. Doran Co., 1921), 24.

[21]James D. G. Dunn, *Jesus and the Spirit* (Philadelphia: Westminster Press, 1975), 243.

[22]See especially Robert H. Gundry's often-cited article in which he attacks the translation found in the New English Bible "'Ecstatic Utterance' (N.E.B.)?" *Journal of Theological Studies,* n.s., 17 (1966): 299–307. Gerhard Delling sees a radical disjunction between New Testament glossolalia and Dionysian ecstasy in *Worship in the New Testament,* trans. Percy Scott (Philadelphia: Westminster Press, 1962), 39.

Archaic Expressions

Liddell and Scott's *Greek-English Lexicon* gives, as one meaning of *glōssa,* "an *obsolete* or *foreign word,* which needs explanation." The lexicon by Bauer-Arndt-Gingrich-Danker suggests a similar meaning for the tongues phenomenon.[23] Related to this is the concept of cryptomnesia, which says that in a state of ecstasy or unusual excitement, or even drunkenness, people may blurt out foreign words or phrases unknown to them, which are somehow in their memory bank. Commenting on the Pentecost glossolalia, Cyril G. Williams says that sounds uttered by the disciples seemed to some Jewish hearers to be "identifiable words in languages dimly recalled." He goes on to suggest the possibility that "interspersed among inarticulate utterances would be actual identifiable words."[24]

It is difficult to understand how such a psychological approach, whatever its merits, can adequately explain all the biblical data dealing with the gift. It takes a rather rare use of the word *glōssa* and imposes it on the New Testament. It is much better exegesis to understand a Greek word or term in its most common, face-value meaning, unless compelling evidence exists to interpret it otherwise.

Language

Perhaps the most widely held opinion, at least among those committed to a high view of Scripture, sees glossolalia as a speaking in different languages.[25] It holds, in general, that the "kinds of tongues" (1 Cor. 12:10,28) are types, or species, of languages.

[23]Henry George Liddell and Robert Scott, *A Greek-English Lexicon,* 8th ed. (Oxford, England: Clarendon Press, 1897), 312, emphasis in original; BAGD, 162.

[24]Cyril G. Williams, "Glossolalia as a Religious Phenomenon: 'Tongues' at Corinth and Pentecost," *Religion* 5 (spring 1975): 25–26.

[25]For a defense of glossolalia meaning languages, I suggest the following articles by classical Pentecostals: (1) Jon Ruthven, "Is Glossolalia Languages?: A Survey of Biblical Data," *Paraclete* 2, no. 2 (spring 1968): 27–30; (2) William G. MacDonald, "Biblical Glossolalia: Thesis Four," *Paraclete* 27, no. 3 (summer 1993): 32–45.

This view is held for two basic reasons:

1. Even though the Greek word *glōssa* often means the physical organ of speech or, in a technical sense, a poetic or archaic expression, the meaning which most readily comes to mind in connection with glossolalia is that of language. The word is used in the Septuagint in the account of the confusion of tongues (Gen. 11:1,6–7,9) and is a translation of the Hebrew *lashōn*. It is used further to translate the Hebrew *saphah* (Gen. 10:5,31) to indicate the language or languages spoken by the different families of the earth after the dispersion of chapter 11. One occurrence of the word that is decidedly to the point is found in Isaiah 28:11, which Paul quotes in 1 Corinthians 14. Reference is to the Assyrians, whose language the Israelites would not understand.

2. A further consideration is that the Greek word *hermēneia* and its cognates imply the meaning of "language" for *glōssa* in 1 Corinthians 12 to 14, and that therefore the verb *hermēneuein* means "to translate" or "to interpret" an unintelligible language. With only one exception (Luke 24:27), and exclusive of 1 Corinthians 12 to 14 where its meaning is being sought, this word and its cognates in the New Testament are used to introduce the meaning of foreign words or expressions (for example, Mark 5:41; 15:34; Acts 4:36). The preponderance of evidence in the New Testament, therefore, is that *hermēneia* and its cognates convey the idea of translating, or interpreting, a language unknown to the hearers or readers.

Certainly one's concept of the gift of interpretation of tongues is governed by the concept held of the nature of glossolalia, but the biblical usage of the *hermēneia* family of words is a strong indication that Paul is talking about the translating of languages.

The conclusion that glossolalia is a speaking in languages, however, requires further inquiry. What is the nature of these languages? Two possibilities exist. They may be human, identifiable languages, or they may be some kind of nonhuman, angelic or heavenly language. Some see a contradiction between Luke's presentation (human languages) and Paul's (angelic or heavenly languages), and consequently try to interpret one in terms of the other.[26]

Is glossolalia a spiritual, heavenly language? Those who hold this view say that the general tenor of the teaching of 1 Corinthians 14 suggests it. Tongues seem to be directed at all times to God (v. 2); reference is also made to praying in tongues (v. 14). If, then, this is a means of communication between man and God, and if this speaking is impelled by the Holy Spirit, then a language of heaven is more suited to the occasion than merely another language of men.[27] Further appeal is made to the "tongues . . . of angels" mentioned in 1 Corinthians 13:1.[28]

Is glossolalia a speaking in a human language *(xenolalia)?* Acts 2 is certainly decisive as to this possibility. In addition, there is a linguistic affinity between Acts 2:4 ("other tongues"—*heterais glōssais*) and Paul's quotation of Isaiah 28:11, which contains the compound form *heteroglōssois,* which also means "other tongues."

The most tenable position is that glossolalia must be understood as a speaking in languages, but that the languages may be either human or angelic/heavenly.[29]

[26]The matter is not so clear-cut, however. There is no indication in the Acts 10 and 19 accounts of tongues that they were human languages; and Paul gives sufficient indication, especially in citing Isaiah 28:11, of a view that would at least include human languages.

[27]See, for example, Johannes Behm, *"glōssa, heteroglōssos,"* in *TDNT,* 1:726; and F. W. Grosheide, *Commentary on the First Epistle to the Corinthians* (Grand Rapids: Wm. B. Eerdmans, 1953), 288–89.

[28]Of interest are extracanonical allusions to "tongues of angels" such as Ethiopic Enoch 40 and The Testament of Job 38 to 40. In the latter passage the three daughters of Job are enabled to speak in the languages of angels. The idea of angelic languages was at least present in first-century Judaism.

[29]The following are representative of this inclusive understanding of the nature of glossolalia: Gordon D. Fee, *God's Empowering Presence* (Peabody, Mass.: Hendrickson Publishers, 1994), 890; E. E. Ellis, *Interpreter's Dictionary of the Bible Supplementary Volume* (Nashville: Abingdon, 1962), 908b; M. Max B. Turner, *Holy Spirit and Spiritual Gifts,* 229 ("Paul probably thought of tongues-speech as xenolalia and [possibly] heavenly languages."); Robert Banks and Geoffrey Moon, "Speaking in Tongues: A Survey of the New Testament Evidence," *The Churchman* 80 (1966): 279.

The gathering of so many representatives from the various nations was providentially timed, so that we see in the glossolalic utterances of the disciples a foreshadowing of their commission to go into all the world (Acts 1:8). Although not all the nations of the world were represented, John R. W. Stott observes that Luke includes in the list descendants of Shem, Ham, and Japheth, and gives us a "'Table of the Nations' comparable to the one in Genesis 10."[30]

The content of the disciples' glossolalia was a glorification of God. They were "declaring the wonders of God" (Acts 2:11). It is clear that they did not preach in the divinely inspired languages. Preaching was done by Peter very shortly in the commonly understood Aramaic language. Their utterances were on the order of praise and worship.

For the specific purpose of this chapter, a most significant observation in Acts 2 is that the word "all" in verse 4 is the subject of both main clauses: All were filled with the Spirit, all spoke in tongues. To rephrase it: *All* who were filled with the Spirit spoke in tongues—there were no exceptions.

Fulfillment of Joel's Prophecy

Peter, in his inspired address to the crowd, identified the disciples' experience as the fulfillment of Joel's prediction that the Lord would pour forth his Spirit upon all humankind (Acts 2:16–21). Variations exist between Peter's understanding of the Joel passage and the passage itself. At least two are significant:

1. The "afterward" of Joel 2:28 becomes "in the last days" (Acts 2:17). In the Jewish frame of reference, there were to be only two ages, divided by the coming of the Messiah. The latter age was identified as the Age of the Spirit, the Messianic Age, the last days, etc. Peter says on this occasion that the Messianic Age, with its promised outpouring of the Spirit, has arrived.

[30]John R. W. Stott, *The Spirit, the Church, and the World: The Message of Acts* (Downers Grove, Ill.: InterVarsity Press, 1990), 68; see also J. W. Packer, *Acts of the Apostles* (Cambridge, England: University Press, 1973), 27; William Neil, *The Acts of the Apostles* (London: Oliphants, 1973), 73.

2. Joel's prophecy said, "Your sons and your daughters will prophesy." Yet Peter, after mentioning the Spirit's work in young men and old men, and upon male and female servants, inserted into the prophecy the words, "and they will prophesy" (end of v. 18). Some say the words were added by Luke, but there is no reason why Peter, speaking under the inspiration of the Spirit, could not himself have added them. Clearly, from among all the elements in Joel's prediction, Peter stressed prophetic utterance as the key feature of the fulfillment.

But is speaking in tongues the same as prophesying? It will help to consider how both prophecy and tongues operate. Both oral prophesying and speaking in tongues involve the Holy Spirit coming upon a person and prompting the person to speak out. The basic difference is that prophesying is in the common language, whereas speaking in tongues is in a language unknown to the speaker. But the mode of operation of the two gifts is the same. Speaking in tongues could be called a specialized type of prophesying with respect to the manner in which it functions.[31] In this sense, in view of the fact that God had ordained for something unique to happen on that day, the disciples' speaking in tongues was indeed a fulfillment of Joel's prediction that the Lord's people would prophesy.

Cornelius's Household at Caesarea (Acts 10:44–48)

Several observations in this narrative are pertinent:

1. Peter clearly identifies the experience of Cornelius's household with that of the disciples on the Day of Pentecost. "'God gave them the same gift'" (Acts 11:17). God gave them the Holy Spirit, "'just as he did to us'" (15:8). In addition, common terms like "baptized in the Holy Spirit," "poured out," and "gift" appear in both accounts.

2. The outward, observable manifestation of glossolalia

[31]Don A. Carson, *Showing the Spirit: A Theological Exposition of 1 Corinthians 12–14* (Grand Rapids: Baker Book House, 1987), 140–41; I. Howard Marshall, *The Acts of the Apostles* (Grand Rapids: Wm. B. Eerdmans, 1980), 73; Menzies, *Empowered for Witness*, 186 n. 3.

convinced Peter's Jewish-Christian companions that the Spirit had indeed fallen on these Gentiles, "for they heard them speaking in tongues and praising God" (10:46). However one expresses it, glossolalia was the evidence, or sign, of the Gentiles' baptism in the Spirit.

3. These Gentiles were "speaking in tongues and praising *[megalunō]* God." Very likely, "praising [or exalting] God" indicates what they were saying in tongues (even though, apparently, the glossolalia was not understood). The Greek word for "and" sometimes introduces an explanatory note on what precedes it and may be translated "that is" (technically called the epexegetical use of the word *kai*). They were "speaking in tongues, that is, praising [exalting] God." The related noun form of the verb *megalunō* occurs in Acts 2:11, where the people say, "'We hear them in our own tongues speaking of the mighty deeds *[megaleia]* of God'" (NASB). The verb occurs also in Mary's paean of praise, "'My soul glorifies *[megalunō]* the Lord'" (Luke 1:46), and in Acts 19:17, "The name of the Lord Jesus was being magnified" (NASB). In other words, speaking in tongues often involves prayer or praise to God (1 Cor. 14:2,14–15). Don A. Carson says, "It is not entirely certain whether the praise constituted the *content* of the tongues-speaking, or was parallel to it; but the former is marginally more likely."[32]

Once again, the historical-redemptive aspect of this narrative cannot be ignored. Minimally, glossolalia was the evidence needed to convince Peter's companions and the Jerusalem leadership that God had indeed accepted the Gentiles *as Gentiles* by pouring his Spirit upon them in Pentecostal fashion.

The two incidents discussed so far (Pentecost in Acts 2 and the Gentiles in Acts 10; 11; and 15) indisputably and unambiguously connect speaking in tongues with the Spirit baptism of the recipients. In fact, the specific terminology "baptized in/with the Holy Spirit" occurs in Acts

[32]Carson, *Showing the Spirit,* 147.

only in connection with these two accounts (Acts 1:5; 11:16). These observations are important because these two incidents bracket two others found in chapters 8 and 9 and will help in understanding them.

The Samaritans (Acts 8:14–20)

The Samaritans had witnessed signs performed by Philip (demon expulsions, healings), had responded in faith to the message about Christ, and had submitted to baptism. But they had not yet received the Holy Spirit (v. 15; see vv. 17,19); He "had not yet fallen upon any of them" (v. 16, NASB). As Luke uses the term "receive the Spirit," it is synonymous with other terminology he uses, such as being "baptized in" the Spirit, the Spirit "falling upon" or "coming upon" people, the "gift of" the Spirit, being "filled with" the Spirit.

In the New Testament, "receiving the Spirit" is a flexible term whose meaning depends upon a particular writer's intent and the context in which it occurs. It is therefore inappropriate, for example, to try to force Luke's meaning of the term on Paul, or Paul's meaning on Luke. This is a valid, but not always observed, principle of biblical interpretation.

The important element in this narrative is that the Samaritan believers had a postconversion experience of the Spirit that was mediated through Peter and John by the laying on of hands. Even a casual reading of the text indicates that something quite unusual took place on that occasion, for why would Simon want the authority to impart such a gift if there was not something very dramatic about it? He had already practiced magic in his preconversion days and had witnessed the unusual signs accompanying the ministry of Philip. What was it that he desired so inordinately?

Details are lacking. Luke simply says that "Simon saw [Gk. *horaō/eidon*] that the Spirit was given at the laying on of the apostles' hands" (v. 18). The Greek verb is very common in the New Testament; its basic meaning is "to see," but it has the meaning also of "perceive." No serious student of Scripture will question that something observable took place when Peter and John laid hands on the Samaritans; it was so unusual that even Simon was singularly impressed. The only thing that could have arrested his attention was the unique phenomenon of speaking in tongues.

In light of the absolutely clear identification of tongues with Spirit baptism in the two major accounts that bracket this one (in chaps. 2 and 10), it hardly seems that Luke would have thought it necessary to mention tongues specifically here. The burden of proof rests with those who insist it was *not* speaking in tongues that gripped Simon's attention. If it was not glossolalia, what was it? Even writers who do not subscribe to the Pentecostal view of Spirit baptism say that glossolalia was manifested here. I quote a number of them to illustrate:

Dunn says that what Simon saw "would presumably have been the sort of manifestations which Luke elsewhere attributes to the gift of the Spirit (2:4; 10:46; 19:6)."[33]

"The text does not explicitly say that this reception of the Spirit was attested by tongues, but it seems likely."[34]

The bestowal of the Spirit is here "recognizable by the sign of glossolalia."[35]

"It is plain that the Samaritans' reception of the Spirit was attended by the same audible signs as had marked his reception by the believers at Pentecost."[36]

"Simon sees the power of the Apostles to bring about an outburst of *glossolalia*."[37]

"It is a fair assumption that for Luke the Samaritan

[33]James D. G. Dunn, *The Acts of the Apostles* (Valley Forge: Trinity Press International, 1996), 111.

[34]Carson, *Showing the Spirit*, 144.

[35]Ernst Haenchen, *The Acts of the Apostles*, trans. Bernard Noble and Gerald Shinn, rev. ed. (Philadelphia: Westminster Press, 1971), 304.

[36]Bruce, "Luke's Presentation," 24.

[37]Neil, *Acts of the Apostles*, 123.

'Pentecost', like the first Christian Pentecost, was marked by ecstatic glossolalia."[38]

The commentators quoted above opt for the *occurrence* of tongues in this incident, but do not accept the Pentecostal interpretation that tongues are a necessary sign of Spirit baptism.

Simon "saw" something; therefore the traditional Pentecostal understanding of this incident is not really an argument from silence. It is based in part on the unambiguous association of tongues with Spirit baptism in the two main accounts that precede and follow this incident.

Saul of Tarsus (Acts 9:17)

One purpose of the laying on of Ananias's hands was that Saul might "'be filled with the Holy Spirit'" (Acts 9:17). This account also falls between the two major narratives which unambiguously associate glossolalia with individuals being initially filled with the Holy Spirit. But Luke does not record any details of Paul's Spirit baptism. It is certain, however, that Paul spoke in tongues regularly and often. "I thank God that I speak in tongues more than all of you" (1 Cor. 14:18). Krister Stendahl calls him "the mighty practitioner of glossolalia."[39]

In the Book of Acts, the experience of speaking in tongues, when it is recorded, first occurs at the time of Spirit baptism. It seems perfectly legitimate and logical for Pentecostals, therefore, to infer that Paul first spoke in tongues at the time Ananias laid hands on him. William Neil comments that "in receiving the gift of the Holy Spirit, Paul experienced the Pentecostal ecstacy."[40]

[38]James D. G. Dunn, *Jesus and the Spirit* (Philadelphia: Westminster Press, 1975), 189. See also C. K. Barrett, *The Acts of the Apostles* (Edinburgh, Scotland: T. & T. Clark, 1994), 412; Marshall, *Acts of the Apostles,* 158; David J. Williams, *Acts* (Peabody, Mass.: Hendrickson Publishers, 1990), 156.

[39]Krister Stendahl, "Glossolalia—The New Testament Evidence," in *Paul Among Jews and Gentiles* (Philadelphia: Fortress Press, 1976), 113.

[40]Neil, *Acts of the Apostles,* 131.

The Ephesian Disciples (Acts 19:1–7)

What did Paul mean when he asked the Ephesian men, "'Did you receive the Holy Spirit when you believed?'" (Acts 19:2). In his epistles, receiving the Spirit is a component of the salvation experience (for example, Rom. 8:15; Gal. 3:2,14). But the question shows that for Paul the expression could have an additional meaning. I am compelled to believe that Luke faithfully records the essence of Paul's question and that he has not (1) put his own words into Paul's mouth, (2) edited or revised the question to conform to his own theological agenda, or (3) created the entire incident to advance his own theological purposes. Luke, we must remember, is a reliable historian.

The narrative is clear about the meaning of Paul's question. The matter of having received the Spirit was to be one of "immediate perception: the Ephesians are expected to know whether or not they did in fact receive the Spirit when they 'believed.'"[41] Turner is alluding to the experience which they will indeed have shortly, when "they began speaking with tongues and prophesying" (v. 6, NASB)—the only other reference to the Spirit after verse 2. The terminology in this account is parallel to that found in previous accounts of people being filled with the Spirit: receiving the Spirit (v. 2), the Holy Spirit coming upon them (v. 6), speaking in tongues (v. 6).

On the basis of verse 6, which says the Ephesians spoke in tongues and prophesied, some assume that not all spoke in tongues—that some spoke in tongues and some prophesied—and that therefore *either* tongues *or* prophecy may accompany the experience. Focusing on this verse, I offer the following observations:

1. If prophesying is an alternative to tongues as an indication of Spirit baptism, this is the only place in Acts that would suggest it. It is not sound hermeneutical practice to base a belief on only one passage of Scripture. If Acts 2 is

[41]Turner, *Power from on High*, 392.

programmatic, as I believe it is, glossolalia fulfills Joel's prediction, not prophecy per se.

2. A closer look at the Greek text suggests the following translation: "The Holy Spirit came upon them. Not only did they speak in tongues, but they also prophesied."[42] Luke, then, is correlating this account with the previous accounts that record speaking in tongues by recipients of the Spirit (2:4; 10:46) and says that the men, in addition to speaking in tongues, also prophesied. Carson is uncertain about whether Luke is speaking about two separate phenomena or whether he is "referring to the same reality."[43] Turner says that "Luke does not say that *each* of the twelve began to speak in tongues and to prophesy, but that the group as a whole manifested these diverse gifts."[44]

Some suggest that Luke means to say, "They spoke in tongues, that is, they prophesied," relating the statement to "they spoke in tongues, that is, they exalted God" (10:46). But the Greek text of 10:46 has only the word *kai* ("and," "that is"); the Greek text of 19:6 reads differently.

Summary and Conclusions

Inspired utterance when the Spirit comes upon people recurs throughout biblical history—in the Old Testament, in the beginning days of the new age (Luke 1 to 4), and in accounts recorded in the Book of Acts.

Speaking in tongues, in one important sense, is a specialized form of prophecy. As such, its occurrence on the Day of Pentecost and on subsequent occasions is indeed a fulfillment of Joel's prediction that all God's people would prophesy.

[42]The Gk. construction *te . . . kai* is common in the Book of Acts. BAGD (807) gives the following as possible translations: "as . . . so"; "not only . . . but also." Some examples in Acts include 1:1,8; 4:27; 8:12; 9:2; 22:4; 26:3. I am indebted to a former colleague, Dr. Raymond K. Levang, for this observation in his "The Content of an Utterance in Tongues," *Paraclete* 23, no. 1 (winter 1989).

[43]Carson, *Showing the Spirit,* 150.

[44]Turner, *Power from on High,* 395.

The narrative of the outpouring of the Spirit on the Day of Pentecost is paradigmatic. It becomes the model, or paradigm, for later outpourings of the Spirit. The term "programmatic" is sometimes used for this concept.

Parallel to the inductive approach, which sees a pattern of glossolalia in Spirit baptisms, is the contribution of a contemporary approach to interpretation sometimes called narrative theology. As it relates to this subject, Donald A. Johns says that a worldwide, common technique in storytelling is to tell things in groups of threes and that "three times should be enough to tell anything. The paradigmatic effect of these stories should lead us to expect the same things in our own experience with the Spirit."[45]

Throughout the Old Testament, the early chapters of Luke's Gospel, and the Book of Acts, there is a pattern of inspired speech when the Holy Spirit comes upon people.

The viewpoint of some is that glossolalia may be the *normal* accompaniment of Spirit-baptism, but that it cannot be considered *normative;* that is, tongues will not occur invariably.[46] It is true, of course, that nowhere in Scripture is there a propositional statement that says Spirit baptism will be accompanied by speaking in tongues. Yet the "all" of Acts 2:4 and the "for" of 10:46 speak tellingly against the position that tongues are not normative. J. Rodman Williams argues that when tongues are explicitly mentioned in Acts, "*all* the people spoke in tongues."[47] It is the only manifes-

[45]Donald A. Johns, "Some New Directions in the Hermeneutics of Classical Pentecostalism's Doctrine of Initial Evidence," in *Initial Evidence: Historical and Biblical Perspectives on the Pentecostal Doctrine of Spirit Baptism,* ed. Gary B. McGee (Peabody, Mass.: Hendrickson Publishers, 1991), 163. The author should be distinguished from his late father, Donald F. Johns, one-time academic dean of Central Bible College in Springfield, Mo.

[46]See, for instance, Larry Hurtado, "Normal, But Not a Norm" in *Initial Evidence,* ed. McGee, 190–210; Turner, *Power from on High,* 447; James B. Shelton, "'Filled with the Holy Spirit' and 'Full of the Holy Spirit': Lucan Redactional Phrases" in *Faces of Renewal,* ed. Paul Elbert (Peabody, Mass.: Hendrickson Publishers, 1988), 106–7 n. 30.

[47]J. Rodman Williams, *Renewal Theology: Systematic Theology from a Charismatic Perspective* (Grand Rapids: Zondervan Publishing House, 1990), 2:211.

tation associated with Spirit baptism in Acts which is explicitly presented as evidence authenticating the experience.[48] Robert Menzies comments, appropriately, that the Pentecostal doctrine of tongues as initial evidence "is an appropriate inference drawn from the prophetic character of the Pentecostal gift and the evidential character of tongues-speech." He says further that glossolalia is especially well suited to serve as evidence because of its unusual and demonstrative character.[49]

It is sometimes objected that Luke records numbers of instances where individuals are said to be filled with the Spirit or full of the Spirit and makes no mention of tongues.[50]

The Pentecostal response is twofold: (1) Luke felt no obligation to mention tongues explicitly even in all those five instances. The cumulative evidence is that there was charismatic accompaniment to the first endowments with the Spirit. If the critics' line of reasoning is applied to *conversion* accounts in Acts, it is readily apparent that Luke does not mention repentance and faith as requirements for salvation in all accounts, nor are the respondents to the gospel message always said to have both repented and believed. (2) The classical Pentecostal doctrine of "initial evidence" applies only to one's initial experience of being filled with the Spirit.

It is often objected that the manifestation of tongues in the Book of Acts must be understood only in a historical-redemptive context; that is, Luke mentions it in conjunction with different people groups responding to the gospel and being incorporated into the Church. But the Pentecostal may respond as follows: (1) If Pentecost was a repeatable event on at least three or four occasions, why should it not continue to be repeatable? (2) If this unique phenomenon

[48]Oss, "A Pentecostal/Charismatic View," 261.

[49]Menzies, *Empowered for Witness,* 251; "Coming to Terms with an Evangelical Heritage—Part 2: Pentecostals and Evidential Tongues," *Paraclete* 28, no. 4 (fall 1994): 6.

[50]Carson, *Showing the Spirit,* 150.

occurred solely for historical-redemptive purposes, it should have been withdrawn by God after the event in Acts 19. On the contrary, Paul continued to speak in tongues and wished that all the Corinthians would do the same.

The traditional Pentecostal position finds an unexpected ally in the writing of James D. G. Dunn, one of the most trenchant critics of the Pentecostal view that tongues are a necessary component of Spirit baptism. He states first, "It is a fair assumption that for Luke the Samaritan 'Pentecost', like the first Christian Pentecost, was marked by ecstatic glossolalia." He goes on to say that in every case where Luke records and describes the giving of the Spirit—he does not include Paul's experience since it is not described—the giving is accompanied and evidenced by glossolalia. He adds, "The corollary is then not without force that Luke *intended* to portray 'speaking in tongues' as 'the initial physical evidence' of the outpouring of the Spirit."[51] Unfortunately, however, Dunn then says that Luke's concept of the Spirit's working "can only be described as fairly crude" and undiscriminating with its emphasis upon signs and wonders. He says further that "Luke's presentation is lop-sided."[52] In effect, he says that Luke's theology is not really dependable. But for those who subscribe to a high view of inspiration, Luke's theology is ultimately not his own; it is only mediated through him—by the Holy Spirit.

One critic of the Pentecostal position, voicing the objection of some others, says it seems "extraordinarily arbitrary *not* to see verses 2–3 [of Acts 2] as *equally* normative."[53] The Pentecostal response is simply that nowhere else are wind and fire mentioned in conjunction with, or prior to, people's reception of the Spirit, whereas glossolalia is both mentioned or strongly implied elsewhere and is also presented as evidence (10:46).

[51]Dunn, *Jesus and the Spirit,* 189–90.

[52]Ibid., 191.

[53]Carson, *Showing the Spirit,* 142.

Does Paul's question in 1 Corinthians 12:30—"Not all speak in tongues, do they?" (my translation)—undermine the Pentecostal position? The answer to his question must be no, based on the Greek form of the question. But Paul, in context, is talking about the manifestation of tongues as it occurs in the assembly of believers. Not all are called upon to give *public* utterances in tongues. This understanding is justified in view of the question that follows: "Not all interpret, do they?" (my translation). Furthermore, Paul himself expresses a wish that all God's people would speak in tongues (1 Cor. 14:5), evidently in private, as a means of spiritual self-edification (v. 4).

In conclusion, the Pentecostal doctrine of "initial physical evidence" is substantiated by an investigation of Scripture.[54] The terminology, though not of course divinely inspired, is an attempt to encapsulate the thought that at the time of Spirit baptism, the believer will speak in tongues. It conveys the idea that speaking in tongues is an immediate, empirical accompaniment of the baptism in the Spirit.

Yet three notes are in order: (1) As Robert Menzies points out, the Pentecostal focus on evidence can lead easily to a confusion of the gift of the Spirit with the sign. "The manifestation of tongues is an evidence of the Pentecostal dimension of the Spirit's work, but not the gift itself." Properly understood, one receives the Spirit, not tongues.[55] (2) "'Initial evidence' should not be so much a sign that 'we have the Spirit', but that the Spirit 'has us' as participants in the work of the kingdom."[56] (3) Pentecostals argue that speaking in tongues is only the *initial* evidence, but that there are, or at least ought to be, evidences in addition to

[54]Two articles of interest from a classical Pentecostal perspective are found in *Dictionary of Pentecostal and Charismatic Movements,* ed. Stanley M. Burgess and Gary B. McGee (Grand Rapids: Zondervan Publishing House, 1988): (1) "Glossolalia," by Russell P. Spittler (335–41); (2) "Initial Evidence, A Biblical Perspective," by Ben C. Aker (455–59).

[55]Menzies, *Empowered for Witness,* 253.

[56]Frank D. Macchia, "The Question of Tongues as Initial Evidence," *Journal of Pentecostal Theology* 2 (1993): 121.

tongues. Frederick Dale Bruner, a vigorous opponent of the Pentecostal doctrine of initial evidence, nevertheless states accurately the position of responsible Pentecostals on this matter.[57]

[57]Frederick Dale Bruner, *A Theology of the Holy Spirit: The Pentecostal Experience and the New Testament Witness* (Grand Rapids: Wm. B. Eerdmans, 1970), 77, 85. Additional indications of Spirit-fullness will be covered in the following chapter.

Chapter 10

Purposes and Results of Spirit Baptism

This chapter will cover the following topics: Jesus and the Spirit; the results of Spirit baptism; the reception of Spirit baptism; and the New Testament's inclusive use of the terminology "filled with/full of the Holy Spirit."

Jesus and the Spirit-Empowered Life

OLD TESTAMENT PROPHECIES

The Book of Isaiah contains the following prophecies that link the Holy Spirit with the Messiah:

"The Spirit of the LORD will rest on him—the Spirit of wisdom and of understanding, the Spirit of counsel and of power, the Spirit of knowledge and of the fear of the LORD" (11:2).

"'I will put my Spirit on him and he will bring justice to the nations'" (42:1).

"The Sovereign LORD has sent me, with his Spirit" (48:16). Translations vary. The other possibility is, "The Lord GOD has sent Me, and His Spirit" (NASB). In either case, the Spirit and the Messiah are very closely connected.

"The Spirit of the Sovereign LORD is on me, because the LORD has anointed me to preach . . . to bind up . . . to proclaim freedom . . . and release" (61:1).

In addition, Isaiah records the prophecy of the virginal conception of Jesus (7:14). Even though Isaiah does not mention the Spirit in this connection, both Matthew (1:18–20) and Luke (1:35) attribute the miracle to the activity of the Holy Spirit.

The Earthly Ministry of Jesus

Jesus was anointed with the Holy Spirit at His baptism (Luke 3:22). It marked the beginning of His earthly ministry; it was His commissioning for public service. (Recall that both the transliterated Heb. word "Messiah" and the transliterated Gk. word "Christ" mean "anointed one.") The Spirit remained on Him (John 1:33), and furthermore He experienced the Spirit in unrestricted measure (3:34).

Luke's account of Jesus' wilderness temptation is bracketed by two references to the Spirit: He was "full of the Holy Spirit" when He entered the wilderness (Luke 4:1), and after the temptation He returned to Galilee "in the power of the Spirit" (Luke 4:14). It is clear from Luke's recounting of the story that Jesus' successful resistance to temptation was attributable both to the Holy Spirit's fullness in Him and to His expert use of the Scriptures. Very possibly the Spirit guided Him in the selection of the most effective Scripture passages to counteract Satan's suggestions.

At the synagogue in Nazareth, Jesus read the prophecy of Isaiah 61 and applied it to himself. With that, He embarked on His mission of deliverance. Peter later remarked that "'God anointed Jesus of Nazareth with the Holy Spirit and power, and . . . he went around doing good and healing all who were under the power of the devil, because God was with him'" (Acts 10:38). One outstanding example of Jesus' empowerment by the Spirit is His statement that He cast out demons "'by the Spirit of God'" (Matt. 12:28).

Jesus: The Pattern for Believers

By analogy or parallel, Jesus' anointing with the Spirit at the Jordan River sets the pattern for believers' reception of the Spirit.[1] Some do not hesitate to call the Spirit-empowered Jesus a paradigm for believers.[2] Roger Stronstad strongly advocates this position, saying that "Luke parallels the Spirit baptism of the disciples with the inaugural anointing of Jesus by the Holy Spirit." He cites Charles Talbert's fourfold parallelism between the two episodes:

(1) Both Jesus and the disciples are praying; (2) the Spirit descends after their prayers; (3) a physical manifestation of the Spirit takes place; (4) the ministries of both begin with a sermon that is thematic of what follows, appeals to prophetic fulfillment, and speaks of rejection of Jesus.[3]

Stronstad goes a step further and talks about the "transfer motif" found in Scripture. It involves the transfer of the Spirit from one person to another. Examples are Moses and the elders (Num. 11:16–17); Moses and Joshua (Num. 27:18–20; Deut. 34:9); Elijah and Elisha (2 Kings 2:9,15; cf. vv. 8,14); Saul and David (1 Sam. 10:10; 16:13–14). The purpose of the transfer is twofold: "to authenticate or accredit the new leadership, and to endow the appropriate skills for the new leadership responsibilities."[4] He focuses attention

[1]Representative advocates of this position include Robert P. Menzies, *Empowered for Witness: The Spirit in Luke-Acts* (Sheffield, England: Sheffield Academic Press, 1994), 174; I. Howard Marshall,"Significance of Pentecost," *Scottish Journal of Theology* 30, no. 4 (1977): 352; G. W. H. Lampe,"The Holy Spirit in the Writings of Saint Luke," in *Studies in the Gospels,* ed. D. E. Nineham (Oxford, England: Blackwell, 1957), 168; J. Rodman Williams, *Renewal Theology: Systematic Theology from a Charismatic Perspective* (Grand Rapids: Zondervan Publishing House, 1990), 2:169. Dissenters include: M. Max B. Turner, *Power from on High: The Spirit in Israel's Restoration and Witness in Luke-Acts* (Sheffield, England: Sheffield Academic Press, 1996), 188; and Gordon D. Fee, *Gospel and Spirit: Issues in New Testament Hermeneutics* (Peabody, Mass.: Hendrickson Publishers, 1991), 109, who will not even allow for analogy.

[2]Walt Russell,"The Anointing with the Holy Spirit in Luke-Acts," *Trinity Journal,* n.s., 7, no. 1 (spring 1986): 49; James B. Shelton,"Reply to James D. G. Dunn's 'Baptism in the Spirit: A Response to Pentecostal Scholarship on Luke-Acts,'" *Journal of Pentecostal Theology* 4 (1994): 143.

[3]Roger Stronstad, *The Charismatic Theology of St. Luke* (Peabody, Mass.: Hendrickson Publishers, 1984), 51–52. Stronstad cites Charles H. Talbert, *Literary Patterns, Theological Themes, and the Genre of Luke-Acts* (Missoula, Mont.: Scholars Press, 1974), 16.

[4]Stronstad, *Charismatic Theology,* 21.

primarily on the Moses-elders incident, and relates it to Jesus' sending of the Spirit to the disciples (Acts 2:33), saying both accounts involve a transfer of the Spirit from an individual to a group and both transfers result in an outburst of prophecy.[5]

The Results of Spirit Baptism

Power for Witnessing

In Pentecostal circles, no aspect of Spirit baptism's purpose has received more attention than that it is for the evangelization of the world. This is firmly based in Acts 1:8, "'You will receive power . . . and you will be my witnesses . . . to the ends of the earth.'" The Book of Acts is a commentary on these two related themes that the disciples would receive power when the Spirit came upon them and that they would be Jesus' witnesses to all the world.

When Jesus told the disciples they would be His "'witnesses,'" the thought is not so much that they would be His representatives, though that is true, as that they would attest to His resurrection. The thought of witness occurs throughout the Book of Acts; it is applied generally to the disciples (1:8,22; 2:32; 3:15; 5:32; 10:39,41; 13:31) and specifically to Stephen (22:20) and to Paul (22:15; 26:16).

The worldwide evangelization by Pentecostals that has taken place in the twentieth century is testimony to the reality of the Pentecostal experience. Unfortunately, some modern church historians and missiologists have been slow to acknowledge the tremendous contribution the Pentecostal movement has made in the spread of the gospel throughout the world. Pentecostals cannot and dare not deny or overlook the wonderful and often sacrificial work of missionaries throughout the history of the Church who did not experience, or have not experienced, the baptism in the Spirit as understood by Pentecostals. We thank God for all those from other church bodies and missions

[5]Ibid., 77.

agencies who have contributed to the worldwide missionary enterprise. As with other matters previously discussed, the difference between these missionaries and Pentecostals is one of degree. It would be irresponsible for Pentecostals to say that others know nothing of the power of the Spirit.[6]

The association of power (Gk. *dunamis*) with the Holy Spirit is often made in the New Testament, where the two terms are interchangeable (for example, Luke 1:35; 4:14; Acts 10:38; Rom. 15:19; 1 Cor. 2:4; 1 Thess. 1:5). The power of the Holy Spirit given to the early disciples, however, must not be restricted only to power to evangelize.

Power To Perform Miracles

The miracles recorded in Acts most certainly are done by the power of the Holy Spirit. The following is a listing of some unusual events in the Book of Acts. Many are directly attributed to the Holy Spirit; His power is implied in the others.

- Tongues—2:4; 10:46; 19:6
- Prophecy—11:27–28, Agabus and other prophets; 13:1–2, prophets at Antioch; 21:4, disciples at Tyre; 21:11, Agabus
- Word of knowledge/distinguishings of spirits—5:3–4, incident of Ananias and Sapphira
- Word of wisdom—4:8–13, Peter before the elders; 15:28, the Jerusalem Council
- General statements about healings/miracles—2:43, apostles; 5:15–16, Peter's shadow; 6:8, Stephen; 8:6–8, Philip; 14:3 and 15:12, Barnabas and Paul; 19:11–12 and 28:9, Paul
- Healings—3:1–10, lame man at temple gate; 9:33–35, Aeneas the paralytic; 14:8–10,

[6]In line with this and related comments I have made, I highly recommend the following article: "Baptism in the Holy Spirit, Initial Evidence, and a New Model," by Gordon L. Anderson in *Paraclete* 27, no. 4 (February 1993): 1–10.

lame man at Lystra; 28:3–5, Paul and the viper; 28:8, father of Publius
- Exorcisms—5:16; 8:7 (general statement); 16:16–18, slave girl; 19:13–16, incident involving the sons of Sceva
- Raisings from the dead—9:36–42, Tabitha/Dorcas; 20:9–10, Eutychus
- Visions—chap. 10, Cornelius and Peter; 16:9–10, Paul
- Miraculous deliverances—5:19; 12:7–10, Peter; 16:23–26, Paul and Silas; 27:23–25, Paul at sea
- Miraculous transportation—8:39–40, Philip
- "Reverse" miracles—5:1–11, Ananias and Sapphira stricken dead; 12:23, Agrippa I stricken dead; 13:9–12, Elymas (Bar-Jesus) blinded

Ministry to the Church

In addition to the Spirit being given for the personal benefit of the believer and for empowerment for service (both witnessing and miracle working), the Book of Acts also speaks of the Spirit giving the disciples discernment and guidance in church matters (5:3,9 [implied]; 15:28). There are also instances of the Spirit giving encouragement, wisdom, and direction to the church (6:3,5; 9:31; 11:24,28; 13:52; 15:28; 20:28) and also giving personal guidance (20:23; 21:4,11). "We cannot say the Pentecostal gift to the disciples was 'empowering for witness' *alone*."[7]

Speaking in Tongues

The idea that glossolalia is the "initial physical evidence" of the baptism in the Spirit stresses that tongues will occur at the time of the filling and that, by nature, the phenome-

[7]Turner, *Power from on High*, 344, Turner's emphasis. He adds that "the Spirit is an empowering to serve the church as much as it is to serve its mission to outsiders, even if Luke's account of the expansion of Christianity inevitably gives more space to the latter" (416).

non is observable. Speaking in tongues is therefore the immediate, empirical, and external indication that the filling has taken place. It is not the sum total of the experience, however, for in addition to this on-the-spot phenomenon, the Scriptures speak of continuing and internal evidences of the Spirit's fullness. But for the moment, it will be profitable to explore further the implications of glossolalia at the time of Spirit baptism.

The events of the Pentecostal outpouring recorded in Acts 2 must certainly be seen in a historical-redemptive context. Pentecost is the climactic event in the implementation of the new covenant. As such, it was God's gift of the Spirit to the Church. But just as the experience of those disciples was repeated on future occasions for others—even some twenty-five years afterward (Acts 19:1–6) and for an individual (Acts 9:17)—so this outpouring upon the Church transcends time and is both corporate and personal in nature. It is very appropriate, then, to say that Christians today may experience what some call "a personal Pentecost."

There are at least three reasons why God ordained glossolalia for the Day of Pentecost. The first is historical; the other two apply to all believers.

1. The final step in the inauguration of the new covenant was signaled by meteorological and atmospheric phenomena reminiscent of the institution of the old covenant at Sinai. In addition, the Lord chose to add a new element—speaking in tongues—that had not occurred prior to Pentecost in recorded biblical history. While some Old Testament scholars identify the babblings of some Old Testament prophets with glossolalia, such a position cannot be sustained if one takes seriously the New Testament teaching that glossolalia is speaking in languages, not the utterance of nonsense syllables. The introduction of this new phenomenon at Pentecost was designed to draw attention to the new era that was being inaugurated in God's dealings with his people.

2. The occurrence of glossolalia on the Day of Pentecost

highlighted the missiological imperative Jesus had previously given to the disciples. The various languages the Spirit-inspired disciples spoke would have served, indirectly, to remind them of the many language groups that needed to hear the gospel. Unfortunately, some early leaders of the Pentecostal movement mistakenly thought that the bestowal of tongues was the equipping of believers with languages to be used in evangelization. We should observe that the content of the disciples' glossolalic utterances was not a preaching of the gospel but a recital of "'the mighty deeds of God'" (Acts 2:11, NASB)—apparently a recounting of some manifestations of God's power and deliverance in the Old Testament. It may have been similar to some psalms that recount the manifestations of God's power and glory in historical events. Yet the speaking in tongues did arrest the attention of the nonbelievers to the point where they listened to Peter's preaching (Acts 2:14–39).

3. There is also a personal dimension to glossolalia. Paul says that "anyone who speaks in a tongue does not speak to men but to God" (1 Cor. 14:2) and that one "who speaks in a tongue edifies himself" (v. 4). This is one reason why he says, "I would like every one of you to speak in tongues" (v. 5). The Greek present tense of "to speak" suggests the translation "to continue speaking in tongues." Paul's statement that the one who speaks in tongues "edifies himself" must be understood in a positive sense. Glossolalia is a means of spiritual self-edification. Coupled with the gift of the interpretation of tongues, it edifies the congregation. When done in private, it builds up the one praying, in a manner not explicitly stated in Scripture. Since tongues is a means of spiritual upbuilding (what some call a means of grace), it is available to all God's children. Why would God withhold any means of grace from any believer? Closely related to Paul's teaching is Jude's admonition about "building yourselves up in your most holy faith, praying in the Spirit" (v. 20, my translation), as well as Paul's statement elsewhere about prayer in the

Spirit (Eph. 6:18). "Praying in the Spirit" surely includes praying in tongues. Some call glossolalia a "prayer language," a designation which highlights its personal and devotional nature. Paul would agree (1 Cor. 14:15).

In addition, a number of responsible exegetes see glossolalia in Paul's statement that "the Spirit himself intercedes for us with groans that words cannot express" (Rom. 8:26).[8]

Openness to Spiritual Manifestations

The initial experience of speaking in tongues indicates that the recipients are willing to submit themselves to something suprarational. They are willing to "let go" and to allow themselves to be immersed in/overwhelmed by the Spirit of God to the point where their mind does not contribute to what they say (1 Cor. 14:14).

The baptism in the Spirit opens up the receivers to the full range of spiritual gifts. A look at the major lists of spiritual gifts (Rom. 12:6–8; 1 Cor. 12:8–10,28–30; Eph. 4:11) will reveal that most of those gifts had already been manifested in some way both in the Old Testament and in the Gospels. The pre-Pentecost disciples themselves were instrumental in healings and demon expulsions (Luke 10:9,17; see also Matt. 10:8). Furthermore, a study of church history demonstrates that spiritual gifts in their many forms were manifested by Christians in all ages.

In addition, the New Testament shows that among the early disciples there was a higher *incidence* of spiritual gifts after Pentecost than before. For instance, miracles were wrought through nonapostles like Stephen (Acts 6:8) and Philip (8:7), as well as through apostles. Both Peter and Paul were instrumental in healing hopeless cases and in raising the dead. Peter certainly experienced the gift of faith in telling the lame man to walk (3:6), as well as the gift of a word of knowledge in exposing the sin of Ananias and Sapphira (5:1–10).

[8]See Anthony Palma,"The Groanings of Romans 8:26," *Advance* 31, no. 8 (fall 1995): 46–47.

It is a matter of record that those who have championed and experienced Spirit baptism have no reservations about the continuation of the extraordinary gifts. This is largely attributable to their own experience of Spirit baptism in which they have opened themselves up to the unusual working of the Spirit, and consequently have a heightened sensibility to His miraculous working in its many forms.

As with this and the points that follow, these considerations are not a question of the haves versus the have-nots. Pentecostals must resist the temptation to be spiritually elitist in these matters. Rather, whatever they experience from the hand of the Lord should induce greater humility among them.

Righteous Living

Spirit baptism cannot be divorced from its implications for righteous living. It is, after all, an immersion in Him who is called the *Holy* Spirit. The emphasis in the Book of Acts is on the evangelization of the Roman Empire by the power of the Spirit, but that does not eliminate the Spirit's work in the personal life of the believer, which is simply not an emphasis in Acts. One who is indeed filled with/overwhelmed by the Holy Spirit will not live an unrighteous life. Pentecostals must be careful not to identify Spirit baptism only with speaking in tongues and world evangelization. To do so is to exclude or restrict the work of the Spirit in other aspects of a believer's life.

A basic problem with some of the Corinthian believers was that they continued speaking in tongues (whose genuineness Paul did not question) without allowing the Spirit to work internally in their lives. Article 7 of the Assemblies of God "Statement of Fundamental Truths" states, in part, that with the baptism in the Holy Spirit "comes the enduement of power for life and service." I understand "for life" to mean "for righteous living." If people who profess to have been baptized in the Holy Spirit are not living a God-pleasing life, it is because they have not allowed the experience to manifest itself in their lifestyle.

Spirit baptism does not result in instant sanctification (nothing does!), but it ought to provide an added impetus for the believer in pursuing a God-pleasing life.

Reception of Spirit Baptism

If, as Pentecostals believe, Spirit baptism is not synonymous with regeneration or necessarily contemporaneous with it, what is required for one to receive this fullness of the Spirit?[9] The Scriptures do not give a formula, but the following considerations will be helpful.

The Experience Is for All Believers

Joel's prophecy, repeated by Peter on the Day of Pentecost, stresses that this outpouring of the Spirit is for all believers. This is sometimes called the democratization of the Spirit, in distinction to the Old Testament in which the Spirit was for a select few. The Lord now desires to put His Spirit upon all His people (Num. 11:29; Joel 2:28–29). Parallel to this is the idea that the promised outpouring of the Spirit upon individual believers transcends time and race, for the promise is "'for you [Jews] and your children [descendants] and for all who are far off'" (Acts 2:39). The expression "'far off'" is often understood in a geographical sense, which the Book of Acts certainly indicates. But Peter very likely had in mind Gentiles, in distinction from Jews, as the Book of Acts also indicates. This latter view is supported by a similar phrase Paul uses when he distinguishes Gentiles from Jews (Eph. 2:13,17). The individual seeker must be convinced that the experience is indeed for him or her.

Spirit Baptism Is a Gift

A gift, by definition, is not given on the basis of merit. We do not become worthy to receive the fullness of the Spirit, for whatever we receive from God is on the basis of his grace, not our works. If one could be baptized in the Spirit

[9]For a helpful summary, see Williams, *Renewal Theology,* 2:271–306.

on the basis of personal merit, then the troublesome and unanswerable questions are, What constitutes worthiness? and, What degree of spiritual perfection is requisite to qualify one for the experience? At the same time, needless introspection and a sense of unworthiness can be a barrier to being filled with the Spirit. If we must speak of a human requirement, then that requirement is faith.[10]

The Spirit Already Indwells

New Testament imagery for the baptism in the Spirit, if pressed literally, will give the impression that the Spirit is at first external to the individual ("poured out," "baptized in," "falling/coming upon") or that we must think of Him in quantitative terms ("filled with"). But as we have seen earlier, the Spirit indwells all believers at the time of their repentance and faith in Christ. Therefore Spirit baptism is an additional work of the already indwelling Holy Spirit. Some refer to it as a "release" of the Spirit in one's life.

Openness and Expectancy Facilitate Reception

God does not baptize in the Spirit against a person's will. Yieldedness to the Lord, a willingness to submit entirely to Him, will facilitate one's being filled with the Spirit. This is especially true with regard to the glossolalic aspect of Spirit baptism. The recipient must learn to cooperate with, or to be borne along by, the Holy Spirit, for the disciples spoke in tongues "as the Spirit was giving them utterance" (Acts 2:4, NASB). They did not generate the tongues-speaking; they responded, rather, to the impetus and prompting of the Spirit.

[10]See Williams, *Renewal Theology*, 2:271–78, for a treatment of faith as a condition for reception of the Spirit. Bruner misunderstands the position of responsible Pentecostals when he says that Pentecostalism "makes the mastery of what it considers sin to be the condition for the grace of the Holy Spirit." Frederick Dale Bruner, *A Theology of the Holy Spirit: The Pentecostal Experience and the New Testament Witness* (Grand Rapids: Wm. B. Eerdmans, 1970), 233; see also 249.

Prayer and Praise Lead Naturally Into the Experience

Luke, the foremost New Testament writer on Spirit baptism, records the words of Jesus: "'If you then, though you are evil, know how to give good gifts to your children, how much more will your Father in heaven give the Holy Spirit to those who ask [keep asking] him!'" (Luke 11:13). This promise is in a context of Jesus' teaching on prayer in which He speaks of persistence (v. 8), elaborating in verse 9 by saying "keep asking, keep seeking, keep knocking" (the meaning of the Gk. present tense in all three instances). It is worth noting that Jesus says the Spirit will be given by our heavenly Father to those who ask, and that the Father will insure they do not receive some counterfeit or substitute in response to their petition.[11] This ought to encourage some unsure and perhaps overly sensitive believers who fear that what they will receive will not be genuine.[12]

We have noted that glossolalia is an expression of praise for the mighty deeds of God (Acts 2:11; 10:46) and that it is connected with giving thanks to God (1 Cor. 14:16–17). It is therefore very appropriate, during times of prayer in expectation of the infilling of the Spirit, for a person to engage in praise as well as petition. The disciples were praising God during the period preceding the Day of Pentecost (Luke 24:53), and while it cannot be proved or disproved from Scripture, experience shows that praising God in the language at one's command facilitates the transition to praising Him in tongues.

The Laying On of Hands Is Not Necessary

Only three instances in Acts record the laying on of hands in connection with Spirit baptism—the Samaritans

[11]Stronstad comments that prayer is not the means for conferring the Spirit, but "is more properly the spiritual environment in which the Spirit is often bestowed." *Charismatic Theology,* 70.

[12]See Lampe, "Holy Spirit in the Writings," 169.

(chap. 8), Saul (chap. 9), and the Ephesians (chap. 19)—and nowhere is it stipulated as a requirement.

God Is Sovereign

Since the baptism in the Spirit is a gift, the timing of its giving is in the hands of the Giver. The Lord most certainly does respond to believing prayer when the object of the prayer is in accordance with His will. But for reasons which He does not disclose, sometimes the Lord's timing differs from ours. It is evident from the Book of Acts and from church history that outpourings of the Spirit can occur at unexpected times. Consequently, a person who wishes to be baptized in the Spirit must not get under self-condemnation if the experience does not take place when expected. There may be times of special visitation by the Lord during which many people are filled with the Spirit. It is during those times that conditions are optimum for a prospective recipient.

Inclusive Meaning of "Filled With/Full Of the Spirit"

The baptism in the Spirit is not a once-for-all experience; the New Testament does not teach "once filled, always filled."[13] Instead, the widely accepted Pentecostal view is that of "one baptism, many fillings."[14] A review of passages containing the expressions "filled with" and "full of" will demonstrate this.[15]

[13]Howard M. Ervin represents a decided minority who believe in "One Baptism, One Filling," the title of the chap. in his *Spirit Baptism: A Biblical Investigation* (Peabody, Mass.: Hendrickson Publishers, 1987), 49–61. An effective rebuttal to his position is given by Larry W. Hurtado, "On Being Filled With the Spirit," *Paraclete* 4, no. 1 (winter 1970): 29–32. Stronstad concurs in his criticism of Ervin: *Charismatic Theology,* 54.

[14]The same expression is used by many who deny a postconversion experience of Spirit baptism, equating Spirit baptism with the Spirit's work in regeneration or conversion.

[15]The two expressions occur only in Luke's writings, with one exception—Eph. 5:18.

"FILLED WITH THE SPIRIT"

We have already noted that the expressions "baptized in the Holy Spirit" and "filled with the Holy Spirit" are interchangeable (Acts 1:5; 2:4). But in the Book of Acts "filled with the Holy Spirit" is used in two additional ways:

1. Episodic Enduements in Time of Need. Three instances in the Book of Acts bear this out. First, Peter experienced a fresh enablement of the Spirit at the time he and John were brought before the religious authorities following the healing of the lame man at the temple gate. When they were challenged as to the power by which the miracle was performed, Luke records: "Then Peter, filled [lit. "having been filled"] with the Holy Spirit, said to them . . . " (4:8). He was given precisely the right thing to say under those difficult circumstances. This was a fulfillment of Jesus' promise that during such times the Holy Spirit would give believers appropriate words (Matt. 10:17–20; Mark 13:9–11; Luke 12:11–12).

Second, Paul had a similar experience of special enduement when, early in his missionary work, he confronted Elymas the sorcerer. Luke records, "Paul, filled [again, lit. "having been filled"] with the Holy Spirit, looked straight at Elymas" (Acts 13:9). In this "power encounter," the Spirit came upon Paul to enable him to combat one who was a "'child of the devil and an enemy of everything that is right'" (v. 10).

Third, the early believers, in the face of persecution if they continued to proclaim Christ, prayed, "'Enable your servants to speak your word with great boldness'"[16] (Acts 4:29). The Lord's response: "They were all filled with the Holy Spirit" (this Gk. clause is virtually identical with that of 2:4) and they "spoke the word of God boldly" (v. 31).

There may indeed be special fillings of the Holy Spirit after the experience of Spirit baptism, to enable one to cope with a special problem. Additional experiences of this type

[16]Gk. *parrēsia,* a word often used in connection with bearing witness to Christ, often translated "boldness" or "confidence."

are sometimes called "anointings," but the New Testament nowhere uses that word when it records them.[17] The verb "anoint" *(chriō)*, however, is used in connection with Jesus' Jordan experience of the Spirit (Luke 4:16–21; Acts 10:38; some cite Acts 4:26).

Do these three experiences imply that the recipients were not already filled with the Spirit? "Our western logical concept that something which is full cannot be filled any further is misleading if applied to the Spirit. One filling is not incompatible with another."[18] The most widely accepted view is that Pentecostal pneumatology includes room for second, third, fourth, etc., fillings of the Spirit in times of special need.[19]

2. A Continuing, Perhaps Continuous, Experience. Paul encouraged believers to "be filled [lit. "keep on being filled"] with the Spirit" (Eph. 5:18). The verses that follow are of special interest (vv. 19–21). They give several examples of what will demonstrate a Spirit-filled life: (a) speaking to one another with psalms, hymns, and spiritual songs; (b) singing and making music in one's heart to the Lord; (c) always giving thanks to God the Father for everything, in the name of our Lord Jesus Christ; and (d) submitting to one another out of reverence for Christ.[20] Following this last item is an extended treatment of husband-

[17]The verb is used of believers in 2 Cor. 1:21–22 and is in the aorist (past) tense. The cognate noun *chrisma* ("anointing") occurs in 1 John 2:20,27; it is something believers received in the past and which is a present possession. Very likely, Paul and John relate this anointing to the work of the Spirit in regeneration, though some associate it with Spirit baptism. Neither Paul nor John speaks of any additional "anointings."

[18]Marshall, "Significance of Pentecost," 355. He says elsewhere it is possible "that a person already filled with the Spirit can receive a fresh filling for a specific task or a continuous filling." *The Acts of the Apostles* (Grand Rapids: Wm. B. Eerdmans, 1980), 69, 100.

[19]Douglas A. Oss, "A Pentecostal/Charismatic View," in *Are Miraculous Gifts for Today?* ed. Wayne A. Grudem (Grand Rapids: Zondervan Publishing House, 1996), 243.

[20]Translations often obscure the connection of this last clause with being filled with the Spirit, but its grammatical construction (a participial clause) is parallel to that of the three preceding clauses.

wife relations, parent-children relations, and master-slave (employer-employee) relations. It is therefore clear that the truly Spirit-filled life includes encouragement to fellow believers (see the parallel passage in Col. 3:16), genuine worship, a right attitude with regard to circumstances, and proper interpersonal relations.[21] Don. A. Carson comments that Paul's command to be filled with the Spirit "is empty if Paul does not think it dangerously possible for Christians to be too 'empty' of the Spirit."[22] Under different imagery, this appears to be the thought behind Paul's admonition to Timothy to "fan into flame the gift of God, which is in you through the laying on of my hands" (2 Tim. 1:6; see also 1 Tim. 4:14).

This ongoing aspect of the Spirit's filling is also mentioned by Luke when he says that "the disciples were continually filled with joy and with the Holy Spirit" (Acts 13:52, NASB).[23]

"Full Of the Spirit"

The expression "full *(plērēs)* of the Spirit" is used only by Luke (Luke 4:1, of Jesus; Acts 6:3, of a qualification for the seven "deacons"; 6:5 and 7:55, specifically of Stephen; 11:24, of Barnabas). It suggests a state of Spirit-fullness and may not be distinguishable from being continually "filled with the Spirit" (Eph. 5:18; Acts 13:52). But it is instructive that in Luke's writings the completion of the phrase "full of" also includes, from a positive standpoint, wisdom (Acts 6:3), faith (6:5; 11:24), grace and power (6:8), and deeds of

[21]See John R. W. Stott, *The Baptism and Fullness of the Holy Spirit,* 2d ed. (Downers Grove, Ill.: InterVarsity Press, 1976), 54–57.

[22]Don A. Carson, *Showing the Spirit: A Theological Exposition of 1 Corinthians 12–14* (Grand Rapids: Baker Book House, 1987), 160.

[23]The verb is in the Gk. imperfect tense, which indicates continuing action. Luke shows a decided preference for *pimplēmi* when it relates to the Holy Spirit, though he does use *plēroō* in Acts 13:52, as does Paul in Eph. 5:18. I do not see any difference in meaning between the two since they both utilize the *ple-* stem.

kindness and charity (9:36). Negatively, the phrase is completed by deceit and trickery (13:10) and rage (19:28).

Similarly, a rundown of "filled with" clauses in Luke-Acts, apart from those that mention only the Holy Spirit, shows that "filled with" is followed, positively, by wisdom (Luke 2:40, Jesus), joy (Acts 2:28; 13:52), wonder and amazement (3:10). Negatively it is followed by wrath (Luke 4:28, KJV), fear/awe (5:26), rage (lit. "folly," 6:11), jealousy (Acts 5:17; 13:45), confusion (19:29). In addition, there is the statement that Satan had filled Ananias's heart to lie to the Holy Spirit (5:3).

In all these instances where Luke completes "filled with" or "full of" with positive characteristics and virtues, he is making a connection between them and being filled with, or full of, the Holy Spirit. Conversely, the negative words that complete the two expressions highlight the antithesis between the Spirit-filled life and the life that is dominated by a spirit other than the Spirit of Christ. A life "full of" a particular quality is a life that outwardly expresses that quality so that it clearly distinguishes a person.[24]

Concluding Remarks

The Pentecostal understanding and experience of Spirit baptism are firmly grounded in Scripture. Yet a word of admonition is in order. Pentecostals must not, and indeed cannot, rely on a past, initial experience of having been filled with the Spirit. The decisive question is not "When were you filled with the Spirit?" but rather "Are you now filled with, and full of, the Spirit?"

[24]M. Max B. Turner, "Spirit Endowment in Luke-Acts: Some Linguistic Considerations," *Vox Evangelica* 12 (1981): 53. He says further that the criterion for assessing if it is appropriate to call someone "full of the Spirit" is "whether the community of Christians *feel the impact of the Spirit through his life*" (55, Turner's emphasis).

Part 3

Spiritual Gifts

Chapter 11

General Considerations

Hans Kueng, a Roman Catholic theologian, emphasized that spiritual gifts, properly understood, are an indispensable and integral part of Paul's teaching on the Church. He states, "To rediscover the charismata is to rediscover the real ecclesiology of St. Paul."[1] Paul presupposes charismatic phenomena in churches he founded in Thessalonica (1 Thess. 5:19–21) and in Galatia (Gal. 3:5), as well as in the church of Rome (Rom. 12:6–8), which he did not found. Regarding Paul's comments to the Romans, one writer says, "The fact that Paul writes to a church he had not visited about these charismata suggests that this subject appeared normal in his teaching and in that of other early Christian missionaries."[2] Another writer says, "The phenomena Paul calls *charismata* abounded in the Early Church. They were 'normal' experiences for nearly all Christians who wrote and first read the New Testament."[3]

The most extended treatment of spiritual gifts is in Paul's

[1]Hans Kueng, "The Charismatic Structure of the Church," in *The Church and Ecumenism*, in *Concilium* (New York: Paulist Press, 1965), 4:49.

[2]Ernest Best, "Interpretation of Tongues," *Scottish Journal of Theology* 28, no. 1(1975): 55.

[3]John Koenig, *Charismata: God's Gifts for God's People* (Philadelphia: Westminster Press, 1978), 95–96. It should be noted that the author does not identify himself as a Pentecostal or a charismatic.

first letter to the Corinthians (especially chaps. 12 to 14).[4] In opening his extended discussion, Paul tells the Corinthians, "Now about spiritual gifts, brothers, I do not want you to be ignorant" (1 Cor. 12:1). The Greek tense of "to be ignorant" suggests that Paul means, "I do not want you to continue being ignorant." Instead of "ignorant," some versions say "uninformed" (NRSV) or "unaware" (NASB). Paul's wish for the Corinthians is just as applicable today. An intensive study of his teaching on spiritual gifts should, ideally, lessen the ignorance of God's people in this area. It is a study that should prove beneficial to both Pentecostal and non-Pentecostal believers.

It is necessary at the outset to investigate a number of general matters pertaining to spiritual gifts. The remainder of this chapter will cover the areas of basic terminology, the relationship between gifts and the body of Christ, the overall function of the gifts, the distribution of the gifts, and the belief that the so-called extraordinary gifts have ceased (i.e., cessationism).

Terminology

CHARISMATA

The Greek word *charisma* (pl. *charismata*) occurs in the New Testament seventeen times and, with one exception (1 Pet. 4:10), only in Paul's writings (Rom. 1:11; 5:15–16; 6:23; 11:29; 12:6; 1 Cor. 1:7; 7:7; 12:4,9,28,30–31; 2 Cor. 1:11; 1 Tim. 4:14; 2 Tim 1:6). It occurs nowhere in the standard text of the Septuagint or in the writings of Josephus and only twice in the writings of Philo of Alexandria.[5] Consequently,

[4]Eduard Schweizer, "*Pneuma, Pneumatikos* in the New Testament," in *TDNT,* 6:423.

[5]Even in the case of Philo, there is "the possibility of a Pauline reflection upon Philo's editor." See Ziegfried Schatzmann, *A Pauline Theology of Charismata* (Peabody, Mass.: Hendrickson Publishers, 1987), 3. According to Don A. Carson, "There is no textually certain pre-Pauline example." *Showing the Spirit: A Theological Exposition of 1 Corinthians 12–14* (Grand Rapids: Baker Book House, 1987), 19 n. 9. See also Archibald Robertson and Alfred Plummer, *A Critical and Exegetical Commentary on the First Epistle of St. Paul to the Corinthians* (Edinburgh, Scotland: T. & T. Clark, 1914), 263.

it is only in Paul's letters that this concept acquires weighty significance.[6]

The word is used in both a broad and a restricted sense. In its broad meaning it refers to the whole gift of redemption (Rom. 5:15–16; 6:23). Paul uses it also in referring to gifts which God bestowed upon Israel (Rom. 11:29; see also 9:4–5) and when referring to his rescue from mortal danger (2 Cor. 1:11). Of these broad uses, certainly Romans 6:23 is the most important: "The gift of God is eternal life in Christ Jesus our Lord." "Other charismata only exist because of the existence of this one charisma."[7]

In a restricted sense, *charismata* indicates spiritual manifestations which highlight the contribution of a believer to the Christian community. Paul uses the word "to describe gifts of God (not always spectacular) that differentiate individuals from one another for the purpose of enhancing their mutual service."[8] This is especially true of its usage in Romans 12:6 and 1 Corinthians 12:4,9,28,30–31. Paul tells the Corinthians, "You are not lacking in any gift" (1 Cor. 1:7, NASB). This has a direct connection with his extended treatment in chapters 12 to 14. In another passage, in dealing with the matter of sexual abstinence in the unmarried state, he says, "But each man has his own gift from God; one has this gift, another has that" (1 Cor. 7:7).

When he writes to the Romans he says, "I long to see you so that I may impart to [*metadidōmi*, "share with"] you some spiritual gift" (Rom. 1:11).[9] He does not mention the precise nature of this gift,[10] but he must have had in mind

[6]Eduard Schweizer, *Church Order in the New Testament,* trans. Frank Clarke (London: SCM Press, 1961), 99 n. 377. Kueng goes so far as to say it is "a specifically Pauline concept" (*Charismatic Structure,* 58–59).

[7]Ernst Kaesemann, "Ministry and Community in the New Testament," in *Essays on New Testament Themes,* trans. W. J. Montague (London: SCM Press, 1964), 64.

[8]Koenig, *Charismata,* 14.

[9]See also 1 Thess. 2:8 and Eph. 4:28 for other occurrences of the Gk. verb that involve the idea of sharing.

[10]William Sanday and Arthur C. Headlam, *A Critical and Exegetical Commentary on the Epistle to the Romans,* 5th ed. (Edinburgh, Scotland: T&T

the type of gifts he lists in 12:6–8 as well as those in 1 Corinthians 12 to 14. He very possibly possessed many of these gifts to an eminent degree (see also 1 Cor. 14:18). Whatever the precise nature of the "spiritual gift," Paul fully expected that the sharing of gifts would be "reciprocal and mutual," as the context bears out.[11]

The two passages in the pastoral letters (1 Tim. 4:14; 2 Tim. 1:6) are probably related to Timothy's functioning in a leadership role in the church. Peter's usage of the word *charisma* (1 Pet. 4:10) is in complete agreement with Paul's teaching on the more restricted use and meaning of the word.

To summarize: There is a completely nontechnical use of *charismata* to describe any of God's benevolent works in the world and among His people, and there are gifts that He imparts to individual members of the Christian community but which are not necessarily imparted to all.[12]

The related verb *charizomai* ("to give freely or graciously as a favor")[13] may be the basis for the noun *charisma*.[14] The verb, interestingly, occurs in the New Testament only in Paul's writings and in Luke-Acts.

The noun *charisma* indicates the result of the action understood by *charis* ("grace").[15] God's *charis* is the origin of every *charisma*.[16] Grace "takes concrete shape in specific

---

Clark, 1914), 21. Gerhard Delling says that this gift is "undoubtedly primarily teaching" in his *Worship in the New Testament,* trans. Percy Scott (Philadelphia: Westminster Press, 1962), 154.

[11]Schatzmann, *Pauline Theology of Charismata,* 15.

[12]Arthur Carl Piepkorn, "*Charisma* in the New Testament and the Apostolic Fathers," *Concordia Theological Monthly* 42 (1971): 378–79.

For a summary of the New Testament uses of the word *charismata,* see Schatzmann, *Pauline Theology of Charismata,* 4.

[13]BAGD, 876.

[14]See Sanday and Headlam, *Romans,* 99; and M. Max B. Turner, *The Holy Spirit and Spiritual Gifts: In the New Testament Church and Today,* rev. ed. (Peabody, Mass.: Hendrickson Publishers, 1998), 264.

[15]BDF, sec. 109(2).

[16]Arnold Bittlinger, *Gifts and Graces,* trans. Herbert Klassen (Grand Rapids: Wm. B. Eerdmans, 1967), 20.

gifts (Rom. 12:6; 1 Cor. 12:11)."[17] Another writer says *charisma* is "an individuation of the power of grace."[18] In fact, there are times when the two words seem to be used synonymously (2 Cor. 1:11; Rom. 5:15; 6:23).

PNEUMATIKA

The plural neuter form of the Greek adjective for "spiritual" *(pneumatikon)* is sometimes used in close connection with *charismata*. How do the two terms relate to each other? The commentators are not agreed. *Pneumatika* certainly appears to be used interchangeably with *charismata* when one compares the parallel statements, "Eagerly desire the greater gifts *[charismata]*" (1 Cor. 12:31) and "Eagerly desire spiritual gifts *[pneumatika]*" (14:1). *Pneumatika* therefore is used for the totality of spiritual gifts. Consequently the rendering of the NIV for 1 Corinthians 12:1 is correct—"Now about spiritual gifts."[19] In this verse, even though the form of the Greek word may be either neuter or masculine, the neuter meaning is preferable.

Not all agree that the two terms are interchangeable. Some maintain that *pneumatikos,* in its different forms in 1 Corinthians 12 to 14, refers to the Corinthians' erroneous view of spiritual gifts and their reserving the term for those who were experiencing the more unusual gifts such as speaking in tongues. In this view, the "spiritual" person in 14:37 is one who speaks in tongues (see NASB). This view goes on to say that Paul used the term as an accommodation to them and that he really intended to show them the difference between what they considered to be "spiritual," whether gifts or people, and what were truly spiritual gifts

[17]Hans Conzelmann, *"charisma,"* in *TDNT,* 9:403.

[18]Ernst Kaesemann,"Worship and Everyday Life: A Note on Romans 12," in *New Testament Questions of Today,* trans. W. J. Montague (Philadelphia: Fortress Press, 1969), 192–93.

[19]Hans Conzelmann, *1 Corinthians,* trans. James W. Leitch (Philadelphia: Fortress Press, 1975), 241; see also Schweizer,"Pnuema," 6:437.

and people *(charismata)*.[20] To simplify: According to this view, the reader should precede the word "spiritual" with the words "what you Corinthians consider to be."[21]

Related to the above is a view that says the words *pneumatikon* (spiritual gift) and *pneumatikos* (spiritual person) "denote, respectively, gifts of inspired utterance or discernment and men who exercise such gifts."[22]

It seems best to see the two terms, *charismata* and *pneumatika*, as interchangeable.[23] The emphasis of each is different, however. *Charismata* calls attention to the grace aspect involved in the bestowment of the gifts; *pneumatika* directs attention to the Spirit *(Pneuma)* as the giver of the gifts (see also 1 Cor. 12:11).

Special attention should be given to Romans 1:11, where Paul joins the two words in the phrase "spiritual gift." This combination occurs nowhere else in Scripture.[24] The phrase is a link between the list of gifts in Romans 12:6–8 and those in 1 Corinthians 12:8–10. We must note that, strictly speaking, *charisma* means "gift," not "*spiritual* gift," and *pneumatikon* means "spiritual," not "spiritual *gift*."

[20]See Johannes Weiss, *Der erste Korintherbrief* (Göttingen, Germany: Vandenhöck & Ruprecht, 1910), 294; see also Kaesemann, "Ministry and Community," 66.

[21]For sample treatments of this matter, see David L. Baker, "The Interpretation of 1 Corinthians 12–14," *The Evangelical Quarterly* 46 (October–December 1974): 224–34; D. W. B. Robinson, "Charismata versus Pneumatika: Paul's Method of Discussion," *Reformed Theological Review* 31 (1972): 49–55; D. Moody Smith, "Glossolalia and Other Spiritual Gifts in a New Testament Perspective," *Interpretation* 28 (July 1974): 307–20.

[22]E. Earle Ellis, "Spiritual Gifts in the Pauline Community," *New Testament Studies* 20 (January 1974), 128–29; see also Robert P. Menzies, "Spirit-Baptism and Spiritual Gifts," in *Pentecostalism in Context: Essays in Honor of William W. Menzies*, ed. Wonsuk Ma and Robert P. Menzies (Sheffield, England: Sheffield Academic Press, 1997), 57.

[23]Rudolf Bultmann, *Theology of the New Testament*, trans. Kendrick Grobel (New York: Charles Scribner's Sons, 1951), 1:156; James D. G. Dunn, *The Theology of Paul the Apostle* (Grand Rapids: Wm. B. Eerdmans, 1998), 554–55.

[24]Any other passages where the phrase "spiritual gift(s)" occurs are an interpretation, not a translation, of the Gk. The reason is that "spiritual" is an adjective and sometimes, in context, a noun must be provided to complete the idea.

Dōrea and Dōma

Two related words, *dōrea* and *dōma,* interchangeable with the previous two, are basic Greek words for "gift" found in Ephesians 4:7–8. Paul speaks of Christ giving gifts *(dōmata)* to men. The two words are based on the very common Greek word for "give" *(didōmi),* which occurs twice in these verses. The verb and the nouns are so common that they derive special meaning only from their context. Romans 5:15–16 shows the close association of this word group with *charisma.* In Ephesians 4:11 the gifts are comparable to those in 1 Corinthians 12:28, which lists similar leadership roles in a discussion of *charismata* and *pneumatika.*

The Manifestation of the Spirit

In 1 Corinthians 12:7, Paul speaks of "the manifestation of the Spirit." We should note in passing that nowhere does he speak of "manifestations [pl.] of the Spirit," even though that expression is commonly used to refer to certain spiritual gifts. The reason for the singular may be that Paul regards all the gifts as an entity (similar to his usage of the singular "fruit of the Spirit," after which he enumerates nine—Gal. 5:22–23).

The phrase "the manifestation of the Spirit" is best understood to mean that the gifts are the several ways in which the Spirit manifests himself.[25] "The Spirit is not given in an 'invisible way.' He wants to manifest himself visibly."[26]

Gifts of the Holy Spirit?

The question mark is intentional. It will surprise some that this phrase is found nowhere in the Greek text of the

[25]Weiss, *Der erste Korintherbrief,* 298; J. Rodman Williams, *Renewal Theology: Systematic Theology from a Charismatic Perspective* (Grand Rapids: Zondervan Publishing House, 1990), 2:330; James D. G. Dunn, *Jesus and the Spirit* (Philadelphia: Westminster Press, 1975), 212.

[26]Bittlinger, *Gifts and Graces,* 24; see also Williams, *Renewal Theology,* 2:330.

New Testament, even though most English translations seem to read "gifts of the Holy Spirit" in Hebrews 2:4. The Greek word *merismois* does not mean gifts; it is properly translated "distributions" or "apportionments" and conveys the same idea as found in 1 Corinthians 12:11, "distributing to each one . . . " (NASB).[27] The concept of gifts, however, is implied in the Hebrews passage; this accounts for the NIV paraphrase, "gifts of the Holy Spirit distributed according to his will."

Gifts, Services, Workings/Effects

Three terms are found in 1 Corinthians 12:4–6. Paul precedes each with *diaireseis*, "different kinds of." The Greek word may indeed mean "varieties" or "diversities,"[28] but some prefer meanings like "allotments" or "apportionments" or "distributions."[29] This may be a case of both-and, since Paul's extended treatment of spiritual gifts emphasizes both the variety among them and the Lord who distributes them sovereignly as He wills.

Should these three terms be significantly distinguished from one another? It is generally acknowledged that there is no demonstrable difference among them.[30] In other words, Paul is not making a distinction between three dif-

[27]The root of the verb in 1 Cor. 12:11, *diaireō*, is different from the root of *merismois*, but the meanings are virtually synonymous. In the immediate context of Heb. 2:4, which mentions "signs, wonders, and various miracles," the rendering "gifts of the Holy Spirit" is understandable, but it is still an interpretation, not a translation.

[28]For example, see Gordon D. Fee, *The First Epistle to the Corinthians* (Grand Rapids: Wm. B. Eerdmans, 1987), 161 n. 274; Dunn, *Theology of Paul*, 554.

[29]For example, BAGD; Charles K. Barrett, *A Commentary on the First Epistle to the Corinthians* (New York: Harper & Row, 1968), 283; and many other commentators.

[30]Kurt Stalder, *Das Werk des Geistes in der Heiligung bei Paulus* (Zurich, Switzerland: EVZ, 1962), 88 n. 15; Ralph P. Martin, *The Spirit and the Congregation: Studies in 1 Corinthians 12–15* (Grand Rapids: Wm. B. Eerdmans, 1984), 11; Carson, *Showing the Spirit*, 34; F. F. Bruce, *1 and 2 Corinthians* (London: Marshall, Morgan & Scott, 1971), 118; Fee, *Corinthians*, 586–87.

ferent types of manifestation of the Spirit, nor is he providing a threefold categorization scheme for them. Rather, they present different aspects of spiritual gifts in general.

The first term in 1 Corinthians 12:4–6, *charismata* ("gifts"), speaks of the grace nature of the gifts; one cannot earn them. The second term, *diakoniai* ("services" or "ministries"), stresses the basic function and purpose of the gifts; they are meant to be of service or to minister to others. The third term, *energēmata* ("workings" or "effects"), points to God as the source and energizer of the gifts. Paul apparently was less rigid in his employment of terminology than some of us want him to be. For instance, he applies *charismata* to only one gift—the gifts of healings (1 Cor. 12:9). And he applies *energēmata* to only one gift—workings of miracles (v. 10). Yet it would be wrong to say that only one of the nine listed gifts is a *charisma* and only one is an *energēma.*

It is significant that Paul includes all three members of the Godhead in his treatment of spiritual gifts. While in one sense spiritual gifts are attributable to the Holy Spirit, especially those listed in 1 Corinthians 12:8–10, it is noteworthy that in the other two main lists of gifts—Romans 12:6–8 and Ephesians 4:7–11—the Father is the giver in the first and the Son in the second. This three-pronged approach by Paul should remind us of the vertical and horizontal dimensions of spiritual gifts. Vertically, all of them derive ultimately from the Father who alone is the giver of all that is good. Horizontally, a gift has value only as it is finally rooted in the Son's self-giving service for others (Mark 10:45).[31] And, of course, none of this is possible apart from the enabling presence and power of the Holy Spirit.

Spiritual Gifts and the Body of Christ

It is especially significant that in the three major passages in the epistles dealing with the subject of gifts, the body of

[31]Walter J. Bartling, "The Congregation of Christ—a Charismatic Body; an Exegetical Study of 1 Corinthians 12," *Concordia Theological Monthly* 40 (February 1969): 75.

Christ is also mentioned (Rom. 12:4–5; 1 Cor. 12:12–28; Eph. 4:4–6). The gifts consequently are bestowed only within and ultimately for the benefit of the body of Christ.[32] The most extended treatment of this concept of the body of Christ (1 Cor. 12:12–27) occurs between passages dealing with spiritual gifts (12:1–11,28–31). David Lim asks, "Is not Paul talking about the different functions of the gifts in his analogy between believers and the human body?"[33] We must place side by side the two concepts of spiritual gifts and of members of the body of Christ, since individual members of the body represent in a meaningful sense individual members or functions in the Church.[34] Regarding all the gifts in the key New Testament passages, one writer says, "The variety of these gifts [20+] match the diversity of the members of the body of Christ and their assigned function."[35]

The metaphor or simile of the human body was common in antiquity, but the unique element in Paul is that the community of believers is "one body in Christ" (Rom. 12:5, NASB) as well as being the "body of Christ" (1 Cor. 12:27). It is that body into which all believers are baptized (1 Cor. 12:13).

Volumes have been written on the meaning and significance of the Church being the body of Christ, but it may be best to understand the phrase in a metaphorical, rather than a mystical, sense.[36] More than anything else, it illus-

[32]Klaas Runia, "The Gifts of the Spirit," *Reformed Theological Review* 29, no. 3 (1970): 84.

[33]David Lim, *Spiritual Gifts: A Fresh Look* (Springfield, Mo.: Gospel Publishing House, 1991), 66.

[34]Anthony D. Palma, "1 Corinthians," in *Full Life Bible Commentary to the New Testament* (Grand Rapids: Zondervan Publishing House, 1999), 872–73.

[35]Richard C. Ouderluys, "The Purpose of Spiritual Gifts," *Reformed Review* 28 (spring 1975): 218

[36]See Gordon D. Fee, *God's Empowering Presence* (Peabody, Mass.: Hendrickson Publishers, 1994), 177 n. 358.

In traditional theology the concept "body of Christ" has been understood in four ways: (1) Jesus' physical body; (2) Jesus' spiritual, resurrected body; (3) Jesus' eucharistic body (in the elements of the Lord's Supper); and (4) Jesus' mystical body, the Church. See Michel Bouttier, *Christianity According to Paul,* trans. Frank Clarke (London: SCM Press, 1966), 69 n. 23.

trates how the many members of the Church should relate to one another, and ultimately to the Lord. If this is indeed true, then it is not surprising that these very important statements about the body of Christ, especially as they are found in Romans and 1 Corinthians, are presented in contexts that deal with conduct and attitudes.

With this in mind, it is easy to agree with William Barclay that Paul's immediate purpose in using the imagery of the body in the Corinthians passage "has everything to do with the life and spirit of the particular congregation. Within their own assembly the Corinthians had never learned to live as one body."[37] What Barclay says can certainly be extended to include any local body of believers. This may be called "a phenomenological approach to the Body of Christ."[38] Even though one may conceive of the term "body of Christ" as encompassing all believers, this one body "always becomes particularized in the local church."[39]

This local application of the term may be illustrated by Paul's parallel treatment of the concept of the Church as the temple of God. He states, "We are the temple of the living God" (2 Cor. 6:16)—referring to the entire community of believers everywhere as the one temple. But he also says, "Don't you know that you yourselves are God's temple and that God's Spirit lives in you? If anyone destroys God's temple, God will destroy him; for God's temple is sacred, and you [pl.] are that temple" (1 Cor. 3:16–17). In its context, this last passage applies to the specific situation at Corinth, namely, the divisive spirit which permeated the congregation. This divisiveness could very well destroy the local congregation; it is unthinkable that it could destroy the universal temple of God.

As was noted, the concept of the body of Christ is found in direct connection with the subject of spiritual gifts. We

[37]William Barclay, *The Mind of St. Paul* (New York: Harper & Row, 1958), 244.

[38]Bouttier, *Christianity According to Paul,* 61.

[39]Lesslie Newbigin, *The Household of God* (London: SCM Press, 1957), 70.

see, first, that the initial emphasis is upon the unity of the body (Rom. 12:4–5; 1 Cor. 12:12–13; Eph. 4:4). This thought parallels references to the one Spirit (1 Cor. 12:9,11,13). The function[40] of these gifts, therefore, is to promote this unity of the body of Christ in a demonstrable way. The purpose of variety is "to make it possible for the whole body to function as a unit."[41] By their proper functioning within the local congregation, the gifts serve to edify the body.

Second, the concept of the body points out the diversity of gifts within the Christian community (Rom. 12:4–5; 1 Cor. 12:4–20,28–29; Eph. 4:3–13). Yet Paul is careful to state these two points of unity and diversity in precisely that order: first the unity of the body, and only then the diversity of the individual members (1 Cor. 12:27).

Third, Paul stresses the interdependence of the members with one another. Each member, each gift, should exist for the welfare of the others. And finally, there is no room for pride on the part of anyone exercising any particular gift (1 Cor. 12:21–24), nor should any member feel inferior to others who seem to be more gifted (vv. 15–17), for it is God who has "arranged the parts in the body, every one of them, just as he wanted them to be" (v. 18). This same thought is reflected in the later statement that "in the church God has appointed" the various leaders and ministries (v. 28).

The Overall Purpose of Spiritual Gifts

The all-embracing function of the gifts is that they might edify, or build up, the congregation (1 Cor. 14:3,4–5,12, 17,26). The keynote of the entire chapter is found in the words "Let all things be done for edification" (v. 26b, NASB). Earlier in the letter, Paul had made reference to this theme (8:1,10; 10:23).[42]

[40]Paul uses *praxis* ("function") in Rom. 12:4 with reference to the various members of the body. See BAGD, 697; Dunn, *Theology of Paul*, 554–58.

[41]Stanley M. Horton, *What the Bible Says About the Holy Spirit* (Springfield, Mo.: Gospel Publishing House, 1976), 214.

[42]Ferdinand Hahn, *The Worship of the Early Church* (Philadelphia: Fortress Press, 1973), 68.

One writer says, rather sharply, that this concept of edifying others rejects "religious individualism and egoism, which exhausts itself in the production of special phenomena in order to center upon itself." He says, on the other hand, that the concept of edifying expresses the helping of the other person, not only as an individual but also as a member of the church (14:4–5,12).[43]

Some go so far as to say, with some justification, that the gifts are not given primarily to the one who ministers them but to those who are ministered to.[44] It is more accurate to say, however, that God indeed gives gifts to individuals (see 1 Cor. 12:8–10, "to one," "to another," etc.), but that the gifts are *for the benefit of* others. "The charismata are always to be seen as service . . . , *as God's gifts for the body,* given to, or better, *through,* the individual 'for the common good.'"[45] J. I. Packer says that "our exercise of spiritual gifts is nothing more nor less than Christ himself ministering through his body to his body, to the Father, and to all mankind." He continues by saying that Christ, from heaven, uses Christians as "his mouth, his hands, his feet, even his smile."[46]

The biblical concept of the universal priesthood of believers applies here. It is a priesthood "in which every believer offers himself and his gifts in personal ministry to Christ and through Christ to others, both in the body of Christ and out of it."[47]

In the context of a worship service, Paul never speaks about edifying oneself; he speaks only about the edification of others. The goal of the service is not the happiness of the participant, but the upbuilding of the Church.[48] An expres-

[43]Guenther Bornkamm, "On the Understanding of Worship," in *Early Christian Experience,* trans. Paul L. Hammer (New York: Harper & Row, 1969), 163. See also 1 Thess. 5:11 and 1 Cor. 8:11–13.

[44]Bittlinger, *Gifts and Graces,* 63.

[45]Dunn, *Jesus and the Spirit,* 264, Dunn's emphasis.

[46]J. I. Packer, *Keep in Step with the Spirit* (Grand Rapids: Fleming H. Revell, 1984), 83.

[47]Ouderluys, "Purpose of Spiritual Gifts," 215.

[48]Eduard Schweizer, "The Service of Worship. An Exposition of 1 Corinthians 14," in *Neotestamentica* (Zurich, Switzerland: Zwingli Verlag, 1963),

sion parallel to that of edification is found in 1 Corinthians 12:7, "To each one the manifestation of the Spirit is given for[49] the common good." The stress is not on "each one" but on "the common good."[50]

In summary, it must be emphasized that God's purpose in bestowing spiritual gifts upon individuals is that the gifts will be employed in the upbuilding of the body. The common good must not be sacrificed in the interests of any benefit that the individual exercising a gift might receive. The individual member of a body must not attempt to dissociate itself from the body (1 Cor. 12:14–16), since it is an integral part of the organism. So must gift-endowed persons not operate within a sphere bounded by their own interests, doing only what brings personal satisfaction to them. They must contribute to the well-being of the body.

Distribution of the Gifts

Paul speaks three times of "different kinds" *(diaireseis)* of gifts, services, and workings (1 Cor. 12:4–6). These are the only New Testament occurrences of this Greek word. Does it mean "differences" or "varieties," or "distributions"? The entire context emphasizes that there are indeed different gifts given to members of the Christian community, and Paul elsewhere does speak of "different *[diaphora]* gifts" that are given (Rom. 12:6). But it may be preferable to understand the word as meaning acts of dividing, or "dealings out,"[51] without excluding the idea of variety.

337–38. In the felicitous phrase of William D. Davies,"Pneumatic phenomena of whatever kind are to subserve the common weal," in *Paul and Rabbinic Judaism,* 2d ed. (London: SPCK, 1962), 201. See also Koenig, *Charismata,* 82; and Schatzmann, *Pauline Theology of Charismata,* 70.

[49]Gk. *pros* ("tending towards,""leading to"). C. F. D. Moule, *An Idiom-Book of New Testament Greek,* 2d ed. (Cambridge, England: Cambridge University Press, 1959), 53.

[50]Conzelmann, *1 Corinthians,* 208.

[51]Weiss, *Der erste Korintherbrief,* 297. Conzelmann gives it the meaning of "assignments" (*1 Corinthians,* 208).

The word *diairesis* is used frequently in the Septuagint, especially in Chronicles, of the "courses of priests, Levites and troops."[52] The verb form of the word found in 1 Corinthians 12:11 justifies this interpretation: "[The] one and the same Spirit works all these things [the various gifts], distributing *[diairoun]* to each one individually just as He wills" (NASB). This distribution, or "dividing up," of gifts by the Holy Spirit to each member is the opposite of the "factions" (*haireseis;* see 11:19, NASB) which existed at Corinth, for it produces harmony (see 1 Cor. 12:4,11).[53] The Book of Hebrews expresses a similar thought when it speaks of "signs, wonders and various miracles, and gifts [lit. "distributions," Gk. *merismois*] of the Holy Spirit . . . according to his will" (2:4).

Does every Christian possess at least one gift? Certainly the Holy Spirit is the possession of all Christians (Rom. 8:9; 1 Cor. 12:13). This is true whether or not there are any external manifestations of the Spirit in a believer's life. Yet it is also true that the gifts may be thought of as something in addition to the saving work and presence of the Spirit that all believers experience. They are "the distinguishing factors . . . that differentiate the members of the body of Christ from each other."[54] The consensus of New Testament writers, especially Paul, is that every believer is given at least one gift (Rom. 12:6; 1 Cor. 1:7; 3:5; 12:7,11,18; 14:1,26; Eph. 4:7,11; 1 Pet. 4:10; see also Matt. 25:15). But some maintain that no explicit statement may be found to the effect that every member of the congregation receives a gift. One writer says, "Genuine Pauline utterances on this subject are not quite so clear-cut, though their general tendency is undoubtedly in the same direction."[55] But according to

[52]Robertson and Plummer, *Corinthians,* 262.

[53]Edmund P. Clowney, "Toward a Biblical Doctrine of the Church," *Westminster Theological Journal* 31, no. 1 (1968): 77.

[54]Piepkorn, *Charisma,* 379; see also Bultmann, *Theology of the New Testament,* 1:163.

[55]Hans von Campenhausen, *Ecclesiastical Authority and Spiritual Power in the Church of the First Three Centuries,* trans. J. A. Baker (Stanford: Stanford University Press, 1969), 58 n. 15.

majority opinion on this matter, there should be no passive membership in the body of Christ, for every Christian has been equipped and prepared for service.[56]

Clearly, God does not bestow all the gifts on every member of the body. Paul underscores this by the manner in which he enumerates the *charismata* when he uses the expressions "to one . . . to another . . . to another," etc. (1 Cor. 12:8–10). Consequently, Paul counsels his readers not to covet other persons' gifts. Every believer must think within the limits prescribed for him or her by God (Rom. 12:3).[57]

Is it possible for one person to have more than one gift? There is nothing to suggest that more than one function, or gift, could not be exercised by one person,[58] even though no one can claim all the spiritual gifts (see 1 Cor. 12:29–30).[59] For example, it is possible for the glossolalist also to be given the gift of interpretation of tongues (14:5,13).

Paul categorically indicates that no Christian has all the gifts when he poses the succession of questions: "Not all are apostles, are they? Not all are prophets, are they? Not all are teachers, are they? Not all work miracles, do they?" etc. (1 Cor. 12:29, my translation).[60] Yet there are two statements by Paul himself in chapter 14 that seem to contradict the implied response to these questions. First, he says, "I would like every one of you to speak in tongues" (v. 5). One valid interpretation is that this is a gift granted in principle to all Christians and is latent in most people awaiting only to be prompted by the Holy Spirit.[61] It is true, also, that Paul makes a distinction between the private exercise of tongues and its manifestation in a worship service. For

[56]Kaesemann, "Ministry and Community," 73.

[57]Schweizer, *Church Order,* 203.

[58]Barrett, *Corinthians,* 296.

[59]Kueng, "Charismatic Structure," 56.

[60]For the English-speaking reader, this translation best captures the meaning of the Gk. text, which requires a negative answer to the questions.

[61]Bittlinger, *Gifts and Graces,* 100.

their personal spiritual edification, all Christians may have the potential to speak in tongues (v. 4). But only a limited number are enabled to exercise the gift in the assembly of believers, as a means of upbuilding the church.

Secondly, Paul says, "You can all prophesy in turn" (1 Cor. 14:31). Notwithstanding 1 Corinthians 12:29, this means that the prophets "may turn out to be a group coextensive with the church itself (cf. Num. 11:29; Acts 2:16–18)." Yet Paul does not assert that all Christians will necessarily take part in prophetic activity, but only that all may do so.[62]

We have already noted that the gifts are apportioned to each one individually as the Lord wills (1 Cor. 12:11; see also vv. 18,28; and Rom. 12:6; Eph. 4:7–8,11). Since a gift is a concrete and individual expression of grace,[63] it cannot be based on the recipient's merit or desires. Yet this seems to contradict Paul's statements, "Eagerly desire spiritual gifts" (1 Cor. 14:1) and "Be eager to prophesy" (v. 39). In 12:31 he says, "Eagerly desire the greater gifts." It is possible to translate these clauses, especially the last, in the indicative mood rather than the imperative mood; that is, Paul is making a statement of fact concerning the Corinthians. They were, indeed, "eager to have spiritual gifts" (1 Cor. 14:12). The meaning would then be, "continue to desire earnestly (present imperative) the greater gifts. The Corinthians coveted the greater gifts but they had formed a wrong estimate as to which were greater."[64] But the overwhelming majority of commentators view these statements as commands or wishes by the apostle, and it is best to understand them in that sense.

What are the "greater gifts" (1 Cor. 12:31)? In the broad context of the statement, they should be understood as "whatever gifts are most needed and most edifying at the time."[65] Paul stresses "the need for intelligibility in the com-

[62]Barrett, *Corinthians,* 329.

[63]Kaesemann, "Ministry and Community," 73.

[64]Robertson and Plummer, *Corinthians,* 282.

[65]Horton, *What the Bible Says,* 219.

munity; and in the community *all* the intelligible gifts edify the community and [uninterpreted] tongues does not."[66]

There is no contradiction between the concept of the Lord as the sovereign distributor of the gifts and the believer earnestly desiring the gifts. Robertson and Plummer say, "Our earnest desire for the best gifts is one of the things which fits us to receive them, and each person receives in proportion to this desire, a desire which may be cultivated. The Spirit knows the capacity of each."[67]

The clear inference is that one does not receive a spiritual gift against one's will. Because all believers are granted a measure of faith (Rom. 12:3), the individual is in a position to accept whatever bestowment the sovereign Lord grants. A clear implication is that even though one may already have experienced certain spiritual gifts, such as the gift of tongues which was especially prominent at Corinth, one may make oneself available to receive additional gifts. But it is evident in the Corinthian situation that an erroneous concept of and preoccupation with certain gifts may prevent a believer from desiring or receiving other gifts.

Cessationism and Continuationism

Cessationism is the position that the "extraordinary" gifts were temporary, and were withdrawn after the first century. These gifts are often identified as prophecy, tongues, interpretation of tongues, healings, and other miracles. Apostles are sometimes included in this category. One prominent cessationist says that some gifts "continue throughout the present age, but . . . most of the church will agree that certain spiritual gifts were discontinued after the apostolic age."[68]

[66]Gordon D. Fee, "Tongues—Least of the Gifts? Some Exegetical Observations on 1 Corinthians 12–14," *Pneuma* 2, no. 2 (fall 1980): 13, Fee's emphasis. See also Schatzmann, *Pauline Theology of Charismata,* 45.

[67]Robertson and Plummer, *Corinthians,* 268. See also Bultmann's very insightful comments (*Theology of the New Testament,* 1:163).

[68]John F. Walvoord,"The Holy Spirit and Spiritual Gifts," *Bibliotheca Sacra* 143 (April–June 1986): 110–11.

Continuationism maintains that God did not withdraw any of these gifts at any time, and that they are just as valid and as needed today as in the first century. It holds that even apostolic- and prophetic-like ministries can and should exist today, even though apostles and prophets, in the more narrow New Testament use of those terms, had a unique role in the founding of the Church.

Much of the discussion centers around Paul's statements that prophecies will cease, tongues will be stilled, and knowledge will pass away (1 Cor. 13:8). This will happen "when perfection [lit. "the perfect"] comes" (v. 10). The usual cessationist argument is that "the perfect" means the completion of the canon of Scripture. Extraordinary gifts, it is maintained, were needed to authenticate the preaching of the gospel in the first century; they are no longer available because "no one today has the same authority or the experience of receiving normative truth. . . . No one is given truth that is not already contained in the Bible itself."[69]

Wayne A. Grudem, a continuationist, rightly says that "the claim that New Testament prophecy had authority equal to Scripture is the basis of perhaps every cessationist argument written today."[70] The cessationist has an extremely limited view of the gift of prophecy. The continuationist maintains that the gift was not only to reveal truth, but also to edify, encourage, and comfort the Lord's people. And it was (and is), in principle, available to all believers. Until believers no longer need to be edified, encouraged, and comforted, the gift of prophecy will serve a very useful purpose in the Church.

The vast majority of commentators and exegetes interpret "the perfect" to mean the return of the Lord Jesus Christ. At that time, all the gifts, which at best are partial and imperfect, will no longer be needed because believers will be like their Lord (1 John 3:2).

[69]Ibid., 111.

[70]Wayne A. Grudem, *The Gift of Prophecy in the New Testament and Today* (Westchester, Ill.: Crossway Books, 1988), 244. By "New Testament prophecy," he means the gift of prophecy as it functioned in the NT Church.

In response to the cessationist contention that miracles were signs needed to validate the ministry of the apostles, Max Turner says that healings were "part of the scope of the salvation announced, which reached beyond the merely spiritual to the psychological and physical." They were "part of the firstfruits of the kingdom of God, and so as part of the message of salvation which the church announced."[71] And, one might add, "which the church must *still* announce." Healings and other miracles, while they may confirm the ministry of the Word, are also God's gracious provision to help humankind in time of need.[72]

[71]Turner, *Holy Spirit and Spiritual Gifts*, 293.

[72]See Jon Ruthven, "On the Cessation of the Charismata: The Protestant Polemic of Benjamin B. Warfield," *Pneuma* 12, no. 1 (spring 1990): 14–31.

Much has been written from the continuationist viewpoint on this issue. I list some works (including some already cited in this chap.) that are especially helpful:

Don A. Carson, *Showing the Spirit*, 68–72.

Gordon D. Fee, *Corinthians*, 644–45, especially n. 23.

Wayne A. Grudem, *Gift of Prophecy*.

Grudem, ed., *Are Miraculous Gifts for Today?* (Grand Rapids: Zondervan Publishing House, 1996). A symposium of four views: Cessationist, Open But Cautious, Third Wave, Pentecostal/Charismatic.

Jon Ruthven, *On the Cessation of the Charismata: The Protestant Polemic on Postbiblical Miracles* (Sheffield, England: Sheffield Academic Press, 1993).

M. Max B. Turner, *Holy Spirit and Spiritual Gifts*, 286–302.

Chapter 12

Individual Gifts Part 1

Classification of the Gifts

A comparative study of the different lists of spiritual gifts (Rom. 12:6–8; 1 Cor. 12:8–10,28–29; Eph. 4:11) indicates that no one list is complete, nor did Paul intend for it to be so. Each catalog contains gifts not included in any of the others. In addition, it is not necessary to conclude that a composite listing from all the sources is all-inclusive. Scholars are generally agreed that the lists are "sampling" or "exemplary," rather than inclusive.[1]

Furthermore, any attempt to divide the gifts into separate categories can be, at best, only tentative and suggestive. For instance, in the ninefold listing found in 1 Corinthians 12:8–10, Paul uses two synonyms meaning "another," *allos* and *heteros:*

> To one there is given . . . the message of wisdom, to another *[allos]* the message of knowledge . . . , to another *[heteros]* faith . . . , to another *[allos]* gifts of healing . . . , to another *[allos]* miraculous powers, to another *[allos]* prophecy, to another *[allos]* distinguishing between spirits, to another *[heteros]* speaking in different kinds of tongues, and to still another *[allos]* the interpretation of tongues.

[1]For example, James D. G. Dunn, *The Theology of Paul the Apostle* (Grand Rapids: Wm. B. Eerdmans, 1998), 557–58; Stanley M. Horton, *What the Bible Says About the Holy Spirit* (Springfield, Mo.: Gospel Publishing House, 1976), 209; J. Rodman Williams, *Renewal Theology: Systematic Theology from a Charismatic Perspective* (Grand Rapids: Zondervan Publishing House, 1990), 2:347.

One commentator says that even though the enumeration is unsystematic, "a certain grouping can nevertheless be discerned" on the basis of the shifts in *allos* and *heteros:* the first two, the next five, and the last two.[2] But Paul's use of these two synonyms more likely is for stylistic reasons[3] to avoid the monotony of using *allos* all eight times. Furthermore, the two adjectives refer to *persons* to whom the gifts are given, not to the *gifts* themselves.

If a categorization must take place, the following seems more natural (yet still following the order of the listing):

(1) a word of wisdom and a word of knowledge; (2) faith, gifts of healing, working of miracles; (3) prophecy, distinguishing of spirits, tongues, interpretation of tongues. This division is based on the interrelatedness of the gifts in each category, as the following discussion will demonstrate. Nevertheless, it is still not possible to compare this list fully with the gifts listed in Romans 12:6–8; 1 Corinthians 12:28; and Ephesians 4:11.[4]

In addition, it is not Paul's intention in 1 Corinthians 12:8–10 to establish a rating or hierarchy of gifts.[5] Instead, he wishes to show that all gifts, including the "unimportant" and the "obscure," come from the same source—the Spirit.[6] "As tasks given by the Spirit they are all . . . fundamentally equal, and superiority and subordination are to be regarded as only incidental."[7] The overall standard for measuring the relative importance of the gifts is twofold: (1) whether or not they testify to the Lordship of Jesus

[2]Hans Conzelmann, *1 Corinthians,* trans. James W. Leitch (Philadelphia: Fortress Press, 1975), 209; Williams, *Renewal Theology,* 2:347.

[3]BDF, sec. 109(2); Eduard Schweizer, "*pneuma, pneumatikos* in the New Testament," in *TDNT,* 6:315; Herman C. Beyer, "*heteros,*" in *TDNT,* 2:702.

[4]Johannes Weiss, *Der erste Korintherbrief* (Göttingen, Germany: Vandenhöck & Ruprecht, 1910), 299.

[5]Weiss, *Der erste Korintherbrief,* 299; see also Charles K. Barrett, *A Commentary on the First Epistle to the Corinthians* (New York: Harper & Row, 1968), 286; Eduard Schweizer, *Church Order in the New Testament,* trans. Frank Clarke (London: SCM Press, 1961), 100.

[6]Barrett, *Corinthians,* 286.

[7]Schweizer, *Church Order,* 100. The same would apply also to Rom. 12:6–8.

(1 Cor. 12:3), and (2) whether or not they edify the church.[8] One writer says, insightfully, that Paul avoids "a hierarchical or codified arrangement, which in charismatic circles could have been misused."[9]

Consequently, one cannot argue, as do some, that the last gifts in the 1 Corinthians 12:8–10 list (speaking in tongues with interpretation of tongues) are the least important, any more than one can say that the first is the most important. Is the gift of a word of wisdom the most important in the listing because it appears first? Are the gifts of healing and working of miracles more important than the gift of prophecy?[10] In all likelihood, the last four gifts—prophecy, distinguishing of spirits, tongues, and interpretation of tongues—occur last for literary reasons inasmuch as these four are discussed at length in chapter 14, thus providing the reader with easy continuity.

Offices or Functions?

There is no specific New Testament term that differentiates office from ministry (i.e., function).[11] The three most common terms in Greek to designate the concept of office were *archē/archōn, timē,* and *telos.* Yet the New Testament nowhere applies these terms to leaders of the Church.[12] But even though there is no equivalent in the New Testament for this concept of office, the term *charisma* "described in a theologically exact and comprehensive way the essence and scope of every ecclesiastical ministry and function."[13] Some

[8]To be discussed at a later point.

[9]Otto Michel, *Der Brief an die Römer* (Göttingen, Germany: Vandenhöck & Ruprecht, 1966), 298.

[10]Similarly, are we supposed to conclude that "showing mercy" is the least valuable of the gifts listed in Rom. 12:6–8 because this gift appears last?

[11]Schweizer, *Church Order,* 181.

[12]See Schweizer, *Church Order,* 171, for statistical data on these terms. However, the word *episkopē* in 1 Tim. 3:1 seems to convey the meaning of office, and is rendered "office of a bishop" (KJV; cf. NRSV) or "office of overseer" (NASB), and "position of a bishop" in NKJV.

[13]Ernst Kaesemann, "Ministry and Community in the New Testament," in *Essays on New Testament Themes,* trans. W. J. Montague (London: SCM Press,

go so far as to say that Paul makes a deliberate attempt to avoid a clergy-laity distinction.[14]

It is undeniable, however, that there were officebearers in the churches of Paul's time and in the church-at-large. How else can terms like apostle, prophet, and teacher be understood (1 Cor. 12:28; see Eph. 4:11, which mentions also evangelists and pastors)? Yet one group of ministries was not bound necessarily and permanently to an officeholder, while other ministries were exercised only as a specific function for an actual situation.[15] But even when officebearers are mentioned, the emphasis is not so much on their ecclesiastical office as it is on the variety of functions, activities, and ministries in the church.[16]

This emphasis upon function rather than office can be inferred from the way Paul seeks to correct the errors into which the Corinthians had fallen. He does not tell any officials to take action, but rather addresses the congregation as a whole. "The inference is that *there were no officials in the ecclesiastical sense,* although, as in every society, there were leading men."[17]

An attempt to interpret some spiritual gifts as so many clearly defined ecclesiastical offices misses Paul's point, which is to show how the different functions are those which God has assigned to the various members of the Body.[18] To express it another way: The congregations that

---

1964), 64; see also Michel, *Der Brief an die Römer,* 298 n. 2; Hans Kueng, "The Charismatic Structure of the Church," in *The Church and Ecumenism,* in *Concilium* (New York: Paulist Press, 1965), 4:57.

[14]Some maintain there was this distinction at the time, though not to such a marked degree as later. See Joseph Brosch, *Charismen und Aemter in der Urkirche* (Bonn, Germany: Peter Hanstein G.m.b.H., 1951), 162.

[15]Leonhard Goppelt, *Apostolic and Post-Apostolic Times,* trans. Robert A. Guelich (London: Adam & Charles Black, 1970), 183.

[16]Barrett, *Corinthians,* 237; see also Klaas Runia, "The Gifts of the Spirit," *Reformed Theological Review* 29, no. 3 (1970): 84.

[17]Archibald Robertson and Alfred Plummer, *A Critical and Exegetical Commentary on the First Epistle of St. Paul to the Corinthians* (Edinburgh, Scotland: T. & T. Clark, 1914), 284, italics in original.

[18]F. J. A. Hort, *The Christian Ecclesia* (London: Macmillan & Co., 1900), 159. Robertson and Plummer (*Corinthians,* 263) express the same sentiment.

Paul addresses are composed only of laypersons who are all, potentially, also "priests and officeholders, that is, instruments of the Spirit for the enactment of the Gospel in the everyday world."[19]

The question is not so much whether there were recognized leaders in the New Testament churches. Paul himself appointed elders for the churches in Galatia he had established (Acts 14:23), and clearly indicates there were overseers (bishops) and deacons in the church at Philippi (Phil. 1:1). Also, the Pastoral Epistles speak of overseers (known also as bishops or elders) and deacons (1 Tim. 3:1–13; Titus 1:5–9). The question is more that the emphasis is upon the function of these (and other) leaders, rather than on their office or title.

In summary, Paul stresses function, even though the concept of office is in his letters. According to the general teaching of the New Testament, the sovereign working of the Spirit through any believer and the divine appointment of some to positions of leadership are not mutually exclusive, nor should these two concepts be at odds when the New Testament guidelines are observed.

Character and Function of Each Gift

The purpose of this section is to obtain an overview of the different gifts. In order to accomplish this, it will be necessary to investigate the basic nature of each and also its specific function. A more detailed treatment of the gifts especially associated with a service of worship—prophecy, distinguishing of spirits, tongues, interpretation of tongues—will be given in a subsequent chapter.

We have already noted the difficulty in establishing categories to which the various gifts may be assigned. One general suggestion, however, is worthy of note. Based on Peter's statements about gifts (1 Pet. 4:10–11), Richard Gaffin says we have "a two-part profile on the entire range of spiritual gifts. . . . All of the gifts . . . reduce to one of two

[19]Ernst Kaesemann, "Paul and Early Catholicism," in *New Testament Questions of Today,* trans. W. J. Montague (Philadelphia: Fortress Press, 1969), 246.

basic kinds: word gifts and deed gifts." James Dunn concurs, speaking of "charisms of speech" and "charisms of action," especially with regard to the lists in Romans and 1 Corinthians.[20]

The categories I am suggesting for the various gifts are somewhat arbitrary on my part. The division is more for ease in treatment of the various gifts.

GIFTS OF LEADERSHIP

There is little question that the three ministries of the Word mentioned in 1 Corinthians 12:28—apostles, prophets, teachers—enjoy some degree of priority over the other gifts, for by them the Church is founded and built up.[21] In this passage, where they are listed along with other gifts, they are distinguished from them on three points:

(1) By their identification as "first," "second," and "third," they are regarded as "holders of the three chronologically and essentially primary functions for the edification of the body of Christ."[22]

(2) They are separated from the succeeding gifts by the Greek particle *men* ("on the one hand")[23] to introduce the triad and the adverb *epeita* ("then") to introduce the others. The numerical sequence is dropped after the first three.

(3) The triad is presented in terms of persons, whereas the remaining gifts are given in impersonal terms. This is brought out correctly in the *New American Standard Bible:* "God has appointed in the church, first apostles, second prophets, third teachers, then miracles, then gifts of healings, helps, administrations, various kinds of tongues"

[20]Richard B. Gaffin, Jr.,"The Gifts of the Holy Spirit," *Reformed Theological Review* 51 (January–April 1992): 9; Dunn, *Theology of Paul the Apostle,* 555–56.

[21]Barrett, *Corinthians,* 295.

[22]Rudolf Schnackenburg, "Apostles Before and During Paul's Time," in *Apostolic History and the Gospel,* ed. W. Ward Gasque and Ralph P. Martin (Grand Rapids: Wm. B. Eerdmans, 1970), 299.

[23]Even though the correlative *de* is not used with the second grouping. It is often dropped. See BAGD, 503.

(1 Cor. 12:28).[24] But then this type of distinction is basically reversed in the listing of gifts found in Romans 12:6–8, "showing that Paul was concerned rather with gifts and functions than with persons and their status."[25]

Apostles

Paul's writings do not have a uniform concept of apostleship with clear-cut criteria.[26] He does not speak of his calling as an "apostolic office" but rather as an ordinance of God, a ministry, a grace bestowed on him by the exclusive choice of God himself (Rom. 11:13; 12:3; 15:15; 1 Cor. 3:10; 9:17; 2 Cor. 1:1; 3:6; 4:1; 6:3–4; Gal. 1:15–16; Col. 1:25).[27] Because the concept of apostleship was not carefully defined at the beginning, it is pointless, as some do, to play one view against the other, the "institutional" against the "charismatic," or the "office" against the "function."[28]

Paul uses the term *apostolos* (apostle) in a wide sense to denote function (see Rom. 16:7; 2 Cor. 8:23; Phil. 2:25). Don A. Carson says, "There could not have been false apostles (2 Cor. xi.13) unless the number of Apostles had been indefinite."[29] But generally Paul uses the word in the more restricted sense of Christ's witnesses who have seen the risen Lord (see 1 Cor. 9:1) and who have been definitely commissioned by Him.[30] Paul includes himself among the

[24]Some translations obscure this distinction by "personalizing" each term in the second group. The NIV mistranslates when it says, "workers of miracles, also those having gifts of healing, those able to help others, those with gifts of administration, and those speaking in different kinds of tongues."

[25]Barrett, *Corinthians,* 295.

[26]Schnackenburg, "Apostles," 301.

[27]Hans von Campenhausen, *Ecclesiastical Authority and Spiritual Power in the Church of the First Three Centuries,* trans. J. A. Baker (Stanford: Stanford University Press, 1969), 27.

[28]Schnackenburg, "Apostles," 302.

[29]Don A. Carson, *Showing the Spirit: A Theological Exposition of 1 Corinthians 12–14* (Grand Rapids: Baker Book House, 1987), 88.

[30]Schweizer, *Church Order,* 194–97. "The number of eyewitnesses who had seen the Risen Christ ran into hundreds [1 Cor. 15:6]; but the 'apostolic' men of the primitive community had not merely seen him, they had also been constituted by him public witnesses of his resurrection and person" (Campenhausen, *Ecclesiastical Authority,* 23).

apostles in this more restricted meaning of the word. This commission consisted of preaching, which belongs to the essence of apostleship. One writer goes so far as to say that "no apostles are known to us who are not at the same time missionaries."[31] Yet such a statement is based on tradition rather than on the New Testament.

The concept of apostolic authority associates the New Testament *apostolos* ("sent one") with the Jewish *shaliach* ("sent one"), who was an authorized emissary of the Jewish authorities. But the preaching and often missionary ministry of apostles radically distinguishes them from their Jewish counterparts.[32]

In the list of charismata found in 1 Corinthians 12:28–29, perhaps the only distinctive feature of the apostles is that they were itinerant.[33] Unlike prophets, teachers, and other leaders, their ministry was to the church-at-large rather than associated with a specific local congregation.[34] If the term "apostle" in its more restricted meaning implied a nonrepeatable, once-for-all ministry of certain individuals (Eph. 2:20; 3:4–5), in its broader meaning it can be used for those who carry on the work of the apostles, especially that of itinerant preaching. Arnold Bittlinger says that "the New Testament nowhere suggests that the apostolic ministry was intended only for first-generation Christians. On the contrary, we constantly encounter people in church history whom we designate as apostles."[35]

Some suggest that the successors to the apostles might very well be the evangelists (Acts 21:8; Eph. 4:11; 2 Tim. 4:5). One writer says that the term "evangelist" emerged at a time "when the apostles were seen as a separate group

[31]Campenhausen, *Ecclesiastical Authority*, 53.

[32]Karl H. Rengstorf, "*apostolos*," in *TDNT*, 1:432; Campenhausen, *Ecclesiastical Authority*, 22. But not everyone agrees with this connection (see Schnackenburg, "Apostles," 294; Schweizer, *Church Order*, 202).

[33]Barrett, *Corinthians*, 295.

[34]Rengstorf, "*apostolos*," 1:432.

[35]Arnold Bittlinger, *Gifts and Ministries*, trans. Clara K. Dyck (Grand Rapids: Wm. B. Eerdmans, 1973), 77.

belonging to the early days."[36] It is at least interesting, if not instructive, to compare Paul's statement about the "signs of a true apostle" (2 Cor. 12:12, NASB) with Philip's ministry of signs and wonders (Acts 8:4–8). Stanley M. Horton observes, "Apostolic ministry . . . is a church-building, fellowship-building work, exercised with accompanying miracles that are the work of the Spirit."[37]

Prophets

The prophet *(prophētēs)* is a key figure in New Testament congregations. But as with the term *apostolos,* the word *prophētēs,* with its cognates, does not have a uniform meaning. It may represent a distinct group in the church, or it may be used broadly for any believer whom the Spirit moves upon to prophesy. The gift of prophecy can be imparted to any believer, for Paul seems to indicate that it is available to all (1 Cor. 14:5,24,31).

The prophets, in distinction to the apostles, did not move from place to place but appear to be residents of a fixed locality, as in Antioch of Syria (Acts 13:1), even though there are some indications that prophets at times did move about (for example, Matt. 10:41; Acts 11:27–28 with 21:10). Originally each congregation had members who had been endowed with the gift of prophecy (see Acts 13:1; Rom. 12:6; 1 Cor. 12:10; 1 Cor. 14).

Prophets are directly linked with apostles in a number of important passages (1 Cor. 12:28–29; Eph. 2:20; 3:5; 4:11; Rev. 18:20). The two jointly had a unique ministry. For example, they are the "foundation" of the Church (Eph. 2:20),[38] and to them was revealed the fact that Gentiles are "heirs together with Israel, members together of one body, and sharers together in the promise in Christ Jesus" (Eph. 3:5–6). In this association with the apostle, the prophet fulfilled a unique,

[36]Schweizer, *Church Order,* 200; see also Bittlinger, *Gifts and Ministries,* 63.

[37]Horton, *What the Bible Says,* 266.

[38]"The foundation of the apostles and prophets" is best understood to mean that the apostles and prophets are themselves the foundation (in Gk., the genitive of apposition).

historical function in the formative years of the Church. Yet the spirit of prophecy is always present in the Christian community.

As manifested in the local assembly of believers, the gift of prophecy does not coincide, as some maintain, "to a large extent with what we call a sermon today."[39] Such an equation is too simple. Oscar Cullmann has observed that teaching and preaching are based on an intelligible exposition of the Word; the gift of prophecy, on the other hand, is based on revelation *(apokalupsis)*.[40] It is noteworthy that in Paul's extended treatment of the manifestation of the gift of prophecy found in 1 Corinthians 14, he does not use either the word *kērussō* ("proclaim or announce") or the common compounds of the verb *angellō* ("to give a message").[41] One of those compounds would be *euangelizomai* ("to preach the good news").

Preaching, on the one hand, is the *kērugma:* "the announcement of good news of what God *had done* and was prepared to do for those who would hear and believe." Its hearers are usually unbelievers. Prophecy, on the other hand, is "declaratory and imperative" and is concerned primarily with a crisis or need which faces God's people.[42] These revelations of prophecy "proclaimed to the primitive church what it had to do and to know under special circumstances."[43]

The gift of prophecy was not intended either to supersede preaching or to be regarded simply as preaching. In the Early Church, as Cullmann has noted, "there is room alongside preaching for a perfectly free proclamation in the Spirit."[44] Yet of the two, preaching, which is associated with

[39]Jean Hering, *The First Epistle of Saint Paul to the Corinthians,* trans. A. W. Heathcote and P. J. Allcock (London: Epworth Press, 1962), 127.

[40]Oscar Cullmann, *Early Christian Worship,* trans. A. Steward Todd and James B. Torrance (London: SCM Press, 1953), 20.

[41]Ernest Best, "Prophets and Preachers," *Scottish Journal of Theology* 12 (June 1959): 150.

[42]R. B. Y. Scott, "Is Preaching Prophecy?" *Canadian Journal of Theology* 1 (April 1955): 150, Scott's emphasis.

[43]F. W. Grosheide, *Commentary on the First Epistle to the Corinthians* (Grand Rapids: Wm. B. Eerdmans, 1953), 287.

[44]Cullmann, *Early Christian Worship,* 20.

the apostles, receives priority. Prophecy "may offer divine instruction which is helpful *hic et nunc* [here and now], but it is put beneath the apostolic preaching, beneath the gospel, which must occupy the place of honor (cf. 1 Cor. 12:28)."[45] Consequently, a prophet's hearers are believers and only incidentally unbelievers or outsiders (1 Cor. 14:24).

Prophecy is communicated to the prophet by means of revelation *(apokalupsis)*. In 1 Corinthians 14, the terms "prophecy" and "revelation" seem to be interchangeable. It is surprising, for instance, that in verse 26 Paul speaks of "a hymn, or a word of instruction, a revelation, a tongue or an interpretation" but does not mention prophecy. By a process of elimination, and especially in light of verse 30,[46] the conclusion is that the two terms ("prophecy" and "revelation") are to be equated. Even in verse 6, where there is the enumeration of revelation, knowledge, prophecy, and word of instruction, Paul may be speaking of two pairs related to each other on the pattern a-b-a-b.

Prophecy, then, is a supernatural communication designed primarily to help believers in their Christian walk. And it is significant that the classical passage on the gift of prophecy (1 Cor. 14) makes no reference to a predictive element.[47] Prophesying means "translating the Christian faith into the very situation of the hearer . . . , into the life of this very week."[48]

Is a prophet given suprahuman perception? The disclosure of the secrets of an unbeliever's heart (1 Cor. 14:24–25)

[45]Grosheide, *Corinthians,* 337. These general conclusions are also shared by Gerhard Friedrich in "Prophets and Prophecies in the New Testament," in *TDNT,* 6:854–55.

[46]"And if a revelation comes to someone who is sitting down, the first speaker should stop." The context deals with the regulation of the gift of prophecy in the assembly.

[47]This is not to deny that there can be predictive prophecy (see Acts 11:28; 21:10–11; Rom. 11:25–26; 1 Cor. 15:51–52). However, a predictive element is not in focus in Paul's teaching on the subject.

[48]Eduard Schweizer, "The Service of Worship. An Exposition of 1 Corinthians 14," in *Neotestamentica* (Zurich, Switzerland: Zwingli Verlag, 1963), 340.

certainly points in that direction.[49] The Scriptures clearly establish that the Holy Spirit reveals what is secret (for example, John 2:25; 6:64; 13:11; 16:19; Acts 5:3; 1 Cor. 2:11,15; 1 John 2:20–21). Notice also the disclosure by Jesus to the woman of Samaria about her marital status, and her response, "'I can see that you are a prophet'" (John 4:18–19). Because prophecy is mediated by divine revelation and may include the divine impartation of certain facts, it is tempting to see here a connection with the gift of a word (or utterance) of knowledge, to be discussed later, though this would not exhaust the meaning of that gift.

Prophecy is surely one of the "greater gifts" (1 Cor. 12:31) which the Corinthians are urged to desire earnestly (14:1,39). In addition to the prophets being linked closely with the apostles on a number of occasions, the gifts of prophecy or prophet are found in each list of spiritual gifts (Rom. 12:6–8; 1 Cor. 12:8–10,28–29; Eph. 4:11). The thrust of the entire fourteenth chapter of 1 Corinthians is to show the superiority of this gift over the gift of tongues when uninterpreted. Prophecy may be instrumental in the conversion of an unbeliever, in addition to its primary function of serving the needs of the congregation. If degrees of importance may indeed be assigned to the several gifts, it would not be amiss to say that prophecy would be among the most important.

Teachers

Teachers *(didaskaloi)* constituted another leading group in the early congregations. They are spoken of both in personal terms (1 Cor. 12:28–29; Eph. 4:11; see also Acts 13:1; 1 Tim. 2:7; 2 Tim. 1:11; James 3:1) and in impersonal terms (Rom. 12:7, "he who teaches," NASB; and Gal. 6:6, "him who teaches," NASB). In the Pastoral Epistles, elders have the responsibility of teaching (1 Tim. 3:2; 5:17).

[49]Advocates of this view include Arnold Bittlinger, *Gifts and Graces,* trans. Herbert Klassen (Grand Rapids: Wm. B. Eerdmans, 1967), 107; and Jean Hering, *Corinthians,* 152. Opponents include Johannes Weiss, *Der erste Korintherbrief,* 333; and Barrett, *Corinthians,* 326.

Are the "pastors and teachers" (Eph. 4:11) one and the same individuals? Opinion is divided.[50] But there is sufficient indication apart from this passage that teachers constituted a separate class, even though the *function* of teaching is assigned as well to the bishop (elder or pastor). Presumably teachers were mature Christians who instructed others in the meaning of the Christian faith and in the exposition of the Hebrew Scriptures.[51] C. E. B. Cranfield, commenting on Romans 12:7 ("he who teaches," NASB), says that "the teacher based his teaching upon the Old Testament scriptures, the tradition of Jesus and the catechetical material current in the Christian community."[52] In this way the teacher contributes to the edification of the community of believers.

Since both prophecy and teaching are ministries of the Word, how are they related to each other? According to one writer, they are "the two noblest gifts, which Paul himself singles out as such and links with the apostolate."[53] Yet they must be distinguished from each other. The prophet in the Early Church was distinguished from the teacher by the fact of his on-the-spot inspiration by the Spirit. "His utterance was the result of a particular revelation. . . . It was a characteristic of prophecy that it was directed to a particu-

[50]According to Karl H. Rengstorf, the common article *tous* in the phrase *tous poimenas kai didaskalous* makes it plain that they are the same, "for the *poimēn* [pastor, shepherd] is the one who is responsible for the life of the community, and therefore *didaskein* [to teach] in the widest sense is part of his office" (*TDNT,* 2:158). Others argue to the contrary (for example, Joseph Brosch, *Charismen,* 117; Schweizer, *Church Order* 200 n. 750). See article by Daniel B. Wallace in which he argues that the so-called rule of Granville Sharp does not apply to plural nouns: "Granville Sharp: A Model of Evangelical Scholarship and Social Activism," *Journal of the Evangelical Theological Society* 41, no. 4 (December 1998), 604–12. This may be another example of the imprecision with which some charismatic terminology is used.

[51]Barrett, *Corinthians,* 295; Ziegfried Schatzmann, *A Pauline Theology of Charismata* (Peabody, Mass.: Hendrickson Publishers, 1987); Heinrich Greeven, "Propheten, Lehrer, Vorsteher bei Paulus," *Zeitschrift für die neutestamentliche Wissenschaft* 44 (1952–53): 28.

[52]C. E. B. Cranfield, *A Critical and Exegetical Commentary on the Epistle to the Romans* (Edinburgh, Scotland: T. & T. Clark, 1975), 623.

[53]Campenhausen, *Ecclesiastical Authority,* 60.

lar concrete situation."[54] Prophecy may be said to appeal to the heart, while teaching appeals to the understanding.[55] But it would be wrong to classify the prophets as "pneumatics," as some do, and the teachers as "nonpneumatics," since teachers, as well as prophets, are spiritual gifts to the Church who also need the enablement of the Spirit.

Pastors

The Greek word for pastor *(poimēn)* is the common noun for shepherd. It is used figuratively of Jesus (John 10:11,14,16; Heb. 13:20; 1 Pet. 2:25) and only once in the New Testament of leaders in the church (Eph. 4:11). But the concept of leaders feeding the sheep occurs in several passages (for example, John 21:15–18; Acts 20:28; 1 Pet. 5:2), and feeding the sheep is most closely associated with the pastor's ministry of the Word, especially as a teacher.

Pastors are generally identified with elders or bishops (overseers) (as in Acts 20:28; 1 Pet. 5:2). Some also suggest the possibility that they are meant by the gift of administrations (1 Cor. 12:28).

Evangelists

The Greek word for evangelist *(euangelistēs)* occurs only three times in the New Testament (Acts 21:8; Eph. 4:11; 2 Tim. 4:5). "The evangelist did not go to the churches. He went where the sinners were. Prophets went to the churches."[56] The ministry of the evangelist was and is to preach the gospel *(euangelizomai)* to non-Christians, differentiating him from the pastor, whose primary ministry is to expound the Scriptures to believers. However, this does not preclude a pastor from preaching evangelistically (2 Tim. 4:5).

[54]C. E. B. Cranfield, *A Commentary on Romans 12–13* (Edinburgh, Scotland: Oliver & Boyd, 1965), 29.

[55]Ferdinand Prat, *The Theology of Saint Paul,* trans. John L. Stoddard (London: Burns, Oates & Washbourne, 1957), 1:425; see also John Murray, *The Epistle to the Romans* (Grand Rapids: Wm. B. Eerdmans, 1959), 125.

[56]Horton, *What the Bible Says,* 268.

Helps

"Helps" (1 Cor. 12:28, NASB; Gk. *antilēmpseis*) conveys the basic idea of assistance or support.[57] In its verb form the New Testament uses the term in the sense of serious concern for a right relationship to a brother (1 Tim. 6:2) or of regard for the weak (Acts 20:35), what one writer says refers "obviously to the activity of love in the dealings of the community."[58]

Administrations

The gift of administrations (*kubernēseis;* 1 Cor. 12:28) enables a member to serve as a helmsman[59] to the congregation, "a true director of its order and therewith of its life."[60] Very possibly these functions of administration foreshadow the work of bishops,[61] if the term "bishop" is understood to be interchangeable with "elder" or "pastor."

The two gifts of helps and administrations may well indicate the functions of deacons and bishops, who are specifically mentioned for the first time in Philippians 1:1.[62] Yet more than likely they were not fixed offices at the time Paul wrote 1 Corinthians.

He Who Leads

"He who leads" (Rom. 12:8, NASB) may be related to the gift of pastors or elders. The verb *(proïstēmi)* occurs elsewhere, in 1 Thessalonians 5:12; 1 Timothy 3:4,5; 5:17; and

[57]Gerhard Delling, *"antilambanomai, antilēmpsis, sunantilambanomai,"* in *TDNT,* 1:375–76; see also Barrett, *Corinthians,* 295; Hering, *Corinthians,* 133 ("works of charity").

[58]Delling, *"antilambanomai,"* 1:375. Barrett calls them "gifts of support" and suggests they may be the last three in the Romans 12:6–8 listing (*Corinthians,* 295–96).

[59]This personal noun form is *kubernētēs* (Acts 27:11; Rev. 18:17).

[60]Hermann W. Beyer, *"kubernēsis,"* in *TDNT,* 4:1036.

[61]Barrett, *Corinthians,* 296; Hering, *Corinthians,* 133; Robertson and Plummer, *Corinthians,* 281.

[62]James D. G. Dunn, *Jesus and the Spirit* (Philadelphia: Westminster Press, 1975), 253; Barrett, *Corinthians,* 295–96; Ralph P. Martin, *The Spirit and the Congregation: Studies in 1 Corinthians 12–15* (Grand Rapids: Wm. B. Eerdmans, 1984), 33.

Titus 3:8. It is specifically linked with the work of the elder: "the elders who direct the affairs of the church well" (1 Tim. 5:17). It is also used more generally: "Respect those . . . who are over you in the Lord" (1 Thess. 5:12); those who have trusted in the Lord should be careful to "devote" themselves to good works (Titus 3:8).

Proïstēmi has two basic meanings: (1) "to be at the head of, rule, direct"; (2) "to be concerned about, care for, give aid."[63] Especially with regard to Romans 12:8, it is not a matter of choosing one meaning to the exclusion of the other, but rather deciding which of the two is emphasized. Certainly in this verse it does not refer with precision to any office or position.[64] It is best to think more in terms of care and solicitude on the part of leaders.[65] It is important to observe that this gift is the second member of the triad of "he who shares . . . he who gives aid . . . he who engages in acts of mercy" (Rom. 12:8, my translation). The second expression is plainly related to the other two, which refer to works of love. Therefore this person may be part of a special group gifted by the Holy Spirit for the task of caring for others.[66] The person who has received this gift should perform the work diligently, that is, with zeal. "Zeal and energy are the natural gifts required of any ruler."[67]

[63]BAGD, 707; see also Bo Reicke, *"proïstemi,"* in *TDNT*, 6:702; Michel, *Der Brief an die Romer*, 300.

[64]Charles K. Barrett, *A Commentary on the Epistle to the Romans* (London: Adam & Charles Black, 1962), 239.

[65]Greeven, "Propheten," 32 n. 74. Cranfield (*Epistle to the Romans*, 626–27) suggests the possibility that this person is "the administrator in charge of the charitable work of the congregation" or that he is perhaps "the person, who by virtue of his social status was in a position to be, on behalf of the church, a friend and protector for those members of the community who were not in a position to defend themselves (e.g. the widows, orphans, slaves, strangers)." Michel thinks in a similar vein (*Der Brief an die Romer*, 300).

[66]Dunn, *Jesus and the Spirit*, 250–51; Schatzmann, *Pauline Theology of Charismata*, 27.

[67]Reicke, *"proïstemi,"* 6:701.

Chapter 13

Individual Gifts Part 2

GIFTS OF PRACTICAL ASSISTANCE

It is important to notice that of the seven gifts mentioned in Romans 12:6–8, no fewer than four—serving, giving, caring for or giving aid,[1] and showing mercy—are concerned with practical assistance to members of the Christian community who are in need of help and sympathy.

Service

To the surprise of some, service *(diakonia)* is also a gift (Rom. 12:7).[2] Does Paul use the word in a narrow sense "denoting a range of activities similar to that which came to be the province of deacons"?[3] Or does he mean it in a

[1]In the previous chap. under the subheading "He Who Leads," note that one meaning of the verb *proïstēmi* is "to be concerned about, care for, give aid."

[2]A more detailed treatment of the general concept of *diakonia* will be given in the next chap.

[3]C. E. B. Cranfield, *A Critical and Exegetical Commentary on the Epistle to the Romans* (Edinburgh, Scotland: T. & T. Clark, 1975), 622; see also Charles K. Barrett, *A Commentary on the Epistle to the Romans* (London: Adam & Charles Black, 1962), 238; Stanley M. Horton, *What the Bible Says About the Holy Spirit* (Springfield, Mo.: Gospel Publishing House, 1976), 280. Eduard Schweizer suggests the possibility that the deacons were originally the bishops' servants (*Church Order in the New Testament,* trans. Frank Clarke [London: SCM Press, 1961], 199).

broad sense, for any kind of "ministry"?[4] It is best not to confine the meaning to the narrow sense, but to have it include ideas like "ministry to the needy" or "assistance or administration of help to physical needs."[5] At the most, all that can be said is that this may be the beginning of what later came to be deacons as identifiable persons in the churches.

"Let him serve" (Gk. *en tēi diakoniāi*), according to one writer, means that "those who have received this particular gift, the spiritual capacity for practical service, are to give themselves whole-heartedly to the fulfillment of the tasks of which their particular endowment is also their divine function."[6]

He Who Gives

"He who gives" (Rom. 12:8, NASB) indicates a God-given inclination to give one's personal possessions, but it need not be restricted to sharing one's wealth. Significantly, this thought of sharing is repeated by Paul in a charismatic context in the same letter when he writes, "that I may impart to you some spiritual gift" (Rom. 1:11). The Greek verb *metadidōmi* used in both passages (also in 1 Thess. 2:8) more properly means "to share." This sharing must be done generously, or liberally, and without reservation or ulterior motive.[7] It must be done with sincere concern, ungrudgingly, with no strings attached.[8]

He Who Shows Mercy

Conceptually related to "he who gives" is "he who shows mercy *[eleos]*" (Rom. 12:8, NASB). It may take the

[4]See Rom. 11:13; 1 Cor. 3:5; 12:5; 16:15; 2 Cor. 3:6; 6:4; 8:4; 11:23; Eph. 3:7; 6:21.

[5]Ziegfried Schatzmann, *A Pauline Theology of Charismata* (Peabody, Mass.: Hendrickson Publishers, 1987), 23; John Murray, *The Epistle to the Romans* (Grand Rapids: Wm. B. Eerdmans, 1959), 124; Barrett, *Romans*, 238; Hermann W. Beyer, *"diakoneō, diakonia, diakonos,"* in *TDNT*, 2:87–88.

[6]Cranfield, *Epistle to the Romans*, 623.

[7]Otto Michel, *Der Brief an die Römer* (Göttingen, Germany: Vandenhöck & Ruprecht, 1966), 299.

[8]The meaning of the word *haplotēs* in BAGD, 86.

concrete form of distributing alms, for both in Corinth and in Philippi it was necessary for persons to be chosen for this task (1 Cor. 16:3; 2 Cor. 8:19,23; Phil. 2:25). *Eleos* is a broad term that sometimes has the sense of sympathy or pity. The term is used to describe the act of the Samaritan in the familiar parable (Luke 10:37). It could very well include tending the sick, relieving the poor, caring for the aged and disabled, and visiting prisoners.[9]

This ministry is to be done "cheerfully," not grudgingly or perfunctorily. "Cheerfulness in all the paths of life . . . was a special characteristic of the early Christian (Acts 2:46; 5:41; Phil. 1:4,18; 2:18, etc.; 1 Thess. 5:16)."[10]

Gifts of Power

Faith

Faith as a spiritual gift is not possessed by every Christian. Notice the expression, "to another faith" (1 Cor. 12:9). One who has received this gift has a divinely given conviction that God will reveal his power and mercy in a specific case; it is an assurance that draws the supernatural into the natural world.[11] It is wonder-working faith, which manifests itself in deeds rather than in word.[12] It is the type of faith than can move mountains (Matt. 17:20; 21:21; Mark 11:22–24; 1 Cor. 13:2; see also Mark 9:23). This gift of faith may be regarded as the antithesis of the "'little faith'" Jesus spoke of (Matt. 6:30; 8:26; 14:31; 16:8; 17:20; Luke 12:28).

But the gift of faith usually does not function in isolation. It is a means to an end—miraculous healings and displays

[9]Cranfield, *Epistle to the Romans,* 627; Stanley M. Horton, *What the Bible Says,* 281.

[10]William Sanday and Arthur C. Headlam, *A Critical and Exegetical Commentary on the Epistle to the Romans,* 5th ed. (Edinburgh, Scotland: T. & T. Clark, 1914), 358.

[11]Joseph Brosch, *Charismen und Aemter in der Urkirche* (Bonn, Germany: P. Hanstein G.m.b.H., 1951), 50–51.

[12]Archibald Robertson and Alfred Plummer, *A Critical and Exegetical Commentary on the First Epistle of St. Paul to the Corinthians* (Edinburgh, Scotland: T. & T. Clark, 1914), 266.

of divine power (Gal. 3:5). One notable example of the gift of faith in operation is the healing of the lame man at the temple gate (Acts 3:1–10).

Gifts of Healings

Paul uses plural forms for both nouns—"gifts of healings" (1 Cor. 12:9, lit. trans.). The first plural might indicate that every healing is a special gift.[13] The second plural possibly calls attention to different types, or categories, of healings that would involve restoration of the entire person—body, soul, and spirit. The Gospels and the Book of Acts bear ample testimony to the wide diversity of healings effected by Jesus and his followers (see Mark 1:32–34). However, it goes beyond the evidence to maintain, as do some, that the plural "healings" "seems to imply that different persons each had a disease or group of diseases that they could cure."[14]

It is not correct to say that this gift is given to the one needing healing. While it is certainly true that the healed person is the recipient of a healing miracle, the gift is given to the individual whom God uses for its performance. This is the whole tenor of the passage in 1 Corinthians 12:8–10, which focuses on the individual whom God uses in the exercise of the gift. Therefore it is more accurate to say that the gift is given *to* a person *for* the healing of another person.[15]

Stanley M. Horton emphasizes that the gift can be exercised only at the prompting of the Spirit when he says there is "no evidence that the apostles were able to heal whenever they felt like it by some resident power of healing. Nor did they consider healing their chief ministry."[16]

[13]Arnold Bittlinger, *Gifts and Graces,* trans. Herbert Klassen (Grand Rapids: Wm. B. Eerdmans, 1967), 37.

[14]Robertson and Plummer, *Corinthians,* 266; Harold Horton, *The Gifts of the Spirit,* 2d ed. (Springfield, Mo.: Gospel Publishing House, 1975), 116; Don A. Carson, *Showing the Spirit: A Theological Exposition of 1 Corinthians 12–14* (Grand Rapids: Baker Book House, 1987), 39.

[15]Bittlinger, *Gifts and Graces,* 37.

[16]Stanley M. Horton, *What the Bible Says,* 274. Since the matter of divine healing has always been emphasized in the Pentecostal movement, the

Workings of Miracles

Both nouns are plural in the Greek text. This is a second way in which the gift of faith is manifested. "Miracles" (1 Cor. 12:10, NASB) is a translation of the Greek word *dunamis,* which is often translated "power." The concepts of power and Spirit are closely associated in the New Testament.[17] This particular gift appears to have been one of the marks of an apostle (2 Cor. 12:12; see Rom. 15:19; Heb. 2:4), but it was not restricted to them (for example, Acts 8:5–7).

This gift is distinguished from the gifts of healings in that it would include extraordinary demonstrations of God's power apart from miraculous healings, inasmuch as *dunamis* is a general, comprehensive term for wonder-inducing works of all kinds. This is suggested by the use of this word in conjunction with the terms "signs" and "wonders" (*sēmeia* and *terata*), and especially with the latter (see Acts 2:22; Rom. 15:19; 2 Cor. 12:12; Gal. 3:5; 2 Thess. 2:9; Heb. 2:4). One writer states that these miracles are "acts of power invading the kingdom of demons. In *dunameis* [miracles or powers] demonic forces are resisted and vanquished."[18] Exorcism in particular would be one function of this gift, and it could include, as well, events such as the judgment of blindness on Elymas the magician (Acts 13:9–11) and nature miracles.[19] Especially appropriate in this connection is the observation that the noun "working" *(energeia)* is used in the Septuagint and in the New Testament, along with its verb equivalent, almost exclusively for the work of divine or demonic powers.[20]

---

reader's attention is called to the excursus entitled "Healing and the Atonement" at the end of this chap.

[17]Luke 1:35; 24:49; Acts 1:8; 10:38; Rom. 15:19; 1 Cor. 2:4; Gal. 3:5; 1 Thess. 1:5; see also 2 Tim. 1:7.

[18]Walter Grundmann, "The Concept of Power in the New Testament," in *TDNT,* 2:315.

[19]See, for instance, Carson, *Showing the Spirit,* 40; Charles K. Barrett, *A Commentary on the First Epistle to the Corinthians* (New York: Harper & Row, 1968), 286.

[20]Georg Bertram, *"energeō, energeia, energēma, energēs,"* in *TDNT,* 2:652–53. A possible exception would be Phil. 2:13, in which the second occurrence of

Gifts of Revelation

It is virtually impossible to establish a rigid distinction between the gifts of a word of wisdom and a word of knowledge.[21] To the Corinthians, however, among whom the gifts were probably a common occurrence, the difference might have been clear enough. But it is best to follow the advice that "as a rule the distinction between related gifts must not be too precisely made."[22]

A Word of Wisdom

The Greek text does not say "the" word of wisdom.[23] But on the basis of relating the concept of wisdom to what Paul says earlier in 1 Corinthians, especially in chapters 1 and 2, some say it has to do with insight into the plan of salvation.

It is possible, however, to look in a completely different direction for the meaning of this gift. It may be significant that the Greek word *logos* ("word") in this gift and in the following gift is unaccompanied by the Greek article *ho* ("the"). Therefore, this gift could validly be understood as "a wise saying" or "speaking wisely."[24] "In a difficult or dangerous situation a word of wisdom may be given which resolves the difficulty or silences the opponent."[25] The deci-

---

energeō may apply to the believer and not to God. See NRSV, which reads, "enabling you both to will and to work."

[21]Hans Conzelmann, *1 Corinthians,* trans. James W. Leitch (Philadelphia: Fortress Press, 1975), 246; Robertson and Plummer, *Corinthians,* 265; Barrett, *Corinthians,* 285.

Only two revelatory gifts are discussed under this heading, though certainly prophecy, distinguishings of spirits, and exhorting are also revelatory in nature. Some would also include the interpretation of tongues.

[22]Rudolph Bultmann, *Theology of the New Testament,* trans. Kendrick Grobel (New York: Charles Scribner's Sons, 1951), 1:154.

[23]Students of Gk. will understand that the presence of the article may very often be significant, and that the absence of the article very often renders the noun indefinite. Nevertheless, the somewhat common translation "the word of wisdom" is unjustified.

[24]BAGD, 477.

[25]Bittlinger, *Gifts and Graces,* 29. See Luke 11:11–12; 20:20–26.

sion of the Jerusalem council is a case in point: "'It seemed good to the Holy Spirit and to us'" (Acts 15:28). "One might call the council's decision a pneumatic consensus."[26]

Jesus promised the disciples that when they would be brought before the authorities, "'The Holy Spirit will teach you at that time what you should say'" (Luke 12:11–12). Peter's defense before the Jerusalem authorities is one example of the fulfillment of Jesus' promise (Acts 4:8–12). Significantly, the passage begins, "Then Peter, filled with the Holy Spirit, said to them" (v. 8).

Both with regard to this gift and the gift of a word of knowledge, it may be that the gift is not always meant to be vocalized. The Holy Spirit may give a word to a person for guidance or insight into a specific situation which faces him or her, but the Spirit may intend that the word not be expressed to others.[27] "Specific situation" should be understood in a corporate context, since Paul's overriding concern in his treatment of the gifts is the common good of the body of believers (1 Cor. 12:7).

A Word of Knowledge

The meaning of the gift of a word of knowledge is also uncertain. In one view, it is not the kind of knowledge which is the result of instruction guided by reason and which requires no illumination, but rather "the use of this knowledge, in accordance with the Spirit, for the edification of others" which constitutes the gift.[28] Another view argues that it indicates a "higher" knowledge which can be obtained not through teaching or reflection, but only through divine revelation.[29] It is therefore supernatural and revelatory in nature.

[26]John Koenig, *Charismata: God's Gifts for God's People* (Philadelphia: Westminster Press, 1978), 85.

[27]Harold Horton, *Gifts of the Spirit,* 50.

[28]Robertson and Plummer, *Corinthians,* 265.

[29]Johannes Weiss, *Der erste Korintherbrief* (Göttingen, Germany: Vandenhöck & Ruprecht, 1910), 300.

But it is not necessary to confine this gift to mystical or esoteric knowledge. It may include knowledge of facts or events otherwise unobtainable or unknowable by the individual except for a revelatory act of the Spirit. How, for instance, did Peter know that Ananias had withheld part of the money (Acts 5)? In any event, this revelatory aspect tends to associate the gift with the gift of prophecy.[30]

Gifts for Worship

Speaking in Tongues

The Greek term in the New Testament for speaking in tongues, *glōssais lalein,* occurs nowhere else in ancient Greek literature as a technical term for a divinely inspired utterance. Therefore it is necessary to examine the biblical evidence to gain an understanding of the nature of this gift.[31] Apart from Mark 16:17, the term occurs only in the writings of Luke and Paul. Glossolalia in Acts and in 1 Corinthians is a homogeneous phenomenon, for it is highly improbable that the associates Luke and Paul would both use this identical and unique term but with disparate meanings.[32]

Attempts have been made to find a direct correlation of biblical glossolalia with occurrences in Grecian cults.[33] One writer says that "a vigorous infiltration of ideas and customs from pagan Asia Minor is obvious."[34] The ecstasy of

[30]Harold Horton, *Gifts of the Spirit,* 50.

[31]The treatment here is restricted to the nature and character of the gift. The following chap. will discuss its role in the service of worship, together with its corollary, the gift of interpretation of tongues.

[32]See part 2 of this book, chap. 9, pp. 140–49 for initial comments regarding the nature and character of speaking in tongues. Some comments are repeated here for the reader's convenience.

[33]For arguments against this position, see, for example, Koenig, *Charismata,* 90; C. Forbes, *Prophecy and Inspired Speech in Early Christianity and Its Hellenistic Environment* (Peabody, Mass.: Hendrickson Publishers, 1997), 260–68; M. Max B. Turner, *The Holy Spirit and Spiritual Gifts: In the New Testament Church and Today,* rev. ed. (Peabody, Mass.: Hendrickson Publishers, 1998), 235–37.

[34]Paul Volz, *Der Geist Gottes* (Tübingen, Germany: J. C. B. Mohr, 1910), 197.

the priestess of Apollo at Delphi is often cited as a parallel to speaking in tongues inasmuch as the woman, possessed by a god, breaks into uncontrolled speech. Others try to establish a link with the cult of Dionysus (Bacchus), in which the subjects are completely beside themselves. Their outbursts are involuntary, and they emerge from the trancelike state with no recollection of what has happened.

Significantly, the New Testament writers, when speaking of a prophet or a glossolalist, refrain from using Greek terms[35] "whose employment would tend to break down the distinction between heathenism and revealed religion."[36] In classical Greek literature, for instance, the *prophētēs* (prophet) is superior to the *mantis* (one who speaks in a trancelike state), because he interpreted the oracles of the *mantis* which had been given in a frenzied state. When the verb form of *mantis* does appear in the New Testament (Acts 16:16, its only occurrence), it is with reference to the demon-possessed slave girl who had "a spirit of divination" (NASB, NKJV, NRSV). By this spirit she "earned a great deal of money for her owners by fortune-telling *[manteuomai]*."

Very instructive is Paul's statement: "If the whole church comes together and everyone speaks in tongues, and some who do not understand or some unbelievers come in, will they not say that you are out of your mind *[mainomai]*?" (1 Cor. 14:23). Glossolalia may indeed be identified by outsiders with madness, or the frenzied state. But Paul here says, "If . . . everyone speaks in tongues." The prohibition is against all, at one time or in rapid succession, speaking in tongues—with the clear implication that no interpretations are given. It is under these conditions that the charge of madness[37] may be brought against them.

It is also instructive that in Acts 26:24–25, when Festus says that Paul is mad, Paul responds by saying that he is

[35]For example, *mantis, manteuomai, mainomai.*

[36]Richard Chenevix Trench, *Synonyms of the New Testament* (Grand Rapids: Wm. B. Eerdmans, 1958), 19.

[37]"Being possessed" (Barrett, *Corinthians,* 326).

not mad but that what he is saying[38] is true and reasonable. Luke used the same unusual Greek word two other times: in Acts 2:4, which says that the Spirit "enabled," or gave utterance to, the disciples to speak in tongues; and in Acts 2:14, which says that Peter "addressed" the crowd.

Attempts have also been made to establish a link between New Testament glossolalia and the "ecstatic fervor" of early prophets of the Old Testament, "who seem to be robbed of their individuality and overpowered by the Spirit (cf. 1 Sam. 10:5–7; 10–11; 19:20–24; also 1 Kings 18:28–29)."[39] The prophets of 1 Samuel 10:5–6 are sometimes cited as glossolalists: "[I]t may be supposed from the context that they shouted in ecstasy, i.e. were 'speaking in tongues.'"[40]

Phenomenological similarities may indeed exist between the foregoing instances in pagan and Israelite history and the New Testament concept of glossolalia. But "[e]verything turns on the definition of 'ecstatic,'"[41] or an altered state of consciousness. Morton Kelsey has pointed out significant differences between New Testament glossolalia and similar phenomena in ancient times: (1) Tongue-speech is controllable; it is not a frenzy. (2) The experience does not involve a loss of consciousness or a state of trance. (3) It requires interpretation when given publicly, and the ability to interpret can be given.[42]

We observed earlier that the gift of tongues consists of speaking in languages, whether human or angelic.[43] The

[38]The verb is *apophthengomai*—"to speak out or declare," with a connotation of boldness or loudness or enthusiasm. Johannes Behm, "*glōssa, heteroglōssos,*" in *TDNT,* 1:724.

[39]Ibid. Attention is also directed to the prophet who fired Jehu's revolt, especially since he is called a "madman" and reference is made to "the sort of things he says" (2 Kings 9:11).

[40]Maurice Barnett, *The Living Flame* (London: Epworth Press, 1953), 28.

[41]Carson, *Showing the Spirit,* 78.

[42]Morton T. Kelsey, *Tongue Speaking* (Garden City: Doubleday & Co., 1964), 141–42. For a further trenchant statement concerning the radical disjunction between NT glossolalia and Dionysian ecstasy, see Gerhard Delling, *Worship in the New Testament,* trans. Percy Scott (Philadelphia: Westminster Press, 1962), 30.

[43]See part 2, chap. 9, pp. 146–47.

expression "different kinds of tongues" (1 Cor. 12:10,28) may very well involve this idea of both human and non-human languages.[44]

Interpretation of Tongues

A very practical question is sometimes raised concerning a discrepancy in length between a glossolalic utterance and an interpretation[45] that follows. Several explanations exist:

(1) Since the utterance in tongues is not a language, but nonverbal sounds, the interpretation attempts to give meaning to those sounds.

(2) The "interpretation" is not related in content to the glossolalic utterance. It is really a prophetic utterance independent of the glossolalia. Either because of a lack of teaching or because of timidity, some may not share a genuine prophetic utterance until they hear someone speaking in tongues. If this is the case, then the glossolalic utterance remains uninterpreted.

(3) The interpretation is not a translation of the glossolalic language but more an explanation or paraphrase of it. Therefore it may take more time.

(4) Related to the preceding point: The length of the interpretation depends on the ability of the interpreter to express the meaning of the glossolalic utterance. The human factor suggests that some can say much in a few words, while others may require more words to express the same thoughts.

(5) The interpretation is a translation, not an explanation, of the glossolalia. But because of differences in language structure, sometimes even a "literal" translation may be longer or shorter than the first language. Anyone who has

[44]Carson, *Showing the Spirit,* 81–87; Schatzmann, *Pauline Theology of Charismata,* 43; Jon Ruthven, "Is Glossolalia Languages?: A Survey of Biblical Data," *Paraclete* 2, no. 2 (spring 1968): 27–30; Robert Banks and Geoffrey Moon, "Speaking in Tongues: A Survey of the New Testament Evidence," *The Churchman* 80 (1966): 282.

[45]See pp. 242–45 for comments about the nature of the gift of interpretation of tongues.

studied a second language knows that a "literal" or word-for-word translation from one language to another is often confusing.[46]

In my judgment, the ideal is for an interpretation of tongues to be a close rendering of the original language. The verb for "interpret" *(hermēneuō)* and its cognates is used throughout the Septuagint and the New Testament, with very few exceptions, to mean "translate" in the normally accepted meaning of that word.[47] Yet even close translations sometimes (often?) require an element of explanation or interpretation. In addition, allowances must be made for the human factor in making the transition from glossolalia to the common language.

The overarching purpose of spiritual gifts in a worship service is that they may edify the body of believers. This is certainly true of speaking in tongues that is followed by an interpretation. But in 1 Corinthians 14 Paul gives at least three specific functions that are served by glossolalia:[48]

(1) One function is the edification of the glossolalist himself. "He who speaks in a tongue edifies himself, but he who prophesies edifies the church" (v. 4). Even though the speaking in tongues may not be understood by anyone present (v. 2) or by the speaker himself, it nevertheless edifies him. If an interpreter is not present, the speaker is to keep silence in the church and is to speak "to himself and God" (v. 28). The expression "to himself" *(heautōi)* might better be translated "*for* himself," that is, for his own benefit.[49] Yet it is also possible that the words "to himself and

[46]Yet it is possible, as we can observe in our electronic age, for a translation to be virtually concurrent or simultaneous with the original language and therefore just as long (or short).

[47]Ruthven, "Is Glossalalia Languages?" 28–30; J. Rodman Williams, *Renewal Theology: Systematic Theology from a Charismatic Perspective* (Grand Rapids: Zondervan Publishing House, 1990), 2:395 n. 219.

[48]We have previously observed a fourth function of speaking in tongues, based largely on the Book of Acts: It is an indication that one has been initially filled with the Spirit.

[49]See Barrett, *Corinthians*, 321; and F. W. Grosheide, *Commentary on the First Epistle to the Corinthians* (Grand Rapids: Wm. B. Eerdmans, 1953), 319. The declensional form of the pronoun would then be a dative of interest.

God" suggest that under those conditions the person is to speak inaudibly (that is, whisper), so as not to disturb other worshipers.

(2) Tongues are "a sign, not for believers but for unbelievers" (v. 22). This does not mean that tongues have no value for the upbuilding of the congregation. The operative word is "sign." Paul is correcting the Corinthian believers for their unwarranted elevation of this one gift. It is wrong for them, he says, to think that glossolalia *per se* is a mark, or sign, of God's presence (some would say it is *the* mark of God's presence).

This gift is designed to arrest the attention of unbelievers, but its manifestation does not insure that they will believe. We may infer from the context that if they reject the sign, their culpability is increased.[50] This is why Paul quoted Isaiah 28:11 at this point; disobedient Israel would know, when the Assyrians with their "strange tongues" and "lips of foreigners" came upon them, that God had indeed spoken. But in spite of it they refused to repent. Yet it is possible to overemphasize and overapply the Isaiah quotation to the Corinthian situation.

The most common interpretation of 1 Corinthians 14:21–23 is that tongues are a sign of divine judgment on unbelievers in a service. While there is some truth to this, positive value to unbelievers cannot be eliminated. "Signs in Scripture can be either positive or negative, and sometimes both."[51] One writer calls the citation of Isaiah "a Pauline *ad hoc* quotation. To extract significance from every detail of this loose quotation would be misleading. . . . The thought of judgment does not seem to be in his mind."[52] Paul does not say that unbelievers' reaction to corporate

[50]In the words of Robertson and Plummer, *Corinthians,* it is not a convincing or saving sign but "a judicial sign" (316).

[51]Wayne A. Grudem, *The Gift of Prophecy in the New Testament and Today* (Westchester, Ill.: Crossway Books, 1988), 174–77.

[52]Cyril G. Williams, "Glossolalia as a Religious Phenomenon: 'Tongues' at Corinth and Pentecost," *Religion* 5 (spring 1975): 20; see also Peter Roberts, "A Sign—Christian or Pagan?" *Expository Times* 90 (April 1979): 199–203.

tongues-speaking results in God's judgment upon the unbelievers, but only that they will say the believers are out of their mind.

Paul's overriding concern is that utterances in a service, to be meaningful, must be intelligible. At this point he does not seem to be dealing with the increased culpability of the unbeliever who is present. Why should an unbeliever's natural reaction to a succession of uninterpreted tongues condemn him further?

(3) The value of tongues extends to the body, the church, when tongues are accompanied by an interpretation (1 Cor. 14:5). The glossolalist himself may serve as an interpreter, for if no interpreter is present, he "should pray that he may interpret what he says" (v. 13).[53] Paul implies that in a congregation there may be some who regularly exercise the gift of interpretation and who may be regarded as interpreters. But his emphasis is that there must be an interpretation of a glossolalic utterance, either by an "interpreter" or by the glossolalist himself.

The manner in which tongues coupled with an interpretation serves to edify the congregation is not clear. However, the Book of Acts does indicate that the content of a glossolalic utterance may be a praising or an extolling of God (Acts 2:11; 10:46). In line with this, Paul says that glossolalic prayer consists of praising God and giving thanks to him (1 Cor. 14:16–17). When it is interpreted, believers will be edified in much the same way that prayers or ascriptions of praise to God recorded in Scripture build them up. It may be concluded, therefore, that glossolalic prayers, thanksgivings, and songs, when interpreted, have a salutary effect on the body of Christ.[54]

[53]Some translate v. 5 to read "unless *someone* interprets," and v. 13 to read "should pray that *someone* may interpret." While these translations are possible, it is more natural to understand the vv. to mean that the glossolalist ought to interpret when no interpreter is present.

[54]An excursus at the end of this chap. discusses the question of whether speaking in tongues is directed to God or to people.

Prophecy

Prophecy also serves to build up the congregation (1 Cor. 14:4). The prophet speaks to the congregation for their "strengthening [or "upbuilding," NRSV], encouragement and comfort" (v. 3). Some suggest that the last two are the means by which the first is accomplished.[55] Because the second term in Paul's triad (*paraklēsis*, "encouragement") may also mean "comfort," it is natural to seek a distinction between it and the last term (*paramuthia*). But both involve admonition and comfort. In the New Testament, admonition becomes genuine comfort, and comfort becomes admonition, so that it is difficult to find a sure criterion by which such a distinction between the terms can be made. (see Phil. 2:1; Col. 2:2; 4:8; 1 Thess. 5:11).[56]

In many passages the words used with the verb and the noun for "comfort" show that "there is nothing sharp, polemical, or critical in the expressions."[57] There are instances when it is hard to distinguish between exhortation and comfort (see 2 Cor. 1:3–11). Yet it should also be noted that the verb for "exhort" or "comfort" is used in connection with a verb meaning to "admonish, warn, instruct" (*noutheteō*).[58]

In connection with this concept of encouragement as a function of the gift of prophecy, observe that in Romans 12:6–8 Paul makes a distinction between the two.

[55]The prophets Judas and Silas encouraged and strengthened the Antioch congregations (Acts 15:32). These two ministries may be paralleled with the first two of the triad in 1 Cor. 14:3. (The word for "strengthen" in Acts 15:32 is a synonym for the "upbuilding.")

[56]Gustav Staehlin, "*paramutheomai, paramuthia, paramuthion*," in *TDNT*, 5:820–21. But he observes that the terms are not fully interchangeable, for *paramutheomai* (comfort) and its cognates are never used directly for God's comfort.

[57]See Acts 11:23; 14:22; 15:31 with vv. 28,32; 16:40; 20:1–2; 1 Thess. 3:2. These words are used with the verb for comfort—1 Thess. 2:12; the noun for comfort—1 Cor. 14:3; the verb for establish or strengthen—Acts 14:22; 15:32; 1 Thess. 3:2; 2 Thess. 2:17; the verb for ask, request, or beseech—1 Thess. 4:1; the verb for build up—1 Thess. 5:11; the noun for upbuilding—1 Cor. 14:3; the noun for endurance—Rom. 15:4–5.

[58]BAGD, 544; see also Michel, *Der Brief an die Römer*, 290.

Apparently the gift of encouraging is important enough in his thinking to be listed separately, even though it belongs to the sphere of prophesying (1 Cor. 14:3,31). This is another example of overlapping that sometimes occurs in Paul's treatments of spiritual gifts.

The prophet's ministry also impinges at times on the ministry, or gift, of teaching, for Paul says that "you can all prophesy in turn so that everyone may be instructed and encouraged" (1 Cor. 14:31). He also says, "In the church I would rather speak five intelligible words to instruct others than ten thousand words in a tongue" (v. 19). Yet the gifts of prophecy and of teaching are clearly distinguished elsewhere (as in Rom. 12:6–8; Eph. 4:11).

Distinguishings of Spirits

The next chapter will deal with distinguishing of spirits as it relates specifically to prophetic utterances. Its position in the listing of gifts in 1 Corinthians 12:8–10, immediately after prophecy, suggests this. Furthermore, the noun for "distinguishing" *(diakrisis)* occurs in verb form *(diakrinō)* in Paul's statement that prophetic utterances should be weighed carefully (14:29). In my judgment, this is the primary function of the gift of distinguishing of spirits. Many exegetes see a connection between the two gifts. Some see no connection at all.[59]

The close connection of this gift with the gift of prophecy, however, does not exhaust its meaning. It would apply where there is a need to discern in a given situation whether the influence is the Holy Spirit, a demonic spirit, or the human spirit. Biblical illustrations might include the accounts of Ananias and Sapphira (Acts 5:1–9), Elymas the sorcerer (13:6–12), and the demon-possessed slave girl (16:16–18). The functioning of this gift is particularly applicable in cases of physical or mental illness, to enable a

[59]For instance: Carson, *Showing the Spirit,* 120; Wayne A. Grudem, "A Response to Gerhard Dautzenberg on 1 Cor. 12:10," *Biblische Zeitschrift* 22 (1978): 255, 259.

believer to know whether or not the illness is demonically based—and whether to pray for the person's healing or to engage in a "power encounter" with spiritual forces.

Excursus: Healing and the Atonement

This article will examine the key passages of Scripture that make a specific connection between God's healing provision and the redemptive work of Christ. Is there "healing in the Atonement"? And if so, what does the expression mean?

The article will not deal with general matters related to divine healing, since there should be no doubt about the Lord's ability to heal or His provision for healing today. "'I am the LORD, who heals you'" (Exod. 15:26) is amply demonstrated throughout the Old Testament and the New Testament. He has made provision even today through the *charisma* of "gifts of healings" (1 Cor. 12:9, lit. trans.) and ministry in the local assembly (James 5:13–16).

THE KEY OLD TESTAMENT PASSAGE

Numerous incidents could be cited throughout Scripture of the Lord's healing of His people, as well as specific statements like Psalm 103:3b (NASB), that He "heals all your diseases." But the focal point must be Isaiah 53:4, "Surely he took up *[nasa']* our infirmities *[chali]* and carried *[saval]* our sorrows *[makh'ov]*." Each of the Hebrew words is significant.

Unfortunately, the words "infirmities" and "sorrows" do not adequately translate the Hebrew. *Chali* clearly means sickness or disease, as is evident from a number of passages in Deuteronomy 28 (such as vv. 59 and 61). Similarly, *makh'ov* is used of physical pain. "A man may be chastened on a bed of pain" (Job 33:19). These same nouns are used in describing the Messiah as "a man of sorrows *[makh'ov]*, and familiar with suffering *[chali]*" (Isa. 53:3). (The marginal notes of the NASB render these words as "pains" and "sickness" both here and in the following v.)

The Messiah is described in this manner because in His death He took upon himself our pains and sicknesses. The verbs used in Isaiah 53:4 *(nasa'* and *saval)* speak clearly to this point. *Nasa'* means to "lift, carry, bear, take away." Later in the chapter we read that "he bore *[nasa']* the sin of many" (v. 12). This verb, in contexts like Isaiah 53, definitely conveys the idea of the Messiah dying for the sins and sicknesses of His people, and not only *for* them but *in their place.* The imagery of the scapegoat captures this concept of substitution when we read that "the goat will carry *[nasa']* on itself all their sins" (Lev. 16:22).

The verb *saval* speaks of bearing a heavy load. It occurs in Isaiah 53 in the context of the Messiah bearing our pains (v. 4) as well as our iniquities (v. 11). There is no doubt that in the mind of Isaiah the death of the Messiah was for both the sins and the sicknesses of His people.

MATTHEW 8:16–17 AND ISAIAH 53:4

Isaiah 53:4 is quoted only once in the New Testament. After recounting numerous healings and demon expulsions performed by Jesus, Matthew explains, "This was to fulfill what was spoken through the prophet Isaiah: 'He took up *[lambanō]* our infirmities *[astheneia]* and carried *[bastazō]* our diseases *[nosos]*'" (8:17).

The basic meaning of *astheneia* is that of weakness, but it is used often in the New Testament of sickness or disease (e.g., Luke 5:15; Acts 28:9). In its verb form it is used frequently of suffering bodily weakness, that is, being sick (e.g., Matt. 25:39; John 11:1–3,6; James 5:14).

Nosos, a synonym, means "disease" or "illness."[60] It is found with this meaning in passages like Matthew 4:23; 9:35; Luke 7:21; Acts 19:12; and many others.

As for the verbs in Matthew 8:17, *lambanō,* among its many meanings and wide usage, carries the idea of taking away or removing. One suggested meaning is "to take in

[60]Curiously, the Septuagint at this point in Isa. 53:4 unjustifiably translates the Heb. word into *hamartias* (sins).

order to carry away." *Bastazō* means "to remove, to carry away, or to bear"; it correctly conveys the idea of the Isaiah passage.

Appropriateness of Matthew's Quotation

Isaiah 53 focuses on the atoning death of Christ. How then could Matthew say that Isaiah 53:4 was fulfilled at a time prior to the Crucifixion? Several points need to be made.

The New Testament is normative for any interpretation of an Old Testament passage. Even though Jesus had not yet died, we have in Matthew 8 an anticipation of His death and its benefits. God, who is the eternal I AM, does not have a time-space existence. The quoting of the Isaiah passage by Matthew is proleptic (anticipatory) in nature.

In a way perhaps incomprehensible to us, the benefits of the Cross extend back to all people of faith. The salvation of the Old Testament saints, even though they could not have been aware of it, took place on the basis of the yet-to-come sacrifice of Christ on the cross.

God, who may be said to exist in the eternal present, transcends time. Indeed, in His eyes Christ is the Lamb slain "from the foundation of the world"[61] (Rev. 13:8, KJV). Consequently the benefits of the Cross span the entire history of humankind.

Some Conclusions

It is inescapable that there is an important connection between healing and the Atonement. Yet biblical passages which speak specifically and clearly to this issue are quite rare. Even the familiar and oft-quoted "By his wounds we are healed" (Isa. 53:5; see 1 Pet. 2:24) must be understood

[61]The phrase "from the foundation of the world" is taken by some to apply to the time of entering names in the Book of Life (see also Rev. 17:8), but the Gk. word order more naturally suggests that it modifies the participle "slain" (see also 1 Pet. 1:18–20). In either event, the slain Lamb cannot be separated from the slain Lamb's Book of Life.

inclusively, embracing both spiritual salvation and physical healing. Yet we must recognize that the thrust of the great messianic passage of Isaiah 52:13 to 53:12 is upon Christ's dying for our sins. We ought therefore to be cautious about trying to formulate a detailed theology of "healing in the Atonement." Yet we need to be convinced that divine healing is indeed mediated to us through the Cross.

An important aspect of biblical salvation is its holistic nature. Christ died to reverse the curse resulting from the sin of our first parents; He "redeemed us from the curse of the law" (Gal. 3:13). The curse was death—both physical and spiritual. He died for the whole person, not only for the soul. His redemptive work includes salvation for all aspects of humankind's being, however one conceives the interrelationship of body, soul, and spirit.

Physical healing occurs as a result of the atoning work of Christ, but at best it is only a temporary deliverance since all must die. The greater physical deliverance is the redemption of the body, which will undergo not only resurrection but also transformation, never again to be subject to sickness and disease (Rom. 8:23; Phil. 3:20–21). Ultimately the consequences of physical and spiritual death have been overcome by the death of the One who took upon himself both our sins and our sicknesses!

Excursus: Tongues—Godward or Manward?

Whom does the tongues-speaker address?[62] With respect to private, devotional tongues, the answer is obvious. The glossolalist is speaking to God or is in some way declaring the praises of God. Evidence for this is recorded both by Luke and by Paul. On the Day of Pentecost, the disciples

[62]I use the words "Godward" and "manward" because, in my judgment, they capture the point of this article. "Manward" is not intended to be a gender-exclusive word, any more than Paul meant his use of "men" (as in 1 Cor. 14:2–3) to exclude women.

were magnifying God (Acts 2:11); at the household of Cornelius, the recipients of the Spirit were speaking in tongues, that is, magnifying God (10:46). Paul says that the glossolalist is praising God and giving thanks to Him (1 Cor. 14:16–17). In addition, many exegetes and commentators consider "the groans that words cannot express" (Rom. 8:26) to be glossolalic in nature.

Few will question the Godward direction of tongues in one's private devotions. But differences of opinion exist regarding the direction of tongues in public worship. Is its direction still Godward, or does a shift take place so that an utterance in tongues becomes a message from God to the congregation through the glossolalist? The following are the basic viewpoints regarding the direction of tongues in public worship:

(1) The direction is invariably Godward.

(2) The direction is invariably manward.

(3) The direction is manward, but in exceptional cases may be Godward.

(4) The direction is Godward, but there may be exceptions. This is the position which, in my judgment, best reflects the teaching of the New Testament.

I offer the following observations for consideration:

(1) There is no clear indication in Scripture that the direction of tongues undergoes a change from Godward to manward when the gift is manifested in public worship.

(2) The context of Paul's admonition about speaking audibly in tongues in public worship indicates that the speaker, who is indeed speaking to God, should pray that he may interpret (1 Cor. 14:13–17). Since the glossolalia is Godward, then the interpretation will also be Godward.

(3) There is no passage that clearly teaches tongues and interpretation are addressed to believers. Very few exegetes and commentators interpret 1 Corinthians 14:6 to mean that tongues, when interpreted, may take the form of "some revelation or knowledge or prophecy or word of instruction." At best, it is only an inference that some draw. This is an exegetically difficult verse, but the general

thought is for intelligibility in verbal utterances in corporate worship. Some may appeal to verse 21 which, in the quotation from Isaiah, says that through the Assyrians' language God would speak to Israel. But the manner in which God spoke to them was not cognitive, since they did not understand the language. It was the *fact* of the presence of the language, not the *content* of the language, that was the means by which the Lord communicated to Israel.

(4) Regarding tongues, Paul's primary emphasis in 1 Corinthians 14 is on its use in corporate worship. He opens the discussion by saying that one who speaks in a tongue "does not speak to men but to God" and that it is the prophet who speaks "to men" (vv. 2–3).

(5) The form that an interpretation takes may be influenced by what the interpreter has been exposed to, since the human factor often enters into a manifestation of the Spirit. If all an interpreter has heard is interpretations that address men, then that likely is the form his interpretation will take. "Manward" interpretations may really be the interpreter's recasting of a genuine prompting of the Spirit that is in the form of praise or prayer, but because of prior conditioning the person expresses it as an admonition to praise or pray.

(6) Interpretations that are prayer or praise edify the hearers in the same way that many of the psalms and other expressions of praise and prayer in Scripture are edifying. Even though the interpretation is addressed *to* God, in corporate worship it is *for the benefit of* the hearers.

(7) It is wise to maintain some flexibility in these matters. The question is not so much whether an utterance in tongues may be addressed to individuals, but whether that is the biblical rule. Certainly the sovereign Lord can speak directly through one person to others by means of tongues and interpretation, but are we missing something by understanding this to be the rule rather than the exception?

(8) The reader's attention is invited to portions of chapters 13 and 14 in part 3 of this book that deal with various aspects of tongues and interpretation.

Chapter 14

Spiritual Gifts and Worship

General Comments

The subject of worship in the New Testament is too broad to be covered here. This chapter deals primarily with one aspect of that worship—spiritual gifts in worship. Many spiritual gifts may be exercised during a worship service. Especially applicable are tongues, interpretation of tongues, prophecy, and distinguishings of spirits, to which Paul in 1 Corinthians 14 devotes considerable attention. These will be discussed after attention is given to a few introductory matters.

Charismatic activities that may occur in a worship service include revelation (1 Cor. 14:6,26), knowledge (v. 6), prophecy (v. 6), a hymn (v. 26), a word of instruction (vv. 6,26), a tongue (v. 26), and an interpretation (v. 26). However, the activities mentioned in verse 6—revelation, knowledge, prophecy, word of instruction—may not be clearly distinguishable from one another.[1] One suggestion is that it might be helpful to think of revelation and knowledge as specific activities or manifestations of prophecy

[1]"The boundaries between the four named forms of edificatory speech are fluid" (Hans Lietzmann, *An die Korinther I, II* [Tübingen, Germany: J. C. B. Mohr, 1949], 71); see also Charles K. Barrett, *A Commentary on the First Epistle to the Corinthians* (New York: Harper & Row, 1968), 317.

and a word of instruction, respectively.[2] The implication of "everyone has" (v. 26) is that all are expected to contribute to the edification of the body.

Can the singing of a psalm be understood "charismatically"? Certainly there were fixed hymns which were sung by a congregation,[3] but this does not rule out the possibility of spontaneous, improvised singing by a worshiper.[4] This type of singing may be called "hymns of glossolalia,"[5] or a kind of "charismatic hymnody."[6] The psalms here would be "a fresh, perhaps spontaneous, composition, not Old Testament psalms."[7] Even if they were not clearly glossolalic in nature, the entire discussion in verses 13–19 very strongly suggests this possibility. When one prays in a tongue, the mind is unfruitful. When one sings with the spirit, in contrast to singing with the mind, there is no alternative but to accept a clear distinction between the two. It is certainly possible, however, that this inspired singing could at times be in the common language of the congregation, in which case it might be a form of prophecy.

There is a striking parallel between singing with the spirit and the "spiritual songs" of Ephesians 5:19 and Colossians 3:16. The contrast between being drunk with wine and being filled with the Spirit appears not only in Ephesians 5:18 but also in another "charismatic," glossolalic context (Acts 2:4,15). The verb for "sing" *(psallein)* is found in 1 Corinthians 14:15 and Ephesians 5:19. This

[2]See, for example, Johannes Weiss, *Der erste Korintherbrief* (Göttingen, Germany: Vandenhöck & Ruprecht, 1910), 323; Archibald Robertson and Alfred Plummer, *A Critical and Exegetical Commentary on the First Epistle of St. Paul to the Corinthians* (Edinburgh, Scotland: T. & T. Clark, 1914), 308.

[3]See Gerhard Delling, *Worship in the New Testament,* trans. Percy Scott (Philadelphia: Westminster Press, 1962), chap. 6.

[4]Eduard Schweizer, "Worship in the New Testament," *The Reformed and Presbyterian World* 24, no. 5 (March 1957): 199.

[5]Delling, *Worship in the New Testament,* 86 n. 5.

[6]James D. G. Dunn, *Jesus and the Spirit* (Philadelphia: Westminster Press, 1975), 238.

[7]Barrett, *Corinthians,* 327.

singing with the spirit/Spirit[8] may have a bearing on Paul's use of the expression "kinds of tongues" (1 Cor. 12:10,28). Glossolalic prayer may be one kind; glossolalic singing another (1 Cor. 14:14–16). (As noted in chap. 3, however, the expression may mean human languages and heavenly languages.)

Because of the basic edificatory function of glossolalia and prophecy when properly regulated, Paul discouraged their indiscriminate exercise. The Spirit of God is "never a Spirit bursting out in such a way that the speaker is unable to regulate his speech (14:32!). On the other hand, this order is not unalterable." Furthermore, there must be an order "which remains open to the Lord's intervention whenever and wherever he is willing to interfere." Then the church must ascertain whether it is really God's will, whenever this order is broken through.[9]

The congregation has the obligation to regulate the gifts. This is the concern of 1 Corinthians 12 to 14; it is not an incidental thought.[10] Paul gives these commands not because he is critical of the gifts themselves; he gives them "from his view of the nature of Christian service [worship]."[11] In Paul's teaching on self-control in the exercise of the gifts, he parts company with pagan religion in which the person is seized by an invading spirit and has no control over himself. Instead, he teaches that God's Spirit and the human spirit can and must work in cooperation with each other.

Oscar Cullmann has stated so well Paul's position on freedom and order in worship that I here paraphrase as well as quote his comments: The strength of early New

[8]The meaning of *pneuma* is uncertain or ambiguous in some passages. Since the Gk. text does not use capitalization, does the word mean the human spirit or the Holy Spirit in a given passage?

[9]Eduard Schweizer, "The Service of Worship. An Exposition of 1 Corinthians 14," in *Neotestamentica* (Zurich, Switzerland: Zwingli Verlag, 1963), 338–39.

[10]Kurt Stalder, *Das Werk des Geistes in der Heiligung bei Paulus* (Zurich, Switzerland: EVZ, 1962), 87.

[11]Hermann Gunkel, *The Influence of the Holy Spirit,* trans. R. A. Harrisville and P. A. Quanbeck II (Philadelphia: Fortress Press, 1979), 87.

Testament worship is that the free working of the Spirit and liturgical[12] restrictiveness go hand in hand, and both serve the one purpose of building up the community of believers. Paul was able to bring these two elements together because he saw everything in the light of the building up of the church. "It is precisely in this *harmonious combination of freedom and restriction* that there lies the greatness and uniqueness of the early Christian service of worship."[13]

Regulation of Glossolalia

With respect to glossolalia, there is the insistence that the church is not edified if the utterance remains uninterpreted (1 Cor. 14:5). But prior conditions are that these expressions of glossolalia must be given serially, not simultaneously, and that there will be a maximum of three in one worship service (vv. 27–28). If *all* should speak in tongues, either in rapid succession or in unison, the charge of madness may justly be brought against them (v. 23).[14] In addition, "someone must interpret" (v. 27). Some understand this to mean that only one person does all the interpreting in a service, but it is more natural to understand it to mean that each glossolalic utterance must have only one person interpreting it. Otherwise there would be confusion.

Through whom does an interpretation come? The glossolalist ought to interpret his or her own utterance if someone else does not (vv. 5,13).[15] But under normal conditions

[12]The reader should understand this word in a general sense as an adjective form of a Gk. word for worship *(leitourgia),* and not in the sense of a highly structured order of worship (which is a common meaning today for the word "liturgy").

[13]Oscar Cullmann, *Early Christian Worship,* trans. A. Stewart Todd and James B. Torrance (London: SCM Press, 1953), 32–33, Cullmann's emphasis.

[14]Very likely, "all/everybody" *(pantes)* in this v. and in v. 24 has the same meaning, "one after another." See Robertson and Plummer, *Corinthians,* 317.

[15]See Weiss, *Der erste Korintherbrief,* 327; Robertson and Plummer, *Corinthians,* 307, 311. Some argue, however, that in Gk. the subject "someone" *(tis)* or another easily guessed subject is often understood. See, for example, Jean Hering, *The First Epistle of Saint Paul to the Corinthians,* trans. A. W. Heathcote and P. J. Allcock (London: Epworth Press, 1962), 146–47, 149.

the interpreter is someone other than the glossolalist (see 1 Cor. 12:10; 14:28). One source suggests that the interpreter may be analogous to the translator in the synagogue who rendered the Scripture readings into Aramaic from Hebrew and also communicated aloud to the congregation the softly spoken sermons.[16]

An interpretation is needed because of the presence of an "ungifted" *(idiotēs)* person (1 Cor. 14:16, NASB). The identity of such a person is much disputed. Some suggest he may be a proselyte or a catechumen,[17] or a member of the congregation who is not endowed with the gift of tongues or interpretation of tongues.[18] But it does not seem that Paul has in mind only people of those types, for even full-fledged members do not know what the tongue-speaker has said and whether they must respond with the "Amen."[19] A different meaning for *idiotēs* may be present in verses 23–24, however, where Paul speaks of the possibility of such persons and unbelievers entering a service. They would then be no different from the unbelievers, and the two terms would express one idea—unbelieving outsiders.[20]

Paul prefers to speak "five intelligible words" in the course of a service than ten thousand words in a tongue (1 Cor. 14:19). Only when the language is intelligible can the congregation respond by saying "Amen," which was the Jewish and early Christian custom of the congregation to signify its concurrence with the prayer.[21]

Does an interpretation have the effect of converting

[16]See Hermann L. Strack and Paul Billerbeck, *Kommentar zum Neuen Testament aus Talmud und Midrash* (München, Germany: C. H. Beck'sche, 1924–28), 1:579, 3:465–68, 4:161, 185.

[17]BAGD, 370; Weiss, *Der erste Korintherbrief,* 330–31.

[18]Lietzmann, *Korinther,* 72; Heinrich Schlier, *"idiotēs,"* in *TDNT,* 3:217.

[19]Gordon D. Fee, *The First Epistle to the Corinthians* (Grand Rapids: Wm. B. Eerdmans, 1987), 673.

[20]See Schlier, *"idiotēs,"* 3:217; Lietzmann, *Korinther,* 73.

[21]See Deut. 27:14–26; 1 Chron. 16:36; Neh. 5:13; 8:6; Ps. 106:48; Rev. 5:14; 7:12.

tongues into prophecy?[22] Paul says, "He who prophesies is greater than one who speaks in tongues, unless he interprets, so that the church may be edified" (1 Cor. 14:5). He does not say that interpreted tongues become a prophecy, but only that tongues is as valid as prophecy when it is followed by an interpretation. Tongues and interpretation together "are equal in *value* to Prophecy. . . . They are far from identical in purpose."[23] The basic content of each type of utterance may be different. Glossolalia, as we have seen, is God-oriented; it takes the form of prayer or praise, either spoken or sung. Prophecy, on the other hand, is addressed to the congregation. Paul says that prophecy is for edification, exhortation or encouragement, and comfort; he says that tongues plus interpretation is for edification, but does not add any other functions. If interpreted tongues is the same as prophecy, why have tongues and interpretation in the first place?[24] Furthermore, such a position blurs the distinction between the two gifts of tongues and prophecy, a distinction Paul clearly makes throughout.[25]

Are uninterpreted tongues then ever justifiable? The answer is yes, but not in a worship gathering. In one's private devotional life, a believer may indeed experience personal edification thereby (1 Cor. 14:4). Some, however, interpret Paul's statement as sarcastic and not commendatory.[26] But the very real possibility exists that Paul has this private, devotional aspect in mind when he says that "the Spirit helps *[sunantilambanomai]* us in our weakness" and

[22]Yes, according to Barrett, *Corinthians,* 316. But he represents a small minority of exegetes and commentators.

[23]Harold Horton, *The Gifts of the Spirit,* 2d ed. (Springfield, Mo.: Gospel Publishing House, 1975), 189.

[24]J. Rodman Williams, *Renewal Theology: Systematic Theology from a Charismatic Perspective* (Grand Rapids: Zondervan Publishing House, 1990), 2:405–6 n. 276.

[25]David Lim, *Spiritual Gifts: A Fresh Look* (Springfield, Mo.: Gospel Publishing House, 1991), 144.

[26]For example, H. Wayne House,"Tongues and the Mystery Religions at Corinth," *Bibliotheca Sacra* 140 (April–June 1982): 144.

that "the Spirit himself intercedes for us with groans that words cannot express" (Rom. 8:26).[27]

Regulation of Prophecy

The gift of prophecy must also be regulated, notwithstanding its preferential treatment over glossolalia in corporate worship. Potentially, all Christians may prophesy (1 Cor. 14:5,24,31), but as with speaking in tongues, restrictions are imposed on the manifestation of this gift. First, prophecies are to be given "in turn" (v. 31), that is, one by one,[28] thus eliminating confusion (v. 33). The prophet is able to control the impulse to prophesy if the proposed utterance will violate the regulations prescribed by Paul. This aspect of controllability distinguishes genuine Christian "ecstatic" utterances from similar phenomena in other religions. It is precisely because prophets (as well as glossolalists) *can* control themselves that Paul insists that under certain conditions they *must* control themselves. This is the generally accepted meaning of the statement that "spirits of prophets are subject to prophets" (v. 32, my translation).[29] This thesis is "a postulate that represents the needed basis for his commands."[30]

Other interpretations of the word "spirits" (v. 32) are not lacking. One view is that the plural form reflects an ani-

[27]Gunkel, *Influence of the Holy Spirit,* 80–81, and Cullmann, *Early Christian Worship,* 34, unhesitatingly speak of this as glossolalic. Delling is more cautious: "This pneumatic prayer is a charismatic dealing with God like speaking with tongues, whether with or without the corresponding forms" (Gerhard Delling, "*antilambanomai,* etc.," in *TDNT,* 1:376). See also Charles K. Barrett, *A Commentary on the Epistle to the Romans* (London: Adam & Charles Black, 1962), 168; and especially Gordon D. Fee, "Toward a Pauline Theology of Glossolalia," in *Pentecostalism in Context: Essays in Honor of William W. Menzies,* ed. Wonsuk Ma and Robert P. Menzies (Sheffield, England: Sheffield Academic Press, 1997), 24–37.

[28]C. F. D. Moule, *An Idiom-Book of New Testament Greek,* 2d ed. (Cambridge, England: Cambridge University Press, 1959), 61.

[29]The omission of the definite article before each of the nouns—spirits, prophets, prophets—makes the saying more like a maxim or proverb. See Robertson and Plummer, *Corinthians,* 323.

[30]Gunkel, *Influence of the Holy Spirit,* 87. An alternative interpretation will be discussed shortly.

mistic concept of spirit.[31] It is the ancient idea of an individual, foreign spirit in the prophet, and would represent an accommodation to usage by Paul which refers the work of the Holy Spirit to other spirits.[32]

A second interpretation is that "spirits" equal spiritual gifts or manifestations.[33] This would mean that the gift of prophecy is a possession of the prophet and is subject to his or her control.

A final—and in my judgment, correct—interpretation is that prophets are lord over *their own* spirits. The word "spirits" would then be the human spirits of the prophets which are the vehicle and means of prophetic utterances. In effect, this interpretation says that prophets are able to control themselves.

A second limitation is that there must be a maximum of three prophetic utterances in one service (1 Cor. 14:29a). Some, however, interpret the statement "two or three prophets should speak" to mean that there should be a cluster of no more than three prophecies at one point in a service, but that after these prophecies are evaluated, others may prophesy. In other words, there is no limit to the number of prophetic utterances allowed in a service. Appeal is made to verse 31, "You can all prophesy in turn." Most exegetes and commentators, however, say that the maximum of three allowable prophecies applies to an entire service. It is the view that best suits the general tenor of the chapter.

The question must be asked, however, why this numeri-

[31]Rudolph Bultmann, *Theology of the New Testament,* trans. Kendrick Grobel (New York: Charles Scribner's Sons, 1951), 1:156.

[32]See Weiss, *Der erste Korintherbrief,* 326–27, 341. The classical passage is 1 Kings 22:19–23, where a spirit offers itself from the host of Yahweh. This view would attach the same basic meaning to the pl. form of the word in 1 Cor. 14:12, "you are eager for spirits" (my translation). See also 12:10. For a related viewpoint, see Wayne A. Grudem, *The Gift of Prophecy in the New Testament and Today* (Westchester, Ill.: Crossway Books, 1988), 117–19.

[33]Robertson and Plummer, *Corinthians,* 323, also direct attention to 12:10 and 14:12; see also Hans Conzelmann, *1 Corinthians,* trans. James W. Leitch (Philadelphia: Fortress Press, 1975), 279.

cal restriction is imposed, as it is also with glossolalia. The answer is inferential: It appears that throughout the New Testament, the apostles have priority over prophets. In all passages mentioning the two, "apostle" always precedes "prophet." Even that which purports to be a prophetic revelation cannot preempt the apostolic word (see Gal. 1:8–9). These charismatic manifestations are not to be so numerous as to usurp the place of the normal exposition and reading of the Scriptures. The limitation of nine vocal gifts in one service—three each for tongues, interpretation, and prophecy—is to keep these gifts from dominating a service in which other elements of worship ought also to be observed.

A third limitation is mentioned in verse 30: "If a revelation comes to someone who is sitting down, the first speaker should stop." Someone in the process of giving a prophecy should be willing to defer to another person receiving a prophecy. It is not clear how or why this takes place, but it is implied that no one person should monopolize the giving of prophetic utterances.

Distinguishings/Discernings of Spirits

A restriction placed upon prophetic utterances is that "the others should weigh carefully *[diakrinō]* what is said" (1 Cor. 14:29b). Three questions immediately suggest themselves: (1) Who are "the others"? (2) What is the meaning of "weigh"? (3) By what means should this weighing take place?

(1) Opinion is divided on the identity of "the others" (v. 29). It may mean either the rest of the congregation[34] or the other prophets.[35] There is no indication that the weighing

[34]Barrett, *Corinthians,* 328; Lietzmann, *Korinther,* 74; Friedrich Buechsel, *"diakrinō, diakrisis,"* in *TDNT,* 2:947; Don A. Carson, *Showing the Spirit: A Theological Exposition of 1 Corinthians 12–14* (Grand Rapids: Baker Book House, 1987), 120; Grudem, *Gift of Prophecy,* 70–74; Fee, *Corinthians,* 694.

[35]Conzelmann, *Corinthians,* 245; Robertson and Plummer, *Corinthians,* 322; Weiss, *Der erste Korintherbrief,* 340. Campenhausen inclines to this view, but says also that this does not relieve the congregation of responsibility for what happens. Hans von Campenhausen, *Ecclesiastical Authority and*

of prophecies was the prerogative of prophets. The contrary is the case when we observe the listing of spiritual gifts in 1 Corinthians 12:8–10 in which prophecy is given to one and distinguishing between spirits to another.

(2) The word for "weigh" in 1 Corinthians 14:29 *(diakrinō)* is the verb form of the first word of the gift of "distinguishing *[diakrisis]* of spirits" (1 Cor. 12:10, NASB).[36] It is not accidental that in the list of charismata these two gifts occur together, and in logical order—prophecy first, distinguishing of spirits afterward. This latter gift is the ability to differentiate the Holy Spirit not only from an unclean spirit,[37] but also from a human spirit which, according to some, might speak in ecstasy.[38]

A prophet may be neither divinely nor demonically inspired, but may instead speak from his own spirit or thoughts. Or he may indeed be prompted by the Spirit to speak, but knowingly or unknowingly include some of his own thoughts. There is the "inherent temptation to exercise it [prophecy] without *pistis* [faith]."[39] Consequently Paul says that it must be "in proportion to his faith" (Rom. 12:6), for such a prophet should speak only in accordance with the "measure of faith" given to him by God (Rom. 12:3). The need for this type of discrimination is found elsewhere in the New Testament (for example, Matt. 7:15–20; 24:11,24; 1 Thess. 5:20–21; 1 Tim. 4:1; James 3:5; 1 John 4:1–3).

Spiritual Power in the Church of the First Three Centuries, trans. J. A. Baker (Stanford: Stanford University Press, 1969), 62–63.

[36]The rendering "assess" for the verb is suggested by Buechsel, *"diakrinō, diakrisis,"* 2:947. Interestingly, Hering suggests the translation "discuss" and relates the statement to the prohibition of women "to discuss and ask questions" (see vv. 34–35) (*Corinthians,* 153–54). See also David E. Aune, *Prophecy in Early Christianity and the Ancient Mediterranean World* (Grand Rapids: Wm. B. Eerdmans, 1983), 230.

[37]Gunkel, *Influence of the Holy Spirit,* 49.

[38]Lietzmann, *Korinther,* 61.

[39]Gerhard Kittel, *"analogia,"* in *TDNT,* 1:348; see also William Sanday and Arthur C. Headlam, *A Critical and Exegetical Commentary on the Epistle to the Romans,* 5th ed. (Edinburgh, Scotland: T. & T. Clark, 1914), 356. The one prophesying "should not add material of his own to that which has been revealed to him" (Delling, *Worship in the New Testament,* 31).

This insistence upon evaluating prophetic utterances differs from the Old Testament emphasis, though even there the prophet was not always free of criticism (see Deut. 13:2–6; 18:22). But generally speaking, the prophet in Old Testament and Jewish thought had unlimited authority since he alone had the Spirit. In contrast, the New Testament prophet "is not an unrestricted ruler over others. He is subject to their judgment. He does not stand above the community; like all the rest, he is a member of it."[40]

(3) The third question involves how this assessment of prophecies takes place. The gift of distinguishing of spirits may be understood as a subjective means by which other members of the congregation know intuitively by the Spirit whether a prophetic utterance is genuine (in whole or in part). Externally, there may be no discernible difference between a divinely inspired person and a demonically or "self"-inspired person, since unusual or ecstatic experiences in and of themselves are not necessarily Christian in character.[41]

In addition, Paul, following the lead of the Old Testament (Deut. 13:2–6; 18:21–22), says that content, not manner, is the rule by which prophecies must be assessed.[42] The specific criterion Paul mentions is the utterance of the statement "'Jesus is Lord'" (1 Cor. 12:3). Similarly, a truly inspired person cannot say "'Jesus be cursed'" because "[t]he Spirit (who of course is the 'Spirit of the Lord,' 2 Cor. 3:17) cannot contradict himself. He cannot curse Jesus."[43] But at best, this is only a partial criterion, because neither of these two statements may be present in a prophetic utterance.[44] Strikingly parallel is the thrust of 1 John 4:1–3,

[40]Gerhard Friedrich, "Prophets and Prophecies in the New Testament," in *TDNT,* 6:849.

[41]Walter J. Bartling, "The Congregation of Christ—a Charismatic Body; an Exegetical Study of 1 Corinthians 12," *Concordia Theological Monthly* 40 (February 1969): 73.

[42]Barrett, *Corinthians,* 281.

[43]Conzelmann, *1 Corinthians,* 204.

[44]Hering, *Corinthians,* 124–25.

which also poses a doctrinal test—the humanity of Jesus. "Every spirit that acknowledges that Jesus Christ has come in the flesh is from God" (v. 2). We should note that John is writing to combat a form of Gnostic heresy that denied the full humanity of Jesus Christ.

Since the statements by prophets just mentioned are doctrinal in nature, they give us a guiding principle for evaluating prophecies. I have already noted that apostles have priority over prophets, so we may infer from Paul's and John's statements that doctrinal tests must be applied to prophecies. The original word and witness of the apostles finds definitive form in the New Testament canon, so for the present day the New Testament should be the criterion by which all prophetic utterances are evaluated.[45] This is in line with a strict translation (offered as a footnote in the NIV) of the Romans 12:6 phrase quoted earlier, "in proportion to his faith": "in agreement with the faith," meaning the Christian faith, or the body of truth accepted by the Church. This, then, would mean that the prophet "is forbidden to suppress or add anything on his own authority. He stands on the 'ground' of faith which the apostle has laid."[46] But these two interpretations ("*his* faith," "*the* faith") complement, rather than contradict, each other.

Women and Silence in the Church

Paul states that "women should remain silent in the churches" (1 Cor. 14:34). Verses 33b–35 are among the most disputed in all of 1 Corinthians, largely because they seem to contradict earlier statements that women were allowed to prophesy and to pray in the services (11:4–6). I offer the following observations:

(1) Some question the authenticity and genuineness of this passage, saying it was not in the original manuscript.

[45]Campenhausen, *Ecclesiastical Authority,* 23–24.

[46]Ibid., 62; see also Delling, *Worship in the New Testament,* 31. While not necessarily decisive, the presence of the definite article with "faith" may suggest this "objective" nature of the faith.

But the vast majority of authorities consider these verses to be genuinely from the hand of Paul.

(2) One viewpoint says that this passage forbids women to evaluate prophetic utterances. But there is nothing in the context to suggest this. Furthermore, it is not clear precisely how prophecies were evaluated—whether an evaluation was made vocally or even whether it was done during a service.

(3) The command for the women to keep silent in church is not absolute; it applies only under certain conditions. Two other commands in this chapter to keep silent are likewise not absolute (vv. 28,30). The glossolalist is to maintain silence only if an interpreter is not present; a prophesying prophet must be silent only when another prophet must be given an opportunity to speak.

(4) The interpretation of this passage should not be influenced by what Paul says in 1 Timothy 2:12–14, since each passage must be interpreted in the light of the circumstances under which it was written.

(5) It is quite clear that the women must be silent "if they desire to learn anything" (1 Cor. 14:35, NASB). Any interpretation that misses or ignores this important clue cannot be taken seriously. The 1 Timothy passage deals with women who want to teach; this passage deals with women who want to learn.

(6) We must understand Paul's instructions in the general context of his wanting harmony and order in a church service. Since Greek women lived more sheltered lives than the men, it would be natural for them to make inquiries about spiritual matters. But, says Paul, those questions should be asked at home.

Everyday Service

Spiritual gifts perform a vital function in a worship service, but their operation is not restricted to such occasions. It is true that the assembly of believers is the special place of God's presence and that this is the counterpart of God's dwelling among His people Israel.[47] Yet it is remarkable that in passages dealing with the formal, corporate worship of believers, the New Testament avoids using terms which would be reminiscent of Old Testament and Jewish worship and rites.[48] Upon investigation, it is readily apparent that those cultic terms are indeed used in the New Testament, but not in connection with a Christian service of worship.[49]

In Judaism and in paganism there are priests. In the New Testament, all believers are considered to be priests, which automatically rules out a special class within the Church which performs a special cultic service.[50] However, Paul does use this type of cultic language to describe his work in the gospel, which he calls "the priestly duty of proclaiming the gospel of God" and in that connection refers to himself as "a minister [*leitourgos*, that is, "servant"] of Christ Jesus" (Rom. 15:16). He speaks elsewhere of "being poured out like a drink offering on the sacrifice and service *[thusia kai leitourgia]* coming from [the Philippians'] faith" (Phil. 2:17; see 2 Tim. 4:6). He also uses cultic language when he calls their gift of money "an acceptable sacrifice" (Phil. 4:18). Gentile Christians are called upon to be of service *(leitourgia)* to the Jewish Christians in sharing material blessings (Rom. 15:27; see 2 Cor. 9:12; Phil. 2:25).

The other term for service/serve *(latreia/latreuō)* is used by Paul when referring to the ministry of Christians, but not in a formal sense of ceremonial worship (Rom. 1:9; 12:1; Phil. 3:3; compare 2 Tim. 1:3).[51] Like the previous pair of

[47]See extended treatment by Martin H. Scharlemann, "The Congregation: Place of God's Presence," *Concordia Theological Monthly* 35 (November 1964): 613–21.

[48]The key terms in the Septuagint are *latreia/latreuō* and *leitourgia/leitourgeō.* Both pairs of words have the basic meaning of service/serve.

[49]The reader should understand this basic meaning of the word "cultic," which refers to formal religious rites and ceremonies. The term is theologically neutral and should not be confused with its contemporary connotation which associates it with groups such as Jehovah's Witnesses or Mormons.

[50]1 Pet. 2:5,9; Rev. 1:6; 5:10; 20:6.

[51]He also uses it in reference to Israel's worship (Rom. 9:4), and worship by Gentiles (1:25).

words for service, this pair is not used in a context of a Christian gathering for worship, whereas its Old Testament Hebrew equivalent (*'avodah*), when used in connection with God, always signifies cultic or ritual service.[52] We notice also Paul's statement that the self-presentation of believers' bodies to God constitutes a "spiritual act of worship" (Rom. 12:1).

We have seen that in Paul's writings especially there is an abandonment of the cultic, ceremonial aspects of sacrifice. For example, in Romans 12:1–2 Paul has deliberately resorted to cultic language "in order to describe the sanctification of everyday life as the true sacrifice of Christendom."[53] Yet the idea of a moral spiritualizing of the cultus did not originate with him, for the Old Testament and Judaism also speak of inward as well as material sacrifices.[54]

The two word groups discussed above concern the rendering of service. This concept of service is best expressed by another word group which conveys, even more generally, the idea of service (*diakoneō, diakonia, diakonos*—"serve," "service," "servant"). As distinct from the previous two terms for service, this word group has the special quality of a personal rendering of service—approximating a service of active love.[55] With specific reference to the collection being taken up for the church in Jerusalem, Paul emphasizes that it is not to be regarded merely externally but rather as a true act of love.[56] When he goes to Jerusalem

[52]It occurs about ninety times in the Old Testament and, with one exception, denotes "a religious, in fact a ceremonial action" (H. Strathmann, "*latreuō, latreia,*" in *TDNT,* 4:59–60). See also C. E. B. Cranfield, *A Commentary on Romans 12–13* (Edinburgh, Scotland: Oliver & Boyd, 1965), 11.

[53]Ernst Kaesemann, "Ministry and Community in the New Testament," in *New Testament Questions of Today,* trans. W. J. Montague (Philadelphia: Fortress Press, 1969), 78.

[54]Deut. 11:13; Ps. 51:16–17; Hos. 6:6; Testament of Levi 3:6. See also Gerhard Kittel, "*logikos,*" in *TDNT,* 4:143.

[55]Hermann W. Beyer, "*diakoneō, diakonia, diakonos,*" in *TDNT,* 2:81, 85; see also Schweizer, "Service of Worship," 196–97.

[56]Beyer, "*diakoneō, diakonia, diakonos,*" 2:88. See Rom. 15:30–31; 2 Cor. 8:1–6; 9:1,12–13; also Acts 11:29–30; 12:25.

with the gift, he speaks of it in terms of serving *(diakoneō)* the saints (Rom. 15:25; see 2 Cor. 8:19–20). He also regards apostleship as service *(diakonia)*.[57]

We have previously noted that certain spiritual gifts are manifested in overt service, such as liberality, giving aid, showing mercy. Consequently, spiritual gifts include not only those demonstrated in corporate worship, but also those expressed in the everyday life of the community. In referring to all gifts as services or ministries (*diakoniai,* 1 Cor. 12:5; see also Rom. 12:7), Paul's essential point is that everyday service is placed on a par with acknowledged spiritual phenomena.[58]

I come, finally, to the relationship between the concepts of service and of upbuilding of the body. Are the two used interchangeably? The building up of the body is the overall purpose of the gifts. The way this is accomplished is through service. The one is the ultimate aim of spiritual gifts; the other, the means of and motivation for accomplishing it.[59]

Excursus: Spiritual Gifts and the Fruit of the Spirit

A number of questions are often raised concerning the distinction between spiritual gifts and the fruit of the Spirit. They are sometimes put in propositional form. The following are two of them, together with a brief response.

1. "The greatest gift is love. Why seek any other gift?" But the Bible does not speak of love as a gift, and it is not found in any list of spiritual gifts. However, it is clearly identified as a fruit of the Spirit (Gal. 5:22).

2. "The fruit are superior to the gifts." But one does not find this in Scripture. The Scriptures do not pit one against

[57]Rom. 11:13; 2 Cor. 4:1; 6:3–4; 11:8; see also Acts 1:17,25; 20:24; 1 Tim. 1:12.

[58]Conzelmann, *1 Corinthians,* 208.

[59]The excursus at the end of this chap. is on a related topic. It is a comparative study of spiritual gifts and fruit of the Spirit.

the other. God has ordained that both should be demonstrated in the lives of believers, without placing one in opposition to the other.

Overview of the Fruit of the Spirit

The central passage when discussing spiritual fruit is Galatians 5:22–23, which speaks of the fruit *(karpos)* of the Spirit and then gives a suggested list of nine. The expression "fruit of the Spirit" is best understood to mean that the Holy Spirit is the source of the fruit.

It is especially significant that Jesus, in His last discourse, spoke at length about fruit (John 15:1–17) and also about the coming of the Holy Spirit (John 14:16–18,26; 15:26–27; 16:5–15). It is not accidental that in this farewell discourse Jesus speaks also about love, joy, and peace—the first three fruit mentioned in Galatians 5:22–23. A number of other New Testament passages deal as well with the subject of fruit (Matt. 7:15–23; 12:33; Luke 6:43,44; Rom. 6:22, KJV; Eph. 5:9; Phil. 1:11; Heb. 12:11, NASB).

Other terminology related to this concept is found in expressions that speak about being led by the Spirit, walking in the Spirit, and being spiritual. "Those who are led by the Spirit of God are sons of God" (Rom. 8:14; see also Gal. 5:18). Closely related to this concept are Paul's words that we are to live, or walk, by or in[60] the Spirit (Gal. 5:16,25). In verse 16 the verb translated "live" in the NIV is *peripateō,* which was the common Greek word for the activity of the legs and feet in getting a person from one place to another. But in the New Testament the word is used also in the figurative sense of conducting or behaving oneself (Rom. 6:4; Eph. 4:1).

The verb in Galatians 5:25 is *stoicheō,* which is more specialized. The general idea of the word is "to agree with or to follow." In this verse it means to keep in step with the Spirit, to follow Him, to agree with Him (see also Acts 21:24; Rom. 4:12; Gal. 6:16, NASB; Phil. 3:16).

[60]The dative case lends itself to either translation.

The word for "spiritual" *(pneumatikos)* sometimes refers to spiritual gifts, but more generally it has the meaning of Christian maturity (1 Cor. 2:13,15; 3:1; Gal. 6:1).

All these terms are in the immediate context of the passage on fruit of the Spirit (Gal. 5:22,23), indicating they are different ways of expressing the same idea.

Similarities Between Gifts and Fruit

Both groups have several points in common:

(1) Their source is the Holy Spirit. They do not originate with the believer and are possible only by His enabling.

(2) The purpose of both is to edify. The overarching purpose of the gifts is to edify the body of Christ (1 Cor. 12:7; 14:26). Likewise, the purpose of spiritual fruit, epitomized by love, is to edify (1 Cor. 8:1).

(3) Both works of the Spirit are perfectible. In other words, the believer does not receive them in finished form. The thrust of 1 Corinthians 14 is instructional. Paul nowhere questions the genuineness of the gifts claimed by the Corinthians; yet he insists that the gifts need to be developed so as to edify the congregation. Similarly, spiritual fruit must be developed; they must be brought to a state of maturity. This is the thought behind the concepts of Christian maturity and growth—the continuing transformation of the Christian into the image of Christ (2 Cor. 3:18).

Distinctions Between Gifts and Fruit

(1) As to their nature, the fruit are the result of the indwelling Spirit; the gifts, the result of the empowering Spirit. Fruit are ethical in nature, whereas gifts are charismatic in nature.

(2) There is a distinction with respect to the obligation of Christians in appropriating the two. *All* Christians are required to demonstrate *all* the fruit of the Spirit. But God does not require all Christians to have *all* the gifts. The requirement is that of receptivity and earnest desire (1 Cor. 12:31; 14:1), but the distribution of the gifts is the sovereign

work of the Spirit (1 Cor. 12:11).

(3) Believers are *always* required to manifest spiritual fruit, but their manifestation of spiritual gifts is at the bidding of the Spirit.

The Divine Ideal

The Holy Spirit manifests himself in both the gifts He bestows on believers and in the fruit demonstrated by them. Both categories are central to the New Testament teaching on the activity of the Spirit among God's people.

Since both the gifts and the fruit originate with the Spirit, it is wrong to oppose them to each other. The Corinthian Christians were told, "Follow the way of love and eagerly desire spiritual gifts" (1 Cor. 14:1). The two ideas are correlative, but certainly they must be understood in the light of Paul's pointing to "the most excellent way" (12:31). This became necessary because of an abuse of the gifts and not because of any inherent inferiority of the gifts to the fruit of the Spirit.

At Corinth, the gifts were being used in competition instead of in cooperation, for self-gratification rather than for the edification of the congregation. Yet at no time does Paul suggest the gifts are not genuine when manifested in this way. It is the person manifesting the gift, not the gift, that is nothing (1 Cor. 13:1–2). The gift is genuine; the one who exercises it lovelessly may not be. "The most excellent way" is the mediation of the gifts through the fruit of the Spirit, and primarily through love.

Love, as we see in 1 Corinthians 13, is the regulative principle behind spiritual gifts. It is patient and kind; it willingly defers to other gifted members by giving them an opportunity to speak as well (14:30–31). It is not jealous or boastful; it recognizes that the Spirit sovereignly distributes His gifts to whomever He pleases (12:11). Nor does it pride itself in its possession of any gift or gifts (12:21). It is not arrogant or rude; it always considers the welfare of the entire body when expressing itself in the congregation, and is willing to receive correction (14:29–30). It does not insist on its own way; it submits to duly constituted authority in the church (14:37).

Complementariness, not mutual exclusivity, is the New Testament approach to the gifts and the fruit. Together they serve to edify the church. Related to this is the concept of interpenetration, as discussed in the preceding paragraph. The divine ideal is that *both* the gifts *and* the fruit be manifested among believers. We are not called upon to choose one over the other.

Study Questions

PART 1: GENERAL PNEUMATOLOGY

CHAPTER 1: THE SPIRIT AND THE GODHEAD

1. Give five reasons why there is confusion in the minds of some concerning the personhood of the Holy Spirit.
2. List four or five figures of speech found for the Holy Spirit in Scripture.
3. In what ways do the Scriptures clearly show that the Holy Spirit is a Person?
4. Explain the meaning of blaspheming the Holy Spirit.
5. List, and comment briefly on, five biblical lines of evidence that point to the Spirit's absolute deity.
6. Is it proper to offer prayer and praise to the Holy Spirit? Justify your answer on the basis of Scripture.
7. Explain briefly what each of the following creeds of the Early Church says about the Holy Spirit: The Apostles' Creed, the Nicene Creed, and the Athanasian Creed.
8. What was the theological error of each of the following persons with regard to the Holy Spirit: Arius, Macedonius, and Sabellius?
9. What was the *filioque* controversy?

CHAPTER 2: THE SPIRIT IN THE OLD TESTAMENT PERIOD

1. What two things stand out about the Old Testament teaching on the Holy Spirit?
2. In what two ways is the Holy Spirit related to the creation of the world?
3. In what three ways did the Holy Spirit operate in the physical, or natural, realm with respect to persons?
4. Give six Old Testament expressions for the manner in which the Holy Spirit made contact with individuals.

5. In what two important ways does the New Testament differ from the Old Testament concerning the Holy Spirit's activity among God's people?
6. Define what a prophet is and how the prophet's message relates to the future and the present.
7. In the Old Testament, what was the most frequent result of the Spirit coming upon individuals and groups?
8. What main ideas about the Holy Spirit are found in the non-canonical books of intertestamental Judaism?
9. Give some of the main ideas about the Holy Spirit found in the writings of the Qumran community.

Chapter 3: The Spirit and the Messiah

1. Summarize in a paragraph Isaiah's prophecies concerning the connection between the Messiah and the Holy Spirit. Which passage is most significant for an understanding of Jesus' ministry?
2. What events in the life of Jesus show the important connection between Him and the Holy Spirit?
3. Relate the words "Christ" and "Messiah" to each other. What is their basic meaning?
4. Did the eternal Son of God really need the anointing of the Spirit to accomplish His earthly work? Explain.
5. How is the Holy Spirit related to Jesus immediately before, during, and immediately after the temptation in the wilderness?
6. In what two ways did the Spirit move upon the lifeless body of Jesus?
7. After Jesus' resurrection, in what way was there a reversal of roles in the relationship between Him and the Holy Spirit?
8. According to John's Gospel (16:13–14), what three activities of the Holy Spirit relate specifically to Christ?
9. Explain the concept that the Spirit is subordinate to the Father and the Son but not inferior to them.

Chapter 4: The Spirit and the Church

1. What two figures of speech in the New Testament show the intimate connection between the Holy Spirit and the Church?
2. Show how the Church as the temple of the Holy Spirit is the typological fulfillment of the Old Testament tabernacle and temple.

3. Explain how the earthly Jesus is the bridge connecting the Old Testament tabernacle and temple with the Church as God's temple.
4. What two men in the Book of Acts proclaimed that God's presence does not dwell in an actual building?
5. Comment in one paragraph on the concept that believers, corporately, are both the spiritual temple and its priesthood.
6. Explain the importance of 1 Corinthians 12:13 in understanding the nature of the Church as the body of Christ.
7. In what four ways is the Spirit's activity related to the Church as the body of Christ?
8. What are some important lessons to be drawn from Paul's treatment of the Spirit's appointment of members of the body to specific functions (1 Cor. 12:12–27)?
9. What are two acceptable interpretations of the phrase "the fellowship of the Holy Spirit"?

CHAPTER 5: THE SPIRIT AND THE BELIEVER

1. Explain briefly Jesus' statement that the Holy Spirit will convict (convince) the world of sin, of righteousness, and of judgment (John 16:8).
2. What three New Testament expressions for salvation emphasize the work of the Holy Spirit? Comment briefly on each.
3. What are the main interpretations of the words "'born of water and the Spirit'" (John 3:5), and which do you prefer? (Be sure to read the appropriate footnote.)
4. Justify the author's statement, "All Christians are indwelt by the Holy Spirit."
5. In what two ways does the Spirit witness to a person's salvation?
6. What is the basic meaning of the term "sanctification"?
7. What three extreme views of sanctification must be avoided? Explain each briefly.
8. Write a meaningful paragraph on sanctification as a progressive experience.
9. In what three roles does the Holy Spirit function to help believers in their daily spiritual walk?
10. In what three ways is the Holy Spirit related to the resurrection of believers?

CHAPTER 6: THE SPIRIT AND THE WORD

1. In a few sentences, state how the Holy Spirit and the Word of

God relate harmoniously to each other.
2. Define revelation as it applies to Scripture. What is the role of the Spirit in revelation?
3. What do we mean by the inspiration of Scripture, and how is the Holy Spirit related to inspiration? What are two important New Testament passages on this topic?
4. In the matter of inspiration, what is the relationship between the human authors and the Holy Spirit?
5. What is the meaning of illumination as it pertains to Scripture? How does it differ from inspiration?
6. Since Jesus promised that the Holy Spirit would teach us all things, does this rule out human teachers of the Word? Explain.
7. How are the proclamation of the gospel and the power of the Holy Spirit related to each other?

PART 2: BAPTISM IN THE HOLY SPIRIT

Chapter 7: Introductory Matters

1. Give two reasons why serious attention must be given to hermeneutical matters related to the doctrine of Spirit baptism.
2. Explain the following terms and how a Pentecostal believer deals with them: redaction criticism, narrative theology, historical precedent, authorial intent, inductive form of logic.
3. What does the author mean when he says, "A specific biblical writer must be understood on his own terms"? Relate this to Luke's theology of the Holy Spirit.
4. Explain the difference between the promise of the Holy Spirit found in Ezekiel and the one found in Joel. How does Moses' statement recorded in Numbers 11:29 tie in with Joel's prophecy?
5. During what New Testament period was the twofold Old Testament promise of the Spirit fulfilled?
6. List eight other expressions that Luke uses for the experience often called the baptism in the Holy Spirit.
7. Distinguish clearly between being baptized *by* the Holy Spirit and being baptized *in* the Holy Spirit.
8. What are the main interpretations of 1 Corinthians 12:13? Which do you find most acceptable, and why?

Chapter 8: Subsequence and Separability

1. Is it proper to formulate a doctrine of Spirit baptism from incidents recorded in the Book of Acts? Relate this to the ques-

tion of whether Luke is a theologian as well as a historian.

2. What do Pentecostals mean when they teach that the outpouring of the Spirit on the Day of Pentecost is paradigmatic, or programmatic, in nature?
3. What are the main interpretations of Jesus' statement to the disciples to "'Receive the Holy Spirit'" (John 20:22)? What reasons does the author give for not accepting the view that the disciples were born again on that occasion?
4. What is the best explanation for the ten-day waiting period between Jesus' ascension and the outpouring of the Spirit on the Day of Pentecost?
5. Give several reasons why the Samaritans' reception of the Spirit (Acts 8:14–20) must be understood as an experience distinct from their conversion experience.
6. How do the spiritual experiences of Saul of Tarsus (Acts 9:1–17) show a separation between conversion and Spirit baptism and that one is subsequent to the other?
7. Does the experience of Cornelius and his household (Acts 10:44–46) undermine the idea that Spirit baptism is subsequent to the Spirit's work in conversion? Explain.
8. Give several arguments in favor of the position that the Ephesian men (Acts 19:1–7) were Christian believers when Paul first met them.
9. In your own words, explain briefly the position of most Pentecostals that Spirit baptism is distinct from the Spirit's work in regeneration.

CHAPTER 9: INITIAL PHYSICAL EVIDENCE

1. What events in the first four chapters of Luke's Gospel show that the Old Testament promise of the Holy Spirit was being fulfilled?
2. Discuss the important connection between Old Testament people prophesying when the Spirit came upon them and what happened in the New Testament when the Spirit came upon God's people.
3. What is the significance of the phenomena of wind and fire on the Day of Pentecost?
4. What are the different interpretations of John the Baptist's statement that Jesus would baptize in the Holy Spirit and fire?
5. What are some erroneous views about the nature of glosso-

lalia? On what basis can we say that glossolalia means speaking in languages?

6. How could Peter say that Joel's prediction that all God's people would prophesy was fulfilled on the Day of Pentecost, when the disciples did not prophesy but spoke in tongues?
7. How important is it that Luke says "all" the disciples spoke in tongues on the Day of Pentecost?
8. How does the account of the outpouring of the Spirit on Cornelius's household (Acts 10:44–46) strengthen the Pentecostal position that glossolalia will accompany the experience?
9. Can it be inferred that the Samaritans (Acts 8:14–20) and Paul (9:17) spoke in tongues when the Spirit came upon them? Give reasons.
10. Are tongues the *normal* accompaniment or the *normative* accompaniment of the baptism in the Holy Spirit? Explain the difference, and summarize why most Pentecostals say tongues are normative.

Chapter 10: Purposes and Results of Spirit Baptism

1. In what ways is the earthly life of Jesus as a Spirit-anointed Person a pattern for believers?
2. Comment on the view that the only purpose of Spirit baptism is to empower a Christian to witness.
3. List six results of Spirit baptism and make a statement or two about each.
4. What seven suggestions can one make to a person wishing to be baptized in the Spirit?
5. Explain why the terminology of being filled with the Spirit should not be restricted only to being baptized in the Spirit.
6. What are the different ways in which the expression "filled with/full of the Spirit" is used in the New Testament?
7. Comment on the suggestion that the important question is not whether a person had at one time been filled with the Spirit, but whether the person is presently filled with the Spirit.

PART 3: SPIRITUAL GIFTS

Chapter 11: General Considerations

1. What is the meaning of the Greek words *charismata* and *pneumatika* as they apply to spiritual gifts? Are they used inter-

changeably in the New Testament? Explain.
2. When Paul uses the terms "gifts," "services," and "workings" ("effects") in 1 Corinthians 12:4–6, what does each term contribute to our understanding of spiritual gifts?
3. Explain in a few sentences the close connection between spiritual gifts and the body of Christ.
4. What is the overall purpose of spiritual gifts?
5. On what basis does the author believe that every Christian possesses at least one gift?
6. May one Christian exercise more than one gift? Illustrate.
7. How do you bring together the seemingly contradictory statements that we are to seek certain gifts and that the Holy Spirit sovereignly distributes gifts according to His will?
8. Define the terms "cessationism" and "continuationism."
9. What responses may a continuationist make to a cessationist?

CHAPTER 12: INDIVIDUAL GIFTS—PART 1

1. Why is it difficult to come up with a rigid classification of spiritual gifts?
2. What are the key New Testament passages that deal with the subject of spiritual gifts?
3. Explain the idea that the New Testament emphasizes the function of church leaders, not their position or office.
4. Why is it difficult to come up with a clear, ironclad definition of an apostle?
5. Explain how, in the New Testament, the term "prophet" is used in a restricted sense and in a broad sense.
6. Why is it incorrect to say that prophesying and preaching are interchangeable terms?
7. What is the function of teachers in the church? Relate this to the role of a pastor.
8. What other gifts may be the same as the gift of pastor? Give reasons.
9. Explain the role of the evangelist.

CHAPTER 13: INDIVIDUAL GIFTS—PART 2

1. What are the gifts of practical assistance? Explain each in a sentence or two.
2. What are the three gifts of power, and how are they related to one another?

3. In what way does the gift of faith differ from the faith that God requires of all believers?
4. What is the significance of the four plural nouns in the phrases "gifts of healings" and "workings of miracles"?
5. How do the gifts of a word of wisdom and a word of knowledge differ from each other?
6. In what ways does New Testament glossolalia differ from similar phenomena in the pagan world?
7. What are the possible explanations for a discrepancy in length between a glossolalic utterance and its apparent interpretation?
8. According to 1 Corinthians 14, what are three functions of the gift of tongues?
9. In what different ways does the gift of prophecy build up the body of believers?
10. How is the gift of distinguishing of spirits related to the gift of prophecy?
11. Explain why a Christian may say confidently that the atoning work of Christ includes healing for the body.

Chapter 14: Spiritual Gifts and Worship

1. What is the biblical basis for believing in worship music that is charismatic in nature?
2. What restrictions are placed on the audible exercise of tongues in a worship service? Why are the restrictions necessary?
3. Under what conditions are uninterpreted tongues justifiable?
4. What limitations are placed on the exercise of the gift of prophecy in a worship service? Why?
5. In what two ways may prophetic utterances be evaluated?
6. What are the three possible sources of an utterance that seems to be prophetic?
7. What is the best explanation of "Women should remain silent in the churches" (1 Cor. 14:34)?
8. In what different sense does the New Testament use terms that in the Old Testament are associated with worship and rites?
9. In what ways do spiritual fruit and spiritual gifts differ from each other? In what ways are they similar?

Selected Bibliography

Anderson, Gordon L. "Baptism in the Holy Spirit, Initial Evidence, and a New Model." *Paraclete* 27, no. 4 (February 1993): 1–10.

Arrington, French. *The Acts of the Apostles.* Peabody, Mass.: Hendrickson Publishers, 1988.

———. "The Indwelling, Baptism, and Infilling with the Holy Spirit: A Differentiation of Terms." *Pneuma* 3, no. 2 (fall 1981): 1–10.

Baker, David L. "The Interpretation of 1 Corinthians 12–14." *The Evangelical Quarterly* 46 (October–December 1974): 224–34.

Banks, Robert, and Geoffrey Moon. "Speaking in Tongues: A Survey of the New Testament Evidence." *The Churchman* 80 (1966): 278–94.

Barrett, Charles K. *The Acts of the Apostles.* Edinburgh, Scotland: T. & T. Clark, 1994.

———. *A Commentary on the Epistle to the Romans.* London: Adam & Charles Black, 1962.

———. *A Commentary on the First Epistle to the Corinthians.* New York: Harper & Row, 1968.

Bartling, Walter J. "The Congregation of Christ—a Charismatic Body; an Exegetical Study of 1 Corinthians 12." *Concordia Theological Monthly* 40 (February 1969): 67–80.

Bauer, Walter. *A Greek-English Lexicon of the New Testament and Other Early Christian Literature.* Translated by William F. Arndt and F. Wilbur Gingrich. 2d ed. of translation revised and augmented by F. Wilbur Gingrich and Frederick W. Danker. Chicago: University of Chicago Press, 1979.

Best, Ernest. "Interpretation of Tongues." *Scottish Journal of Theology* 28, no. 1 (1975): 45–62.

———. "Prophets and Preachers." *Scottish Journal of Theology* 12 (June 1959): 129–50.

Bittlinger, Arnold. *Gifts and Graces.* Trans. Herbert Klassen. Grand Rapids: Wm. B. Eerdmans, 1967.

———. *Gifts and Ministries.* Trans. Clara K. Dyck. Grand Rapids: Wm. B. Eerdmans, 1973.

Blass, Friederich, and Albert Debrunner. *A Greek Grammar of the New Testament and Other Early Christian Literature.* Trans. and rev. Robert W. Funk. Chicago: University of Chicago Press, 1961.

Bornkamm, Guenther. "On the Understanding of Worship." In *Early Christian Experience,* trans. Paul L. Hammer. New York: Harper & Row, 1969.

Bray, Gerald. "The Double Procession of the Holy Spirit in Evangelical Theology Today: Do We Still Need It?" *Journal of the Evangelical Theological Society* 41, no. 3 (September 1998): 415–26.

Bruce, F. F. *1 and 2 Corinthians.* London: Marshall, Morgan & Scott, 1971.

———. *The Acts of the Apostles: The Greek Text with Introduction and Commentary.* Grand Rapids: Wm. B. Eerdmans, 1983.

———. *The Book of Acts.* Rev. ed. Grand Rapids: Wm. B. Eerdmans, 1988.

———. "Holy Spirit in the Qumran Texts." In *Dead Sea Scrolls Studies.* Leiden, Netherlands: E. J. Brill, 1969.

________. "Luke's Presentation of the Spirit in Acts." *Criswell Theological Review* 5 (fall 1990): 15–29.

Bruner, Frederick Dale. *A Theology of the Holy Spirit: The Pentecostal Experience and the New Testament Witness.* Grand Rapids: Wm. B. Eerdmans, 1970.

Campenhausen, Hans von. *Ecclesiastical Authority and Spiritual Power in the Church of the First Three Centuries.* Trans. J. A. Baker. Stanford: Stanford University Press, 1969.

Carson, Don A. *Showing the Spirit: A Theological Exposition of 1 Corinthians 12–14.* Grand Rapids: Baker Book House, 1987.

Cheung, Tak-Ming. "Understandings of Spirit Baptism." *Journal of Pentecostal Theology* 8 (1996): 115–28.

Clowney, Edmund P. "Toward a Biblical Doctrine of the Church." *Westminster Theological Journal* 31, no. 1 (1968): 22–81.

Conzelmann, Hans. *1 Corinthians.* Trans. James W. Leitch. Philadelphia: Fortress Press, 1975.

Cranfield, C. E. B. *A Commentary on Romans 12–13.* Edinburgh, Scotland: Oliver & Boyd, 1965.

———. *A Critical and Exegetical Commentary on the Epistle to the Romans.* Edinburgh, Scotland: T. & T. Clark, 1975.

Cullmann, Oscar. *Early Christian Worship.* Trans. A. Stewart Todd and James B. Torrance. London: SCM Press, 1953.

Cuming, G. J. "EPOTISTHEMEN (1 Corinthians 12.13)." *New Testament Studies* 27 (1981): 283–85.

Dana, H. E., and Julius R. Mantey. *A Manual Grammar of the Greek New Testament.* New York: Macmillan Co., 1957.

Davies, J. G. "Pentecost and Glossolalia." *Journal of Theological Studies,* n.s., 3 (1952): 228–31.

Davies, William David. *Paul and Rabbinic Judaism.* 2d ed. London: SPCK, 1962.

Delling, Gerhard. *Worship in the New Testament.* Trans. Percy Scott. Philadelphia: Westminster Press, 1962.

Dunn, James D. G. *The Acts of the Apostles.* Valley Forge: Trinity Press International, 1996.

———. *Baptism in the Holy Spirit.* London: SCM Press, 1970.

———. "Baptism in the Spirit: A Response to Pentecostal Scholarship on Luke-Acts." *Journal of Pentecostal Theology* 3 (1993): 3–27.

———. *Jesus and the Spirit.* Philadelphia: Westminster Press, 1975.

———. *The Theology of Paul the Apostle.* Grand Rapids: Wm. B. Eerdmans, 1998.

Ellis, E. Earle. "Spiritual Gifts in the Pauline Community." *New Testament Studies* 20 (January 1974): 128–44.

Ervin, Howard M. *Conversion-Initiation and the Baptism in the Holy Spirit.* Peabody, Mass.: Hendrickson Publishers, 1984.

———. *Spirit Baptism: A Biblical Investigation.* Peabody, Mass.: Hendrickson Publishers, 1987.

Everts, Jenny. "Tongues or Languages? Contextual Consistency in the Translation of Acts 2." *Journal of Pentecostal Theology* 4 (1994): 71–80.

Fee, Gordon D. *The First Epistle to the Corinthians.* Grand Rapids: Wm. B. Eerdmans, 1987.

———. *God's Empowering Presence.* Peabody, Mass.: Hendrickson Publishers, 1994.

———. *Gospel and Spirit: Issues in New Testament Hermeneutics.* Peabody, Mass.: Hendrickson Publishers, 1991.

———. "Tongues—Least of the Gifts? Some Exegetical Observations on 1 Corinthians 12–14." *Pneuma* 2, no. 2 (fall 1980): 3–14.

Gaffin, Richard B., Jr. "The Gifts of the Holy Spirit." *Reformed Theological Review* 51 (January–April 1992): 1–10.

Green, E. Michael. *I Believe in the Holy Spirit.* Grand Rapids: Wm. B. Eerdmans, 1975.

Grosheide, F. W. *Commentary on the First Epistle to the Corinthians.* Grand Rapids: Wm. B. Eerdmans, 1953.

Grudem, Wayne A. *The Gift of Prophecy in the New Testament and Today.* Westchester, Ill.: Crossway Books, 1988.

———. "A Response to Gerhard Dautzenberg on 1 Cor. 12:10." *Biblische Zeitschrift* 22 (1978): 253–70.

———, ed. *Are Miraculous Gifts for Today?* Grand Rapids: Zondervan Publishing House, 1996.

Gundry, Robert H. "'Ecstatic Utterance' (N.E.B.)?" *Journal of Theological Studies,* n.s., 17 (1966): 299–307.

Gunkel, Hermann. *The Influence of the Holy Spirit.* Trans. R. A. Harrisville and P. A. Quanbeck II. Philadelphia: Fortress Press, 1979.

Haenchen, Ernst. *The Acts of the Apostles.* Trans. Bernard Noble and Gerald Shinn. Rev. ed. Philadelphia: Westminster Press, 1971.

Hahn, Ferdinand. *The Worship of the Early Church.* Philadelphia: Fortress Press, 1973.

Hering, Jean. *The First Epistle of Saint Paul to the Corinthians.* Trans. A. W. Heathcote and P. J. Allcock. London: Epworth Press, 1962.

Hoekema, Anthony A. *Holy Spirit Baptism.* Grand Rapids: Wm. B. Eerdmans, 1972.

Horton, Harold. *The Gifts of the Spirit.* 2d ed. Springfield, Mo.: Gospel Publishing House, 1975.

Horton, Stanley M. *What the Bible Says About the Holy Spirit.* Springfield, Mo.: Gospel Publishing House, 1976.

House, H. Wayne. "Tongues and the Mystery Religions at Corinth." *Bibliotheca Sacra* 140 (April–June 1982): 134–50.

Hunter, Harold D. *Spirit Baptism: A Pentecostal Alternative.* Lanham, Md.: University Press of America, 1983.

Hurtado, Larry. "On Being Filled With the Spirit," *Paraclete* 4, no. 1 (winter 1970): 29–32.

Kaesemann, Ernst. *Essays on New Testament Themes.* Trans. W. J. Montague. London: SCM Press, 1964.

———. *New Testament Questions of Today.* Trans. W. J. Montague. Philadelphia: Fortress Press, 1969.

Kittel, Gerhard, and Gerhard Friedrich, eds. *Theological Dictionary of the New Testament.* Trans. Geoffrey W. Bromiley. Vols. 1–9. Grand Rapids: Wm. B. Eerdmans, 1964–74.

Koenig, John. *Charismata: God's Gifts for God's People.* Philadelphia: Westminster Press, 1978.

Krodel, Gerhard A. *Acts.* Minneapolis: Augsburg Publishing House, 1986.

Ladd, George E. *A Theology of the New Testament.* Rev. ed. Grand Rapids: Wm. B. Eerdmans, 1993.

Lampe, G. W. H. "The Holy Spirit in the Writings of Saint Luke." In *Studies in the Gospels,* ed. D. E. Nineham. Oxford, England: Blackwell, 1957.

———. *The Seal of the Spirit.* 2d ed. London: SPCK, 1967.

Levang, Raymond K. "The Content of an Utterance in Tongues." *Paraclete* 23, no. 1 (winter 1989): 14–21.

Liddell, Henry George, and Robert Scott. *A Greek-English Lexicon.* 8th ed. Oxford, England: Clarendon Press, 1897.

Lim, David. *Spiritual Gifts: A Fresh Look.* Springfield, Mo.: Gospel Publishing House, 1991.

Longenecker, Richard N. *The Acts of the Apostles.* Grand Rapids: Zondervan Publishing House, 1981.

Lyon, Robert W. "John 20:22, Once More." *Asbury Theological Journal* 43 (spring 1988): 73–85.

Ma, Wonsuk, and Robert P. Menzies, eds. *Pentecostalism in Context: Essays in Honor of William W. Menzies.* Sheffield, England: Sheffield Academic Press, 1997.

Macchia, Frank D. "The Question of Tongues as Initial Evidence." *Journal of Pentecostal Theology* 2 (1993): 117–27.

Marshall, I. Howard. *The Acts of the Apostles.* Grand Rapids: Wm. B. Eerdmans, 1980.

———. *Luke: Historian and Theologian.* Grand Rapids: Zondervan Publishing House, 1971.

———. "The Meaning of the Verb 'To Baptize.'" *The Evangelical Quarterly* 45 (1973): 130–40.

———. "Significance of Pentecost." *Scottish Journal of Theology* 30, no. 4 (1977): 347–69.

Martin, Ralph P. *The Spirit and the Congregation: Studies in 1 Corinthians 12–15.* Grand Rapids: Wm. B. Eerdmans, 1984.

McGee, Gary B., ed. *Initial Evidence: Historical and Biblical Perspectives on the Pentecostal Doctrine of Spirit Baptism.* Peabody, Mass.: Hendrickson Publishers, 1991.

Menzies, Robert P. "Coming to Terms with an Evangelical Heritage—Part 1: Pentecostals and the Issue of Subsequence." *Paraclete* 28, no. 3 (summer 1994): 18–28.

———. "Coming to Terms with an Evangelical Heritage—Part 2: Pentecostals and Evidential Tongues." *Paraclete* 28, no. 4 (fall 1994): 1–10.

———. "The Distinctive Character of Luke's Pneumatology." *Paraclete* 25, no. 4 (fall 1991): 17–30.

———. *Empowered for Witness: The Spirit in Luke-Acts.* Sheffield, England: Sheffield Academic Press, 1994.

———. "Luke and the Spirit: A Reply to James Dunn." *Journal of Pentecostal Theology* 4 (1994): 115–38.

Moule, C. F. D. *An Idiom-Book of New Testament Greek.* 2d ed. Cambridge, England: Cambridge University Press, 1959.

Murray, John. *The Epistle to the Romans.* Grand Rapids: Wm. B. Eerdmans, 1959.

Neil, William. *The Acts of the Apostles.* London: Oliphants, 1973.

O'Donnell, John. "In Him and Over Him: The Holy Spirit in the Life of Jesus." *Gregorianum* 70, no. 1 (1989): 25–45.

Oss, Douglas A. "A Pentecostal/Charismatic View." In *Are Miraculous Gifts for Today?* ed. Wayne A. Grudem. Grand Rapids: Zondervan Publishing House, 1996.

Ouderluys, Richard C. "The Purpose of Spiritual Gifts." *Reformed Review* 28 (spring 1975): 212–22.

Packer, J. I. *Keep in Step with the Spirit.* Grand Rapids: Fleming H. Revell, 1984.

Packer, J. W. *Acts of the Apostles.* Cambridge, England: University Press, 1973.

Palma, Anthony D. "1 Corinthians." In *Full Life Bible Commentary to the New Testament,* 799–913. Grand Rapids: Zondervan Publishing House, 1999.

———. "The Groanings of Romans 8:26." *Advance* 31, no. 8 (fall 1995): 46–47.

Petts, David. "Baptism of the Spirit in Pauline Thought: A Pentecostal Perspective." *European Pentecostal Theological Association Bulletin* 7, no. 3 (1988): 88–95.

Piepkorn, Arthur Carl. "*Charisma* in the New Testament and the Apostolic Fathers." *Concordia Theological Monthly* 42 (1971): 369–89.

Robertson, Archibald, and Alfred Plummer. *A Critical and Exegetical Commentary on the First Epistle of St. Paul to the Corinthians.* Edinburgh, Scotland: T. & T. Clark, 1914.

Robinson, D. W. B. "Charismata Versus Pneumatika: Paul's Method of Discussion." *Reformed Theological Review* 31 (1972): 49–55.

Rogers, E. R. "EPOTISTHEMEN Again." *New Testament Studies* 29 (1983): 139–42.

Runia, Klaas. "The Gifts of the Spirit." *Reformed Theological Review* 29, no. 3 (1970): 82–94.

Russell, Walt. "The Anointing with the Holy Spirit in Luke-Acts." *Trinity Journal,* n.s., 7, no. 1 (spring 1986): 47–63.

Ruthven, Jon. "Is Glossolalia Languages?: A Survey of Biblical Data." *Paraclete* 2, no. 2 (spring 1968): 27–30.

———. "On the Cessation of the Charismata: The Protestant Polemic of Benjamin B. Warfield." *Pneuma* 12, no. 1 (spring 1990): 14–31.

Sanday, William, and Arthur C. Headlam. *A Critical and Exegetical Commentary on the Epistle to the Romans.* 5th ed. Edinburgh, Scotland: T. & T. Clark, 1914.

Scharlemann, Martin H. "The Congregation: Place of God's Presence." *Concordia Theological Monthly* 10 (November 1964): 613–21.

Schatzmann, Ziegfried. *A Pauline Theology of Charismata.* Peabody, Mass.: Hendrickson Publishers, 1987.

Schnackenburg, Rudolf. "Apostles Before and During Paul's

Time." In *Apostolic History and the Gospel,* ed. W. Ward Gasque and Ralph P. Martin. Grand Rapids: Wm. B. Eerdmans, 1970.

Schweizer, Eduard. *Church Order in the New Testament.* Trans. Frank Clarke. London: SCM Press, 1961.

———. "The Service of Worship. An Exposition of I Corinthians 14." In *Neotestamentica.* Zurich, Switzerland: Zwingli Verlag, 1963.

———. "Worship in the New Testament." *The Reformed and Presbyterian World* 24, no. 5 (March 1957): 196–205.

Scott, R. B. Y. "Is Preaching Prophecy?" *Canadian Journal of Theology* 1 (April 1955): 11–18.

Shelton, James B. "'Filled with the Holy Spirit' and 'Full of the Holy Spirit': Lucan Redactional Phrases." In *Faces of Renewal,* ed. Paul Elbert. Peabody, Mass.: Hendrickson Publishers, 1988.

———. *Mighty in Word and Deed.* Peabody, Mass.: Hendrickson Publishers, 1991.

———. "Reply to James D. G. Dunn's 'Baptism in the Spirit: A Response to Pentecostal Scholarship on Luke-Acts.'" *Journal of Pentecostal Theology* 4 (1994): 139–43.

Smith, D. Moody. "Glossolalia and Other Spiritual Gifts in a New Testament Perspective." *Interpretation* 28 (July 1974): 307–20.

Stendahl, Krister. "Glossolalia—The New Testament Evidence." In *Paul Among Jews and Gentiles.* Philadelphia: Fortress Press, 1976.

Stott, John R. W. *The Baptism and Fullness of the Holy Spirit.* 2d ed. Downers Grove, Ill.: InterVarsity Press, 1976.

________. *The Spirit, the Church, and the World: The Message of Acts.* Downers Grove, Ill.: InterVarsity Press, 1990.

Stronstad, Roger. *The Charismatic Theology of St. Luke.* Peabody, Mass.: Hendrickson Publishers, 1984.

Thomas, W. H. Griffith. *The Holy Spirit of God.* 4th ed. Grand Rapids: Wm. B. Eerdmans, 1963.

Trench, Richard Chenevix. *Synonyms of the New Testament.* Grand Rapids: Wm. B. Eerdmans, 1958.

Turner, M. Max B. "The Concept of Receiving the Spirit in John's Gospel." *Vox Evangelica* 10 (1997): 24–42.

———. "'Empowerment for Mission'? The Pneumatology of Luke-Acts: An Appreciation and Critique of James B. Shelton's *Mighty in Word and Deed* [1991]." *Vox Evangelica* 24 (1994): 103–22.

———. *The Holy Spirit and Spiritual Gifts: In the New Testament Church and Today.* Rev. ed. Peabody, Mass.: Hendrickson Publishers, 1998.

———. *Power from on High: The Spirit in Israel's Restoration and Witness in Luke-Acts.* Sheffield, England: Sheffield Academic Press, 1996.

———. "The Significance of Receiving the Spirit in Luke-Acts: A Survey of Modern Scholarship." *Trinity Journal,* n.s., 2 (fall 1981): 131–58.

———. "Spirit Endowment in Luke-Acts: Some Linguistic Considerations." *Vox Evangelica* 12 (1981): 45–63.

Wallace, Daniel B. "Granville Sharp: A Model of Evangelical Scholarship and Social Activism." *Journal of the Evangelical Theological Society* 41, no. 4 (December 1998): 591–613.

Walvoord, John F. "The Holy Spirit and Spiritual Gifts." *Bibliotheca Sacra* 143 (April–June 1986): 109–22.

Williams, Cyril G. "Glossolalia as a Religious Phenomenon: 'Tongues' at Corinth and Pentecost." *Religion* 5 (spring 1975): 16–32.

Williams, David J. *Acts.* Peabody, Mass.: Hendrickson Publishers, 1990.

Williams, J. Rodman. *Renewal Theology: Systematic Theology from a Charismatic Perspective.* Vol. 2. Grand Rapids: Zondervan Publishing House, 1990.

Scripture Index

OLD TESTAMENT

1 Corinthians

1 Corinthians *(cont.)*

Subject Index